Testimonial Advertising in the American Marketplace

Testimonial Advertising in the American Marketplace

Emulation, Identity, Community

Edited by
Marlis Schweitzer and
Marina Moskowitz

palgrave
macmillan

TESTIMONIAL ADVERTISING IN THE AMERICAN MARKETPLACE

First published in 2009 by
PALGRAVE MACMILLAN®
in the United States—a division of St. Martin's Press LLC,
175 Fifth Avenue, New York, NY 10010.

Where this book is distributed in the UK, Europe and the rest of the world, this is by Palgrave Macmillan, a division of Macmillan Publishers Limited, registered in England, company number 785998, of Houndmills, Basingstoke, Hampshire RG21 6XS.

Palgrave Macmillan is the global academic imprint of the above companies and has companies and representatives throughout the world.

Palgrave® and Macmillan® are registered trademarks in the United States, the United Kingdom, Europe and other countries.

ISBN: 978–0–230–61560–1

Library of Congress Cataloging-in-Publication Data

Testimonial advertising in the American marketplace : emulation, identity, community / edited by Marina Moskowitz and Marlis Schweitzer.
p. cm.
Includes bibliographical references and index.
ISBN 0–230–61560–0
1. Advertising—United States—History. 2. Advertising—United States—Psychological aspects. I. Moskowitz, Marina, 1968– II. Schweitzer, Marlis.

HF5823.T37 2009
659.1—dc22 2009021748

A catalogue record of the book is available from the British Library.

Design by Newgen Imaging Systems (P) Ltd., Chennai, India.

First edition: November 2009

10 9 8 7 6 5 4 3 2 1

Printed in the United States of America.

Previous publications:

By Marina Moskowitz

Standard of Living: The Measure of the Middle-Class in Modern America. Baltimore: Johns Hopkins University Press, 2004.

Cultures of Commerce: Representation and American Business Culture, 1877–1960. Edited with Elspeth Brown and Catherine Gudis. Palgrave Macmillan, 2006.

By Marlis Schweitzer

When Broadway Was the Runway: Theater, Fashion, and American Culture. University of Pennsylvania Press, 2009.

Contents

Acknowledgments vii

Introduction: "The Spirit of Emulation" 1
Marina Moskowitz and Marlis Schweitzer

1 Testimonials in Silk: Juba and the Legitimization of American Blackface Minstrelsy in Britain 23
Stephen Johnson

2 The Testifying Subject: Reliability in Marketing, Science, and Law at the End of the Age of Barnum 51
Michael Pettit

3 "After a Season of War": Sharing Horticultural Success in the Reconstruction-Era Landscape 79
Marina Moskowitz

4 "The Ten Year Club": Artificial Limbs and Testimonials at the Turn of the Twentieth Century 95
Edward Slavishak

5 "The Mad Search for Beauty": Actresses, Cosmetics, and the Middle-Class Market 123
Marlis Schweitzer

6 "I am Kay and I Prefer Modern": Bridal Testimonials and the Rise of Consumer Rites, 1920s–1950s 151
Vicki Howard

7 "Dear Friend": Charles Atlas, American Masculinity, and the Bodybuilding Testimonial, 1894–1944 173
Dominique Padurano

8 "For Us, By Us": Hip-Hop Fashion, Commodity Blackness and the Culture of Emulation 207
Mary Rizzo

Notes on Contributors 231

Index 233

ACKNOWLEDGMENTS

This book has been many years in the making. It began in the summer of 2002 while the two of us, along with our colleague Elysa Engelman, were Fellows at the National Museum of American History. Over a series of coffee meetings we discovered our mutual interest in testimonial advertising and began to dream about the possibility of putting together a collection examining the subject. Now, seven years later, we are thrilled to see that what was once a far-off dream has become a reality.

A number of people have been instrumental in bringing us to this point. First and foremost, the authors who joined this project not only shared their intellectual gifts, but have been professional, patient, and very gracious during the lengthy process; it has been a true pleasure to work with them. Many thanks to our earliest supporter, Charles McGovern, who mentored us at the NMAH with his encyclopedic knowledge of American advertising practices and offered helpful comments on individual essays at the Organization of American History conference in 2003. Thanks as well to Jean-Christophe Agnew and Sara Alpern who made thoughtful and insightful suggestions at various conferences along the way; Pamela Walker Laird offered her support and profound insights from the early days to the very end of this project, for which we are extremely grateful.

We would like to extend a special thank you to Elysa Engelman, who was unable to stay with us on the lengthy journey from seed idea to publication, but who nevertheless played an important role in the early planning of this book. A special thank you also to Elspeth H. Brown for reading our introduction and making helpful recommendations for improvement, and to York University graduate student Pola Tumarkin for research assistance.

At Palgrave Macmillan, Chris Chappell, our editor, and Samantha Hasey, our editorial assistant, have helped shepherd this project along; Rachel Tekula at Palgrave and Maran Elancheran at Newgen oversaw its production. We are grateful for their encouragement and support. Thanks as well to Palgrave's readers, who offered incredibly helpful comments to all of our authors. Their generosity has made this a much stronger volume.

Finally, many thanks to our families and loved ones (especially Simon, Dan, Marcus, and Isaac), who have lived with this project almost as long as we have, and have remained faithful cheerleaders to the end. We could not have done it without you.

Introduction: "The Spirit of Emulation"

Marina Moskowitz and
Marlis Schweitzer

In the premiere episode of the acclaimed AMC series *Mad Men,* a glamorous look at postwar Madison Avenue, senior advertising executive Donald Draper faces a crisis with one of his most lucrative accounts. For years he has relied on reassuring testimonials from doctors to promote Lucky Strike cigarettes and quell public concerns about the risks of tobacco addiction. Now pesky questions from the Federal Trade Commission and damning reports from *Reader's Digest* on the relationship between smoking and cancer have effectively nullified the campaign. A continued reliance on these medical testimonials, Draper realizes, would be tantamount to professional suicide.[1]

That testimonial advertising should drive the plot in the opening moments of a twenty-first-century representation of American commerce is itself a testament to the historical importance of this marketing practice. Testimonial advertisements insert into the negotiation between buyer and seller the words of a third party, presented as disinterested in the commercial transaction but in some way knowledgeable about the product at hand and willing to share that knowledge. Testimonials for consumer goods and services are given all the time, in the form of informal recommendations or advice, but testimonial advertising places these personal views into the public realm by disseminating them through a variety of contemporary media. Though the writer or speaker of the testimony is not involved in the actual commercial exchange, his or her words are packaged and publicized by the producer, retailer, or service provider and used as part of a marketing campaign. Testimonials might come from people with a specialized knowledge that grants authority in a particular sector of the market—such as the doctors Draper had previously called upon—or people considered typical consumers whose experience will be widely recognized and shared. As developments in print technology and subsequent forms of media, such as television, allowed for greater reliance on visual imagery, the verbal basis of testimonials was sometimes eclipsed by pictorial associations. Endorsements, the close cousin of testimonials in the realm of commerce, might suggest a particular person's use of a particular product through one powerful photograph or illustration of the product in use, without any explanatory text or narrative; the testimonial is implicit.

Draper's experience with the Lucky Strike campaign highlights both the greatest strengths and the greatest weaknesses of testimonial advertising as a marketing strategy. In the right situation, a well-worded testimonial from highly respected experts can help to sway consumer opinion, boost product sales, and establish a strong brand identity; but if those experts are somehow disgraced or proven wrong, the company with whom they are associated stands to lose much more than consumer trust. Yet despite these risks, testimonial advertising has remained a prominent and popular marketing strategy, even today as consumers become increasingly savvy about the industry's manipulative practices. Why? For 1920s ad man Stanley Resor, the answer was fairly simple: "People like to read about other people." In his view, the testimonial's human element was its greatest selling point "because people *understand* other people. Before printing was invented, even before language was evolved, people were thrown in contact with other people. People understood personalities before there was any social structure or code of laws."[2] Speaking to agency executives in March 1929 in his capacity as President of the J. Walter Thompson Company, Resor went on to identify three additional reasons for the testimonial's success. First, he explained, people were drawn to testimonials out of sheer "curiosity—love of gossip—desire to know 'how the other half lives.'" Second, testimonials played into the "spirit of emulation," arousing consumer desires "to copy those whom we deem superior in taste or knowledge or experience" and thereby enact some form of self-transformation. Finally, testimonials work because "people are eternally searching for authority. Democracy, even in name, is new. Royalty, aristocracy, feudalism, dominated the world for scores of centuries, instilling in the masses a sense of inferiority and an instinctive veneration for 'their betters.'"[3]

While Resor's pop psychology assessment of consumer behavior may raise eyebrows today, his general observations remain compelling. Testimonials offer consumers an opportunity to learn about what other people are doing, to put their trust in experts, or to emulate the appearance and practice of success. Although they bear striking similarities to brand names and trademarks in that they help to bestow distinction upon advertised goods and promise consumers that their purchases will not be in vain, testimonials are a unique advertising phenomenon. Whereas brand names and trademarks—the names and visual symbols by which products are recognized and valued—represent their makers, testimonial advertising represents *consumer experience*, giving prospective purchasers an opportunity to hear directly from their predecessors in the marketplace. Indeed, satisfied consumers hold one key to a successful sale that producers and marketers do not: they can give a firsthand narrative of the product in use without (theoretically) the interference and clever wordsmithing of an advertising team. Of course, there is no doubt that those responsible for advertising carefully edit and select consumer testimonials; testimonials nonetheless carry an aura of authenticity for many readers and viewers that sets them apart from other advertising strategies. For while all advertisements offer the promise of the product in some form or another, testimonials confirm that this promise *comes true*.

The essays in *Testimonial Advertising in the American Marketplace: Emulation, Identity, Community* explore the history and practices of testimonial advertising in the United States from the mid-nineteenth century to the present day, addressing a surprising lack of scholarship on this enduring and pervasive marketing tool. Treating consumers as neither the victims nor the empowered foes of corporate practices, the authors gathered here contribute to new scholarship at the intersection of cultural and business history by examining how testimonials mediate negotiations between producers and consumers and shape modern cultural attitudes about social identity, advice, community, celebrity, and the consumption of brand-name goods and services.

The specific power of testimonial marketing depends on who is offering support. One kind of campaign features "experts"—doctors or financial planners, movie stars or professional athletes, even the Pope (figure I.1)—whose opinions carry weight because of occupational knowledge, established talent, or simply life lived in the public eye. These individuals are the descendents of "royalty" and "aristocracy" who, in Resor's terms, satisfy the general public's desire to learn from "their betters." Testimonials from these experts imply that by using a particular product, consumers will attain similar prestige, success, or glamor. In contrast, testimonials from "average consumers" claim authority based solely on small-scale successes with the advertised product; in such cases, the endorsers' similarity and familiarity to the prospective consumer provides the appeal. These advocates share with most consumers a lack of fame or prestige, along with a shared desire to sleep better, be thinner, or have cleaner bathrooms with less work. Their testimony implicitly promises that the consumer will achieve similar success with the product or service in question and also gain membership in a community of buyers with some shared attributes or goals.

Although testimonials to a particular product offer an obvious benefit to the producers or retailers who sell it, and potentially to consumers looking

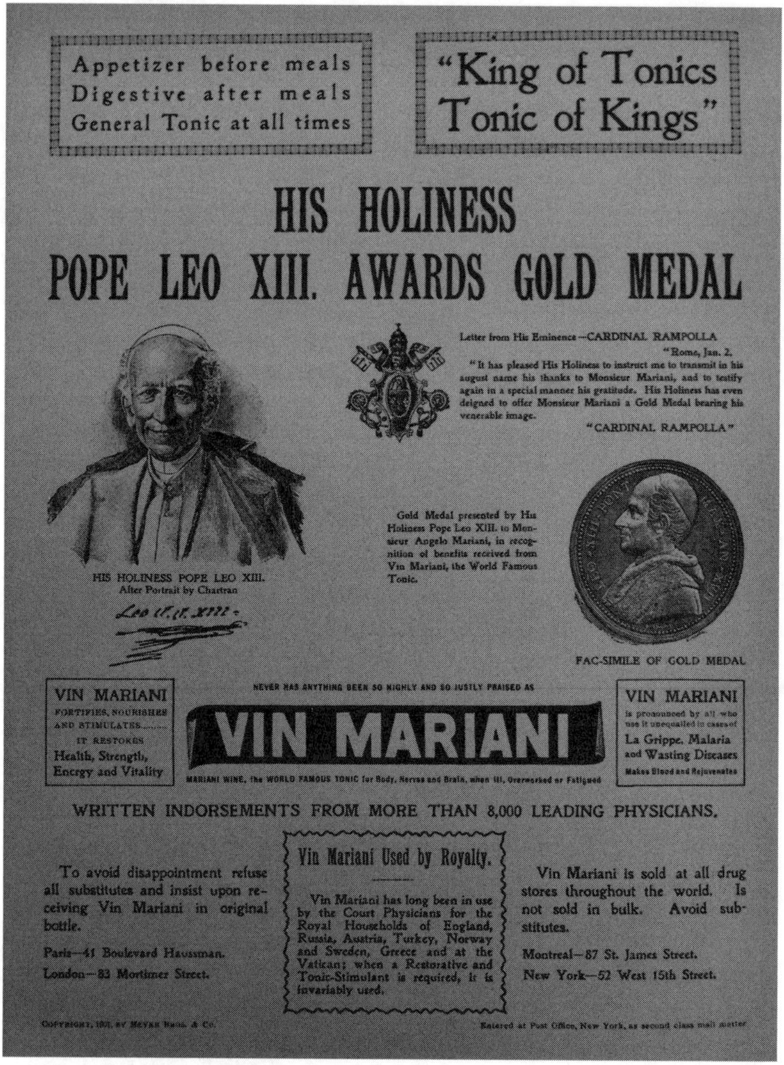

Figure I.1 In this advertisement for Vin Mariani, the Pope testifies to the quality of the wine and offers a special medallion as further proof of his approval.

Source: *Theatre Magazine* (October 1901): inside cover.

for advice, the person offering the words of praise can also find advantages. Experts who are willing to lend their names, and sometimes their stories, to particular brand-name products find that their media appearances not only build upon but also enhance their fame. In today's multimedia and cross-promotional marketplace, celebrities from David Beckham and Michael Jordan to Gwyneth Paltrow and Beyoncé construct their own images through the products they endorse or (to borrow a term from Naomi Klein) "co-brand."[4] The money these celebrities receive for product endorsements often surpasses their other income, making them financially dependent on promotional contracts; for example, the tennis player Anna Kournikova famously (or infamously) found that the recognition she received from billboards was of greater value than her success on the courts. In fact, the financial remunerations sometimes offered for such endorsements have fostered a new industry unto itself.[5] By contrast, everyday testimonial givers rarely receive money for their statements; indeed, one of the main features distinguishing endorsements from testimonials is whether or not the individual speaking to the value of the advertised product has received remuneration. In the purest sense, then, testimonials are statements freely given by happy consumers without any expectation of financial gain. Of course, this is not to suggest that testimonial givers do not benefit in some way from their willingness to share their stories; such individuals often gain a taste of minor celebrity by seeing their name or picture in print, and by imagining that their successes will impress and influence their peers. Testimonials, therefore, both derive from and confer the prestige and authority of those who testify to the worthiness of a brand-name product, service, or experience.

In the realm of the marketplace, personal and corporate identities overlap. This convergence is strengthened by the mechanisms of branding, not the least of which is testimonial marketing. These practices may seem modern phenomena but in fact date back to the middle of the nineteenth century, with even earlier precursors for somewhat different forms. The term "testimonial" was used as early as the sixteenth century as a personal introduction, reference, or commendation, often in the context of the search for employment. American letter writing manuals from the nineteenth century offered models for how best to endorse the character and skills of other people, showing the importance, and frequency, of this particular form of communication.[6] Over time, such personal testimonials shifted from the private realm of correspondence between two parties to small-scale, often local, advertisements. In mass-circulated testimonial advertising, the commendation is transferred from an individual to a firm or corporation, or even more abstractly, to the consumer goods and services. Of course, historically, the word "testimonial" also had legal ramifications, implying in the commercial sector the honesty and veracity one would expect under oath in a court of law.

Beyond the term itself, the practice of offering support for the labor and produce of another's hand is linked to other traditions as well. As Resor's words suggest, the granting of royal warrants to a variety of tradespeople, recognizing the patronage of particular members of a royal family, has for centuries been used to distinguish specific artisans, purveyors, or services. In the context of the British Commonwealth, this practice continues to the present day, with specific seals used as logos of the royal warrant status; the twenty-first-century incarnation is the Web site of the Royal Warrant Holders Association, which allows visitors to search for the patronage of Queen Elizabeth, Prince Philip, and Prince Charles in dozens of trades.[7] As the American context expanded and democratized the profile of those whose trade preferences might carry weight with other consumers, other public means of endorsing products emerged with the increasing dissemination of print culture. The practice of ordering printed works in advance of their actual publication allowed for the inclusion of subscriptions lists. Printers incorporated into the publication a list of those people who had already committed to purchase a text or portfolio, which served to flatter both printer and purchaser.[8] As developments in print technology led to a wider dissemination of the printed word and visual culture, the simple lists of names that endorsed a publication were expanded into quotations and even letters addressing a host of products and services. Printed matter became not just the subject of but also the vehicle for early use of testimonial advertising.

Testimonials became increasingly important in the United States toward the end of the nineteenth century, when producers expanded their market reach across the country, gaining a broader consumer base but losing face-to-face knowledge of and influence on their prospective purchasers. Commodity chains lengthened by phased production processes and new webs of distribution separated producers from their ultimate consumers. Rapidly expanding transportation technology allowed salesmen from particular firms to crisscross the country in search of new customers, often through commercial layers of wholesalers and retailers, while agents working for a variety of firms were responsible for the distribution of other products. But even retailers were no longer necessarily local merchants with face-to-face contact with their consumers; through the new mechanism of mail-order sales, retail giants such as Sears Roebuck and Montgomery Ward set the standard for conducting business by correspondence with consumers across the country.[9] In an effort to bridge the expanding divide between producer and consumer while fostering repeat purchases, manufacturers adopted a range of strategies, everything from introducing catchy jingles and slogans to creating amusing and readily identifiable trade characters.[10] Of these, testimonial advertising proved one of the most promising tactics for reintroducing a personal touch to mass marketing, in that it offered genuine statements from satisfied consumers on the value of a specific good and the company that produced it. Early testimonials were used primarily to sell consumable goods bought on a regular basis,—for example, alcohol, cigarettes, and medicine—and were later extended to the sale of durable goods ranging from pianos to cars, as well as the promotion of the service sector. By codifying word-of-mouth recommendations, American businesses hoped to establish a personal relationship with consumers that would build brand loyalty and make both their products and themselves appear personable, familiar, and trustworthy.

More than building brand loyalty for individual companies, however, the essays in this collection show that testimonials also helped American consumers define individual and collective subjectivities by inviting them to join, through consumption, a community of famous or otherwise familiar faces. For those overwhelmed by the alienating forces of modernity—brought about by a host of factors including rapid urbanization; mass immigration; the rationalization of manufacturing processes and the deskilling of labor; the expansion of corporate entities and the increase in white collar, middle management positions; and the swift movement of goods, people, and ideas across national and international borders—the person-to-person communication that testimonial advertising invited was understandably appealing. Amid growing fears of lost individuality and fractured community, advertisers used statements from satisfied consumers to urge Americans to equate consumption with a coherent, sustainable identity and membership within an established, recognizable community.[11] It is this aspect of the testimonial, in particular, that makes it a valuable subject of inquiry for cultural as well as business historians.

In the twentieth century, testimonial advertising became a standardized marketing tool as leading advertising agencies such as the J. Walter Thompson Company devoted considerable resources to attracting testimonials from reputable people for everything from mattresses and yeast to laundry detergent and face cream. Minutes for an April 5, 1928 meeting on "Personality Advertising" identify over sixteen different accounts for which the J. Walter Thompson Company was responsible for securing testimonials, including such major brands as Pond's, Simmons, Libby, Lux, Maxwell House, and Fleischmann.[12] As Stanley Resor and his agents were well aware, the challenge facing the Company was "to be ingenious enough to keep the campaigns different—and to make them acceptable to personalities and ring true with the public."[13] To that end, the Company adopted a range of strategies for gathering and presenting testimonials. For the Lux Toilet Soap campaign, for example, agents worked with motion picture magazine *Photoplay* to distribute free samples to all "important motion picture actresses" in Hollywood as a preliminary step to approaching the women for a testimonial statement. Within months, 414 of these actresses had agreed to commit to using Lux for a three-year period and submitted statements testifying to the quality and uniqueness of the product without requesting any form of remuneration (figure I.2).[14] That these statements were freely given, albeit in response to the gift of Lux soap, was one of the major selling points for the product. The actresses themselves and the evidence of their use of the product were other obvious factors in the campaign's success. In figure I.2, for

Figure I.2 Advertisement for Lux Toilet Soap featuring actress Ann Sheridan, c. 1940. In the 1920s, 1930s, and 1940s, the J. Walter Thompson Company led the way in securing testimonials for a variety of advertising campaigns.

Source: Author's collection.

example, actress Ann Sheridan not only invites women to share her beauty regime but demonstrates in a series of cartoonlike panels how specifically she uses the product.

The J. Walter Thompson Company took a slightly different tact for Pond's Cold Cream and Simmons mattresses, enlisting the services of prominent society women to recruit their friends and relatives.[15] In exchange for their "contacts," these society "agents" received a commission ranging between $1,000 and $2,000, depending on the reputation and status of the endorsee, who was similarly paid between $1,000 and $5,000 for her statement.[16] With its innovative take on the pyramid scheme, the agency managed to attract such high-profile targets as Mrs. Franklin Delano Roosevelt, Mrs. Charles Tiffany, and Mrs. Morgan Belmont.[17] Not surprisingly, the J. Walter Thompson Company did not reveal to the public that these women had been compensated for their efforts, presumably hoping that readers would believe that such testimonial statements were spontaneous expressions of consumer delight. For years, the J. Walter Thompson Company used these and dozens of other campaigns to bestow otherwise commonplace goods with an aura of glamor and sophistication, appealing to the average consumer's desire to read about other people and emulate their lifestyles and shopping habits. In the 1930s, however, the agency encountered some difficulty when the Federal Trade Commission (FTC) turned its attention toward the problem of "tainted testimonials," particularly false or fabricated testimonials and the practice of paying "widely known people" for their statements. What the public had assumed was a gift freely given to a company, an act of enthusiasm or goodwill, was now revealed to be a commodity exchange, a service rendered for a fee. In the face of this challenge, the J. Walter Thompson Company redoubled its efforts to verify all statements used in testimonial advertising, reexamined its practice of paying for statements, and opted to play it safe in situations where other advertising strategies could work just as well.[18] Despite pressure from the FTC, advertising agencies like the J. Walter Thompson Company continued to use testimonials to promote a range of products but did not devote as much attention to the practice as they had previously.

Today advertising agencies continue to solicit testimonials for their corporate clients, often working in concert with agencies that specialize in finding endorsement opportunities for elite athletes, film and television actors, pop stars, and a host of other celebrity clients. Ad execs looking to hire an Olympic athlete to promote their client's latest power bar need look no further than Gold Medal Greats, an agency that represents American Olympic champions, from Janet Evans and Mark Spitz to Bruce Jenner and Larry Bird.[19] Other advertising agencies are foregoing celebrity altogether, opting to hire unknown athletes to wear uniforms emblazoned with corporate logos at major sporting events.[20] Significantly, whereas the J. Walter Thompson Company came under fire for paying for testimonials, most agencies today work from the assumption that public figures will *only* endorse a product if they receive some form of payment, and consumers are (to all appearances) willing to accept this commercial practice. Yet while testimonial advertising has undergone some dramatic changes in recent years, it nevertheless continues to play an important role within the American marketplace. How, then, can we explain the apparent hesitancy with which historians of advertising and consumer culture have treated this particular marketing phenomenon?

Testimonial advertising has been studied little, perhaps because it has sometimes received a bad rap, whether from industry executives debating its value; skeptical consumers who believe the testimonies are at best solicited and at worst fabricated; and even historians who, faced with those debates, are uncertain how best to use sample letters or promotions as source material. Indeed, this project grew out of the editors' failure to find any in-depth studies of the subject that would help to contextualize the copious testimonial advertising we were finding in our individual research projects. Although, as we discovered, many historians of advertising and consumer culture reference testimonials in their work, and some devote entire sections to discussing particular testimonial campaigns, few offer sustained analyses of the subject.[21] The recent proliferation of texts on the historical and contemporary practices of marketing, such as Douglas Holt's *How Brands Become Icons*, Nancy Keohn's *Brand New*, Naomi Klein's *No Logo*, Pamela Laird's *Advertising Progress*, and Jackson Lears' *Fables of Abundance* all provide helpful starting points for thinking about corporate and consumer identification through marketing.[22] But it seems that some mechanisms of branding, such as the use of visually identifying logos or the use of multimedia campaigns, have received more attention than others, and we have not found any cohesive treatment of the use of testimonials.[23] Scholars working within the burgeoning field of celebrity culture have gone further to examine the cultural work of testimonials; however, the majority of this research has looked at contemporary examples and, in keeping with the focus on celebrity, all but ignores the practice of soliciting testimonials from "average" men and women.[24]

Testimonial Advertising in the American Marketplace addresses this gap in the scholarly and popular literature on advertising, marketing, and branding by examining a broad range of testimonial advertisements from both experts and everyday consumers, beginning in the mid-nineteenth century and continuing through the late twentieth century. Not surprisingly, this development mirrored the rise of nationally distributed goods, as well as the mass media that provided venues for their promotion. One of our underlying assumptions, then, is that fully appreciating the cultural significance of testimonials today requires understanding the role that testimonials have played historically within the American marketplace. Key framing questions for our study therefore include: What cultural work do testimonials perform and how has this shifted over time? What kinds of debates have testimonials provoked? Were there periods when testimonials were outright dismissed or denigrated? If so, why did advertisers later resume using them? How and to what extent do testimonials facilitate relationships between advertisers and consumers, between advertisers and the personalities giving testimonial statements, and between the personalities giving testimonials and the consumers reading them? In what way, if at all, have testimonials supported and/or challenged ideologies of gender, sexuality, race, class, and physical ability? How does a historical analysis of testimonial advertising complicate the way we think about the American marketplace as a site for the production and circulation of business practices, commodities, relationships, and culture?

We use the term marketplace to draw upon both historical and contemporary aspects of commercial endeavour. The marketplace is a site of exchange, encompassing fixed geographical points, whether a nineteenth-century produce market or a twenty-first-century big box store, as well as more abstract systems of commerce, such as the mail-order trade that has at various points in history been conducted by post, telegraph, or Internet. But the marketplace is not only the site of an economic exchange of goods or services for money or in-kind equivalents. It is also the commercial realm in which cultural exchanges educate, influence, and determine what goods and services are both produced and consumed. In this more abstract sense, the marketplace encompasses documented means of influence from a wide variety of parties, both interested and disinterested in commercial exchange—such as lifestyle magazines, product placement in film, or even negative messages such as the Surgeon General's warnings decried by the real-life counterparts of *Mad Men*'s Don Draper. But there are also inaccessible channels of influence that occur between consumers—letters, conversations, or simply the practice of viewing one another's houses, cars, or haircuts. Testimonial advertising is an attempt to harness these personal opinions and make them public.

In this broad frame of the marketplace, the only boundary placed in this volume is a national one; the essays focus on the United States, though some do consider transnational promotion and reception of goods and services. In limiting the parameters of this project to the American marketplace, we do not mean to imply that the practices of offering and publicizing testimonials are uniquely American. Rather, a geographic focus allows for greater concentration and elaboration on the mechanics of testimonial use and specific cultural circumstances such as the emergence of the culture of personality or the effects of internal migration, minimizing the need for extensive focus on national or regional contexts. Indeed, we hope that *Testimonial Advertising in the American Marketplace* might inspire further research that expands the view we have taken to include other nations, or transnational marketing efforts.

Over the past decade, cultural and business historians, social theorists, and other scholars of the humanities and the social sciences have looked more frequently at the marketplace as an important site of human behavior, social identification, and cultural construction. A new generation of scholars has answered the challenge put forward by Kenneth Lipartito's groundbreaking essay, "Culture and the Practice of Business History" (*Business and Economic History*, Winter 1995), by examining not just corporate or consumer culture but a broader *commercial* culture, existing *between* the realms of production and consumption.[25] At the same time, business studies have explored the workings of social and cultural conditions as critical for the understanding of financial and economic trends. Authors such as Malcolm Gladwell (*The Tipping Point, Blink*), Jim Surowiecki (*The Wisdom of Crowds*), and Steven Levitt and Stephen Dubner (*Freakonomics*) have proven the broad public interest in this nexus of culture and the market.[26]

As *Testimonial Advertising in the American Marketplace* demonstrates, testimonials, perhaps more than any other advertising medium, not only shed new light on the many negotiations, collaborations, and exchanges that occur in the marketplace but they also offer a fascinating perspective on how commodities, corporations, and consumers participate in processes of identity-formation. Essays on actresses' endorsement of cosmetics, industrial workers' testimony to the benefits of prosthetics, and audience reception of minstrel shows demonstrate the incredible range that personal experience of products, and the forms of authority deriving from those products, can take. From a farmer's routine annual purchase of seeds to a bride's (presumed) once-in-a-lifetime gift registry, numerous forms of consumption invited the opinions of others. Consumers might encounter this varied commercial testimony in catalogues, magazines, television commercials, or even in the flesh, as people offered their word on a product's worth in settings that were increasingly designed and mediated by corporations. Thus, testimonial marketing can be classified in a variety of ways, from the techniques whereby endorsers derive authority, to the types of commodity being discussed, to the media in which the testimony appears, to the collective relationships and individual subjectivities it fosters.

As these examples suggest, the use of testimonials in the marketplace both informs and is conditioned by other forms of testimony. Public interest in issues of witnessing and sharing of personal experience, indeed *testimony* in the broadest sense of the word, has also risen in the recent past, evidenced in, and spurred on by, wildly disparate cultural phenomena ranging from the outpouring of reaction surrounding 9/11 to the popularity of reality TV shows. Developments within such fields as Holocaust studies and trauma studies have similarly complicated the way we view testimony today, offering a number of productive methodological and critical frameworks for thinking about testifying as a performative act.[27] Certainly the varied roles of the expert and the everyday bystander (and the blurring between these roles) are not confined to the commercial realm. The public is familiar with witnesses appearing in a courtroom, before a government committee, or on the nightly news, and people apply similar, if often imperceptible, processes of evaluating these witnesses' credibility, as they do in the consumer arena. The varied motives and strategies used by lawyers, government officials, television producers, and indeed those willing to offer testimony, are augmented by those of producers, marketers, agents, and endorsers. Yet while we recognize the multiple meanings and associations that come into play whenever the word "testimonial" is used, and acknowledge that much is to be gained by thinking through and across these associations, our primary goal here is to explore one highly prevalent facet of these public exchanges of opinion and its role within the commercial and cultural sectors.

Despite these qualifications, we nevertheless wish to identify other lines of inquiry for students and scholars of business and culture to consider when thinking about testimonials and testimonial advertising practices. While the following questions are beyond this volume's deliberately narrow focus, we raise them here as both an invitation and provocation for future research: How does the history of testimonial advertising in the United States compare with the history of testimonial advertising elsewhere in the world? How have testimonials been used by international corporations to appeal to different markets worldwide and what kinds of responses have these advertisements elicited? Which faces, names, and images have travelled across national borders? Which have not? Focusing now on more contemporary developments in testimonial advertising: How has the testimonial changed in response to the overwhelming popularity of social networking sites such as Facebook and MySpace and the introduction of innovative viral marketing techniques? Is the testimonial a genre unto itself, comparable to the soap opera, the Shakespearean sonnet, or indeed any other cultural and literary form? If so, might it be possible to develop a poetics of the testimonial? Have American producers and consumers developed a dependency on testimonials as proof of a product's worth, and if so, can American culture be defined as a "testimonial culture"?

As these questions suggest, the testimonial is a rich and deserving subject for academic inquiry; it is our hope that this collection will initiate new discussions about the testimonial as both a historical and contemporary phenomenon in the United States and abroad.

* * *

The eight essays in *Testimonial Advertising in the American Marketplace* have been organized in loose chronological order to allow readers to trace the testimonial's genealogical development, although we should emphasize that it is not our goal to present a linear narrative of the testimonial's evolution or suggest that one form of testimonial necessarily gave way to another. To further aid readers, the essays have been paired according to the particular themes they address in order to highlight certain characteristic features of testimonial advertising. We nevertheless expect that readers will find many overlapping connections between essays not already grouped together, as central issues such as authority, emulation, identification, and individual subject formation run through most contributions.

The relationship between corporations and consumers may seem distant or obscure without some intermediary figure or representative. One of the primary purposes of testimonial marketing is to forge a personal connection with the consumer to promote trust in goods, services, and other commodities, such as entertainment and spectacle. Interestingly, some of the earliest examples of testimonial use in the United States appear in the context of marketing performance and spectacle. As consumers grew more familiar with testimonial advertising in later years, the evaluation and veracity of the testimony was often called into question. But ironically, testimonials in this earlier period were often employed specifically to lend credence to commercial pursuits that were themselves suspect or unreliable in some way. The essays in the first section of this volume examine the marketing of performance and the ways in which testimonials have been used to legitimate and even dignify certain forms of spectacle.

In "Testimonials in Silk: Juba and the Legitimization of American Blackface Minstrelsy in Britain," Stephen Johnson examines the shift from working-class to middle-class audiences for blackface entertainment in the mid-nineteenth century. He argues that this remarkable—and remarkably swift—transformation was in part facilitated by a well-organized advertising campaign, which used a variety of means to make minstrelsy "safe" for a new clientele. At the center of this transformation was William Henry Lane, touring as "Boz's Juba," the only performer of color in this context. His difference both emphasizes and naturally questions the means used to "sell" minstrelsy. Juba was advertised as the same figure described by Charles Dickens in his *American Notes*, though there was no corroboration, and Dickens was oddly silent on the ubiquitous use of his words as testimonial.

The Dickens association was only one of the ways in which British opinion was used for "legitimacy" before American audiences. Johnson shows that the advertisements for Juba placed him "on exhibition" rather than "in performance," using this distinction to differentiate edification from entertainment, while the shows themselves actually sought to combine the two. This relationship between entertainment and education is also present in Michael Pettit's essay, "The Testifying Subject: Reliability in Marketing, Science, and Law at the End of the Age of Barnum." Pettit shows the relationship between the idea of witness testimonials in law, science, and marketing, and the different ways in which authority was derived in each arena. Pettit focuses on the use of eyewitness testimonials in the promotion of the 1869 spectacular exhibit, the Cardiff Giant. The promotional materials encouraging people to visit the giant included eyewitness accounts from many local elites, who provided testimonials on the giant's behalf. Due to the giant's fraudulent nature, the reliability of testimony grounded in the moral character of the observer was challenged. This case study illuminates the ways in which witnessing and testifying function in marketing strategies and the legal regulation of commercial fraud.

The next two essays consider the use of testimonial advertising for quite prosaic products in the late nineteenth and early twentieth centuries. Although focused on two very different commodities—seeds and artificial limbs—the essays in this section show the importance of the testimonial not only to producer and consumer but to those writing the letters, often former consumers themselves. These testimonials were usually letters from satisfied consumers to the companies with which they traded, and which were later printed in advertisements, trade catalogues, and even special supplements to such catalogues. In their personal address, these testimonials retain and promote elements of gift exchange or informal trading within the increasingly rigid confines of modern business practice. These essays share a focus on the networks of consumers fostered by the use of testimonial marketing, exploring the appeal of testimonial letters to those who write them, read them, and place them in their business ephemera. The specific context of postbellum American society and culture suggests the role that commerce may have played in promoting national, rather than regional, identities. Although some household names featured in these early testimonials, the main emphasis in both of these case studies is on the shared successes of everyday Americans, even those who were gravely affected by the recent Civil War.

In "'After a Season of War': Sharing Horticultural Success in the Reconstruction-Era Landscape," Marina Moskowitz argues that the seed trade used testimonial advertising to develop national markets. Because it straddled the sectors of agriculture and industry, the seed trade was uniquely positioned to appeal to a range of markets that might otherwise have been starkly divided by economic pursuit in the years leading up to and encompassed by the Civil War. The inclusion of testimonial letters in promotional materials both encouraged and asserted the existence of a broad community of consumers, and fused local landscapes into a national one. By writing to seed firms and allowing their letters to be published, consumers indirectly corresponded with one another. Horticultural success came in a variety of forms: financial gain from prolific crops with good market value, prizes for horticultural specimen deemed the best at county or state fairs, neighborhood acclaim for an abundant garden, or even tales of survival in a time of national turmoil. But perhaps no one experienced the hardship of the Civil War more directly than those who fought in its battles. In "'The Ten Year Club': Artificial Limbs and Testimonials at the Turn of the Twentieth Century," Edward Slavishak explores the use of testimonials in the national prosthetics industry, which emerged after the Civil War as a patriotic supporter of veterans. As the nineteenth century gave way to the twentieth, the trade harnessed the post-Civil War spirit of sacrifice and applied it to their new clientele, who were more frequently workers who had suffered industrial accidents. Crucial to the selling power of this marketing tableau were the words of admiration and encouragement from satisfied customers. Their voices were meant to calm accident victims' fears that dismemberment was a trauma from which they could not recover. Most catalogues ended with lengthy collections of customer commendations that welcomed active correspondence. The pinnacle of these attempts came from the J.F. Rowley Company of Chicago. Rowley established a "Ten Year Club" for individuals who had worn a Rowley leg for a decade and wanted to correspond with veterans and newcomers. In these two very different case studies, the companies employing testimonials are nonetheless fulfilling a similar role; on the one hand, they use testimonials to educate and influence prospective consumers, but on the other, they offer a space within their trade literature for these consumers to commune with one another.

Testimonials play a central role in shaping individual consumer behavior and creating new patterns of consumption within specific demographic groups. This was particularly true in the first half of the twentieth century when advertising agencies fully embraced their role as creators and manipulators of American markets, focusing specifically on the figure of the female consumer. Beginning in the 1910s and 1920s, reports that women were responsible for 80–85 percent of all consumer purchases guided advertising agencies and their clients to reorient their business practices toward women's perceived interests and desires.[28] To that end, newspapers, magazines, department stores, mail-order catalogues, theatres, beauty salons, and numerous other businesses swapped display strategies and formed collaborative relationships to stimulate the imagination of female consumers and promote consumption as a uniquely female activity.[29] Some agencies, most notably the J. Walter Thompson Company, formed special departments staffed by female copywriters who presumably had an "insider" perspective on what women wanted.[30] Still, controlling and shaping female desires and behavior was a difficult job, especially where new product categories and consumer practices were concerned. Advertising agents, magazine editors, and department store managers often had to adopt a range of techniques to convince female consumers to follow their advice or, in the case of testimonial advertising, the advice of other women.

The next two essays explore the advertising industry's attempt to influence the female imagination, looking specifically at how the cosmetics and bridal industries sought to provide a template for new consumer rituals and ease class anxieties about products previously associated with working-class women. In "'The Mad Search for Beauty': Actresses, Cosmetics, and the Middle-Class Market," Marlis Schweitzer analyzes how beauty product manufacturers in the 1910s used their association with Broadway stage stars to build, reinsure, and sustain a white, middle-class market. Acknowledging the class-based prejudices that continued to surround cosmetics, manufacturers emphasized how products such as cold cream could be used to enhance rather than transform an individual woman's "natural" beauty. Central to their argument, Schweitzer suggests, was the revelation that Broadway actresses were not "naturally more beautiful" than the average woman but rather the beneficiaries of careful use of cosmetics. Assisted by actresses' testimonials, advertisers implied that all women had the right, the capacity, and the obligation to make themselves as beautiful as possible by incorporating creams and other "invisible" cosmetics into their everyday beauty regimes. In "'I am Kay and I Prefer Modern': Bridal Testimonials and the Rise of Consumer Rites, 1920s–1950s," Vicki Howard similarly investigates how the burgeoning American wedding industry used testimonials to shape consumer behavior by promoting a particular vision of the ideal wedding. Although some advertisers relied on testimonials from Hollywood stars or beauty contest winners, others preferred to use testimonials from engaged women or newly married women. By the 1930s and 1940s, Howard shows, bridal testimonials for everything from towels and toasters to cigarettes and automobiles became embedded in the editorial advertising that dominated *Bride's Magazine* (1934) and *Modern Bride* (1949). By 1950, a whole range of prefabricated bridal identities emerged in editorial advertising articles, in which engaged women belonging to different social situations testified about their brand preferences and gift registries. Such testimonials offered readers a range of consumer types, from the small-town girl to the campus wife to the career woman, with whom they could identify and (hopefully) emulate.

While mainstream advertising agencies devoted their attention to women, other twentieth-century advertisers used testimonials to offer special products and services to men, often challenging or reworking traditional perceptions of masculinity to encourage male consumers to experiment with new ways of using their bodies and performing their identities. Taking up these themes, and with a particular focus on the intersection of race, class, and gender, the last two essays in the collection consider how testimonials have been used to address traditionally disadvantaged groups of men and offer, via consumption, opportunities for social, economic, and bodily transformation. Although separated by almost fifty years, the two campaigns explored here share striking similarities in the way that they make the endorsers' personal attributes and constructed identities attainable to average consumers through the commodity form.

In "'Dear Friend': Charles Atlas, American Masculinity, and the Bodybuilding Testimonial, 1894–1944," Dominique Padurano analyzes how advertisements for Charles Atlas' mail-order fitness course offered a definition of masculine success that would increasingly be accepted as standard during the twentieth century. Appearing in working-class men's periodicals by the 1930s and comic books by the 1940s, these ads promised to transform ninety-seven-pound weaklings into "power-muscled he-men" like Atlas himself. Like the promise of salvation in the seventeenth century or undreamed-of wealth in the nineteenth, Padurano concludes, bulging biceps and tight abdominals became symbols of discipline as much as of one's ability to attract the attention of others, and thus predict men's future success, in the increasingly "outer-directed" twentieth. In "'For Us, By Us': Hip-Hop Fashion, Commodity Blackness and the Culture of Emulation," Mary Rizzo similarly explores the promotion of hypermasculine ideals through the medium of the celebrity endorsement, offering a well-considered critique of the hip-hop fashion company FUBU ("For Us, By Us") and its apparent reliance on racialized stereotypes. As Rizzo explains, FUBU's major marketing technique has been celebrity endorsements from such recognizable celebrity icons as LL Cool J, the Wayans Brothers, Will Smith, and Brandy. In addition to these endorsements, FUBU markets its brand through the images of the founders who are depicted as hip-hop insiders who are close to "the street." Yet despite FUBU's undeniably positive emphasis on successful black artists and entrepreneurs, its ads also reproduce images of black hypermasculinity, toughness, and ghetto authenticity, playing into longstanding stereotypes. These stereotypes become all the more troubling in light of the growing number of young white males who purchase FUBU's clothes. Rizzo argues that as suburban white youth adopt the markers of urban blackness associated with FUBU, blackness is reduced to a commodity that can be worn and then just as easily tossed aside.

Together, the essays gathered in this collection offer a fresh perspective on the multivalent relationships that exist between producers and consumers by focusing on testimonials as sites of cultural and commercial exchange. These essays highlight the myriad ways that testimonials and the commodities they promote operate within the American marketplace to facilitate the formation of individual and collective identities. Over time, testimonials themselves have become objects of commodification, granted in exchange for financial remuneration in the form of endorsements, as well as offered freely as outgrowth of customer satisfaction. Whether promoting the shared goals of a community of consumers or the aspirational acquisition of goods and services identified with celebrity sportsmen, performers, and other public figures, testimonial advertising to this day captures the "spirit of emulation" noted by advertising executive Stanley Resor in the 1920s. Even in the media-saturated twenty-first century, in which magazine readers know that the familiar faces looking up at them from print ads are likely being handsomely recompensed and favorite television commercials featuring "on the street" testimony are replayed on YouTube, testimonial advertising remains big news and big business. The essays in this volume outline the historical development and entrenchment of this common practice, which is now so often taken for granted as an inevitable part of any marketing campaign.

NOTES

1. "Smoke Gets in Your Eyes," Season 1, Episode 1, *Mad Men,* Dir. Alan Taylor. AMC. July 19, 2007. For plot synopsis, see http://www.amctv.com/originals/madmen/episode1. Accessed January 18, 2009.
2. Stanley Resor, "Personalities and the Public: Some Aspects of Testimonial Advertising," *New Bulletin* 138 (April 1929), 1. J. Walter Thompson Information Center Records, Box 4, Testimonial Advertising, 1928–1977. John W. Hartman Center for Sales, Advertising, and Marketing History, Rare Book, Manuscript, and Special Collections Library, Duke University [hereafter Hartman Center].
3. Resor, "Personalities and the Public," 2–3.
4. See Naomi Klein, *No Logo: No Space, No Choice, No Jobs* (New York: Picador, 2002).
5. Chris Isidore, "Anna Can Keep Winning Off the Court," *CNN/Money*, July 8, 2002, http://money.cnn.com/2002/07/05/commentary/column_sportsbiz/anna/, accessed January 8, 2009.
6. See, for example, Thomas Hill, *Hill's Manual of Social and Business Forms* (Chicago: Moses Warren and Co., 1878), vi, 92, 94; and *A New Letter Writer for the Use of Gentlemen* (Philadelphia: Porter and Coates, 1877), 26, 28.
7. http://www.royalwarrant.org/

8. *A New Letter Writer for the Use of Gentlemen*, 59–60. See also Adrian Johns, *The Nature of the Book: Print and Knowledge in the Marking* (Chicago: University of Chicago Press, 1998), 450–451; and Hugh Amory and David D. Hall, *A History of the Book in America: vol. 3: The Industrial Book, 1840–1880* (Chapel Hill: University of North Carolina Press, 2007).
9. On the development of American business practices, see Boris Emmet and John E. Jeuck, *Catalogues and Counters: A History of Sears, Roebuck and Company* (Chicago: University of Chicago Press, 1950); David Hounshell, *From the American System to Mass Production, 1800–1920* (Baltimore: Johns Hopkins University Press, 1984); William Leach, *Land of Desire: From the Department Store to the Department of Commerce: The Rise of America's Commercial Culture* (New York: Pantheon Books, 1993); Timothy Spears, *100 Years on the Road: The Traveling Salesman in American Culture* (New Haven: Yale University Press, 1995); Susan Strasser, *Satisfaction Guaranteed: The Making of the American Mass Market* (New York: Pantheon Books, 1989); Olivier Zunz, *Making America Corporate, 1870–1920* (Chicago: University of Chicago Press, 1990).
10. Stephen Fox, *The Mirror Makers* (Champaign: University of Illinois Press, 1997) 44, 46–47; Strasser, *Satisfaction Guaranteed,* 89–103; Charles W. Hurd, "Different Uses of the Testimonial: Several Varieties of the Real Thing and a Few of the Imaginary Ones," *Printers' Ink* (August 28, 1913), 40.
11. On the role of advertising and other forms of consumer culture in mediating experiences of modernity, see T. J. Jackson Lears, *No Place of Grace: Antimodernism and the Transformation of American Culture: 1880–1920* (Chicago: University of Chicago Press, 1981); T. J. Jackson Lears, "From Salvation to Self-Realization: Advertising and the Therapeutic Roots of the Consumer Culture, 1810–1930," in *The Culture of Consumption: Critical Essays in American History, 1880–1980*, ed. T. J. Jackson Lears and Richard Wightman Fox (New York: Random House, 1983), 3–38; Warren I. Susman, "Personality and the Making of Twentieth Century Culture," in *Culture as History: The Transformation of American Society in the Twentieth Century* (New York: Pantheon Books, 1984 [1974]), 271–285; Roland Marchand, *Advertising the American Dream: Making Way for Modernity, 1920–1940* (Berkeley, Los Angeles, and London: University of California Press, 1985); T. J. Jackson Lears, *Fables of Abundance: A Cultural History of Advertising in America* (New York: Basic Books, 1994); Benjamin Singer, "Modernity, Hyperstimulus, and the Rise of Popular Sensationalism," in *Cinema and the Invention of Modern Life*, ed. Leo Charney and Vanessa R. Schwartz (Berkeley: University of California Press, 1995), 72–99.
12. "Company Meeting on 'Personality Advertising,' Mr. Stanley Resor, Chairman," April 5, 1928, 3, J. Walter Thompson Company Information Center, Box 4, Testimonial Advertising, 1928–1977, Hartman Center.
13. Ibid.
14. "Production and Representatives Meeting—April 9, 1928," 6–8. J. Walter Thompson Staff Meeting Minutes, 1927–1929 April, Minutes of representatives' Meetings, Box 1, January 5–April 18, 1928, Hartman Center.

15. Ibid, 4.
16. For more on the Simmons campaign, see the J. Walter Thompson Company papers for Lucile Turnblach Platt, Box 1, Women Endorsers, 1926–1927, Hartman Center.
17. Memo to Mr. Fowler from Esther Eaton, June 8, 1927. JWT Lucile Turnblach Platt, Box 1, Women Endorsers, General, Lists, 1926–1929, Hartman Center.
18. "The Federal Trade Commission and the Tainted Testimonial, by Mr. Earle Clark," Staff Meeting, August 4, 1931, 2–11, J. Walter Thompson Staff Meetings, June 1931–February 1932, Minutes of Representatives' Meetings, Box 4, August 4–August 25, 1931.
19. http://www.goldmedalgreats.com/aboutus.html. Accessed 24 Nov. 2008.
20. R. M. Schneiderman, "Fighting for Endorsements," *New York Times*, October 6, 2008, http://economix.blogs.nytimes.com/2008/10/06/fighting-for-endorsements/. Accessed November 24, 2008.
21. The following books include brief discussions of testimonial advertising: Robert Jay, *The Trade Card in Nineteenth-Century America* (Columbia: University of Missouri Press, 1987); Charles Goodrum and Helen Dalrymple, *Advertising in America: The First 200 Years* (New York: Harry N. Abrams, 1990); Jennifer Scanlon, *Inarticulate Longings:* The Ladies' Home Journal, *Gender, and the Promises of Consumer Culture* (New York: Routledge, 1995); Lears, *Fables of Abundance*; Marchand, *Advertising the American Dream.*
22. Douglas Holt, *How Brands Became Icons: The Principles of Cultural Branding* (Cambridge, MA: Harvard Business School Press, 2004); Nancy Keohn, *Brand New: How Entrepreneurs Earned Consumers' Trust from Wedgwood to Dell* (Cambridge, MA: Harvard Business School Press, 2001); Klein, *No Logo*; Lears, *Fables of Abundance*; Pamela Walker Laird, *Advertising Progress: American Business and the Rise of Consumer Marketing* (Baltimore and London: The Johns Hopkins University Press, 1998).
23. One notable, if rather questionable, exception is William M. Freeman's 1957 book *The Big Name*, commissioned by Printers' Ink Books primarily as a resource for advertising agents. William M. Freeman, *The Big Name* (New York: Printers' Ink Books, 1957), 183. However, a memoranda sent by Miss Florence Baldwin, a J. Walter Thompson employee, to Mr. Stanley Resor in January 1958 calls into question the quality and veracity of the book, particularly its treatment of Thompson campaigns. As Baldwin concluded, "There is much exaggeration in the book, and sensationalism, and inaccuracy, and some truth." Memorandum from Florence Baldwin to Mr. Stanley Resor, Stanley Ralph Bernstein Company History Files—Box 4—Resor, Stanley, February 1936–February 1964, n.d.
24. See for example, Joshua Gamson, "The Negotiated Celebration," 698–720; Rosemary Coombe, "Author(iz)ing the Celebrity: Engendering Alternative Identities," 721–769; and Graeme Turner, Frances Bonner, and P. David Marshall, "Producing Celebrity," in *The Celebrity Culture Reader*, ed. P. David Marshall (New York and London: Routledge, 2006), 770–798; Rachel Moseley, ed. *Fashioning Film Stars: Dress Culture & Identity* (London: British Film Institute, 2005); Chris Rojek, *Celebrity* (London: Reaktion Books, 2001), esp. ch. 2.

25. Examples include Regina Blaszczyk, *Imagining Consumers: Design and Innovation from Wedgwood to Corning* (Baltimore: Johns Hopkins University Press, 2000); Elspeth Brown, *The Corporate Eye: Photography and the Rationalization of American Commercial Culture* (Baltimore: Johns Hopkins University Press, 2005); Sally Clarke, *Trust and Power: Consumers, the Modern Corporation, and the Making of the United States Automobile Market* (New York: Cambridge University Press, 2007); Catherine Gudis, *Buyways: Billboards, Automobiles, and the American Landscape* (New York: Routledge, 2004); Marina Moskowitz, *Standard of Living: The Measure of the Middle Class in Modern America* (Baltimore: Johns Hopkins University Press, 2004); Shelley Nickles, "Object Lessons: Household Appliance Design and the American Middle Class, 1920–1960" (Ph.D. diss., University of Virginia, 1999).
26. Malcolm Gladwell, *The Tipping Point: How Little Things Can Make a Big Difference* (Boston: Back Bay Books, 2002); Gladwell, *Blink: The Power of Thinking Without Thinking* (Boston: Back Bay Books, 2007); Jim Surowiecki, *The Wisdom of Crowds* (New York: Doubleday, 2004); and Steven Levitt and Stephen Dubner, *Freakonomics: A Rogue Economist Explores the Hidden Side of Everything* [revised and expanded] (New York: William Morrow, 2006).
27. See, for example, Zoe Vania Waxman, *Writing the Holocaust: Identity, Testimony, Representation* (New York: Oxford University Press, 2008); Suzette A. Henke, *Shattered Subjects: Trauma and Testimony in Women's Life-Writing* (New York: Palgrave Macmillan, 2000); Leigh Gilmore, *The Limits of Autobiography: Trauma and Testimony* (Ithaca, NY: Cornell University Press, 2001).
28. See William Leach, "Transformations in a Culture of Consumption: Women and Department Stores," *The Journal of American History* 71 (September 1984): 319–342; Strasser, *Satisfaction Guaranteed*; Roger Miller, "*Selling Mrs. Consumer:* Advertising and the Creation of Suburban Socio-Spatial Relations, 1910–1930," *Antipode* 23.1 (1991): 263–301; Lears, *Fables of Abundance*; Scanlon, *Inarticulate Longings*.
29. On the gendering of consumption, see Elaine S. Abelson, *When Ladies Go A-Thieving: Middle-Class Shoplifters in the Victorian Department Store* (New York and Oxford: Oxford University Press, 1989); Ellen Gruber Garvey, *The Adman in the Parlor: Magazines and the Gendering of Consumer Culture, 1880s to 1910* (New York and Oxford: Oxford University Press, 1996); Scanlon, *Inarticulate Longings*.
30. See Scanlon, *Inarticulate Longings*, 169–198.

CHAPTER 1

Testimonials in Silk: Juba and the Legitimization of American Blackface Minstrelsy in Britain[1]

Stephen Johnson

In the Dance Collection of the Library and Museum of the Performing Arts, New York Public Library, there exists a rare document of the history of advertising. It is a large piece of a lightweight and delicate silk, approximately 18 by 24 inches, containing printed black ink text and the vestiges of a gold-leaf filigree that identify it as a souvenir from the 1848 appearance of the African-American dancer Juba at Vauxhall Gardens, London, England (figure 1.1).[2] The silk is impressive, first of all, because it is an unusually well-preserved example of this easily-degraded material, and one of the best of a number of extant silk souvenirs in the New York Public Library, printed for theatrical special occasions.[3] Its survival is astonishing. In the rarified world of nineteenth-century popular performance, for which evidence is so scarce, its mere existence makes it valuable, and the fact that it is a physical document, handled by people who witnessed the performance, creates an almost fetishistic response to its examination.

This particular object, however, is unusual in a number of other ways. It is the largest example of its kind in the New York Public Library system, and most likely one of the largest extant anywhere. It is a souvenir of a nondramatic dance performance from a less-than-polite circus-oriented venue. It pays tribute to a performer of color in a performance idiom that was aggressively racist. And it is also strangely unattractive. The "Vauxhall Silk" has no illustration at all, let alone of Juba. There is none of the playfulness of typography available to the typesetters of the day, or on view in other examples of silk souvenirs.[4] There is nothing that catches the eye. It

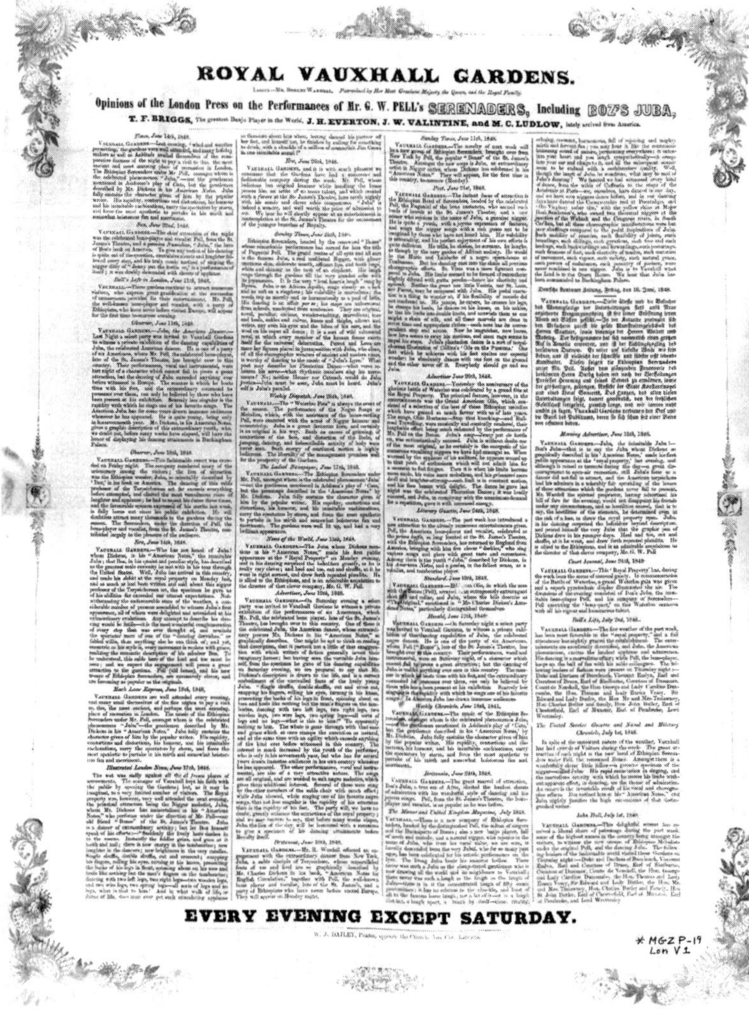

ROYAL VAUXHALL GARDENS.

Opinions of the London Press on the Performances of Mr. G. W. PELL's SERENADERS, Including BOZ'S JUBA, T. F. BRIGGS, The greatest Banjo Player in the World, J. H. EVERTON, J. W. VALINTINE, and M. C. LUDLOW, lately arrived from America.

EVERY EVENING EXCEPT SATURDAY.

Figure 1.1 "The Vauxhall Silk." Royal Vauxhall Gardens: Opinions of the London press on the performances of Mr. G. W. Pell's Serenaders, 1848.

Source: Courtesy Jerome Robbins Dance Division, The New York Public Library for the Performing Arts, Astor, Lenox, Tilden Foundations.

consists of the most ordinary of newspaper type, in column upon column of excerpted reviews describing and praising one performer. It is visually boring—or at least that is my judgment looking back from the twenty-first century. What could have convinced publicity-obsessed performers and company and venue managers to settle on this design?

This artifact constitutes what in microhistory is called the "exceptional normal," or the attribute that appears unusual to the historian but not, apparently, to the subject-culture.[5] It stands out as too large, too "popular" in subject, and too mundane in its design; but in this respect, form fits function, since the purpose of the Vauxhall Silk is as "testament" to the art of "Boz's Juba," who as a performer of color in an otherwise racially segregated form of entertainment, the minstrel show, can also be described as an "exceptional normal." I will attempt in this essay to get past the visceral response to the silk and its subject in order to "get to" an understanding of their exceptional characteristics. I believe the Vauxhall Silk, in particular, represents an attempt to utilize the testimonial to authorize the presence of this unusual dancer (and dance) on the bourgeois stage. More generally, the use of such testimonials appears to have been an important part of an effort by American blackface minstrels and minstrel companies to gain a foothold in Britain.

Making Minstrelsy Safe for the Middle Classes

The American blackface performer was not new to the British stage in 1848, but the idea of a full evening dedicated to such entertainment was. A number of individuals, most notably T. D. Rice, had been successful on tavern, circus, and variety stage from the 1830s. In their act, these white performers appeared in blackface, in the alleged costume of a southern plantation slave and speaking with an (again, alleged) authentic dialect, in a performance combining song, dance, comic monologue, and parody. It was a kind of Americanized version of the much earlier Elizabethan jig: chaotic, clown-like, topically political and salacious, and (unsurprisingly) intensely racist. Rice in particular had a large following in Britain, and many imitators, both American and British. From 1843, however, a variation on this character took hold in America with the formation of the Virginia Serenaders in New York, a group of four solo artists who booked a small venue and presented a stand-alone full evening's entertainment. This was unheard of for blackface performance, and relatively uncommon for popular performance generally. Although this event may seem a minor development, it was in fact a notable event. In effect, the act of booking a venue and advertising a full evening's entertainment set these minstrels, clown-like mainstays of the circus, saloon, and theatrical entr'acte, in opposition to their former employers. Their immediate and unqualified commercial success in New York and other American urban areas established minstrelsy as a separate genre of performance altogether. Ultimately, blackface minstrelsy became among the most popular genres of entertainment in nineteenth-century America, persisting as a major commercial vehicle until the 1920s, and continuing much longer in amateur cultures.[6] But in the 1840s, it was a rebel form that was not supposed to exist.

There is a generally stated model for the minstrel show that includes a three-part structure—performances by urban black characters in dandy costume, a variety "olio," and a rural plantation finale. The early years of minstrelsy had no such rigidity, although there were some common attributes. Performers were white Anglo-Americans who "blacked up" with burnt cork, or by other means. They purported to be imitating (or "delineating") the authentic culture of southern plantation slaves, in dress, speech, song, and dance. This conceit appears to have provided a license to enact mutual disagreements with cultures of power through parody, while at the same time disempowering through ridicule a growing population of runaway and freed slaves. Despite this mimetic veneer, however, strong evidence of a clown culture persisted. Some performers wore long, oversized clown shoes, some the large, extravagant collars that could hide the entire head. The dress was typically ragged, whether vaguely rural or urban, with outlandish colors and patches variously defended as authentic, but at times almost harlequin-like.

In general the party sat in a line or semicircle, holding an array of instruments. The two "endmen" were the most essential feature, one played the tambourine (which was more like an Irish borrin), and the other played the "bones" (related to the Spanish castanets and Anglo-folk "spoons"). The third essential instrument was the quite new and exotic banjo—recently commercialized from an instrument common in southern slave culture, and in this early incarnation unfretted and comprised of five strings. Other instruments included the fiddle and (less often) the accordion. The entertainment included a range of popular dialect songs, which might be topical, sentimental, highly sexual, or entirely nonsensical; they were interrupted or accompanied by raucous dances, comic monologues, burlesques, and dialogues dependent on the bad pun. Overall, the troupe appeared to be wild, nearly out of control during performances, and, because of the inferiority of their "black" personae, incapable of formal structure. The genre was in some measure a parody of the polite concert format of groups like the Hutchinson family, who were American concert singers popular at the time.[7]

A good deal has been written about the complexities of this new performance genre, emphasizing the difficult-to-read attitudes toward race, class, and gender, often contradictory and embedded in the same imagery.[8] What is significant for this discussion is that at its inception it was a working-class entertainment and in general pitched at a male audience. Early success, however, led to a proliferation of troupes and greater competition. This in turn initiated an effort to broaden the audience. To some extent this was an act of reclamation: minstrels had performed at circuses, frequented by children, and variety houses had at least some women audience members. Most important, however, was the effort by minstrelsy to accommodate the middle classes.[9] During the first ten years of minstrelsy, we can see a stabilization and gentrification of the venues leased and rented, from basements and saloons to "mechanics halls" and legitimate (if lesser) theatres. The nature of the entertainments, though still raucous, were self-censored for obvious reasons; the references were less sexual, the lyrics more sentimental. If the minstrel performer still defined the body out of control, and the roots of the form were still clearly from urban streets, ports, and levees, ways were found to make that body safe.[10]

Nowhere is this shift more evident than in the early tours to England. British culture held an ambivalent place in American culture, at once resented and imitated. American performing arts relied heavily on imported British plays, songs, and entertainers, who appealed to a middle-class belief in European cultural superiority, and to still-strong immigrant ties across all classes. In return, American performers regularly traveled to Britain, because the superior ease of touring and relative density of population created financial opportunities, and because (then as now) it carried a critical cachet back home. The ambivalent longing-and-resentment of such cultural dependency is exemplified by the pioneering American showman P. T. Barnum, who toured Britain in the mid-1840s with the young midget "General Tom Thumb." Barnum implemented an aggressive campaign to pitch his *protegé*—both as exhibition of difference and as exhibition of skilled performer—to the British middle classes and aristocracy, while at the same time writing regularly published letters home pitching American values and skills at the expense of the anti-democratic, class-oriented British. His triumphant tour abroad increased his respectability (and breadth of audience) back in New York; his pro-American letters maintained his working-class popularity. This was still necessary in an America that had not yet reached the population watershed that would allow for the segregation of its performance venues along class lines.[11] Economic prosperity was most fully assured by an appeal "across the board." Not surprisingly, Barnum's lessons were not lost on the early minstrel troupes; the Virginia Serenaders traveled to Britain only months after they "invented" the form, and in the ensuing years dozens of imitators landed at Liverpool and Dover. The British press regularly announced a glut of such "delineators" and a (hoped for) decline in their appeal, but they kept coming, until finally they were both accepted and thoroughly anglicized.[12]

Playing to Everyone: The First Ethiopian Tour

The effort to broaden the public viewership of the American minstrel show in Britain is nowhere better expressed than in the 1846 tour of the Ethiopian

Serenaders, which in effect made minstrelsy safe for mass consumption.[13] That tour began with a testimonial distributed in advance of the troupe's initial appearance, promoting their quality. An early critic reports as follows:

> We perused with intense pleasure the diplomatic document, politely transmitted to us by Mr. Germon, who acts as the Ethiopian Chief. First, there is a protocol, signed by L. C. F. Fatio, captain of the U.S. Maine, of such an unprecedented nature, that we feel convinced it must create an immense sensation in the musical world, and we hasten to submit it to our readers:—
>
> Washington City, United Stages Treasury Department, Sept. 12, 1844.
>
> Sir—It is with great pleasure I forward to you the letter of the Honourable Charles Wickliffe, the Postmaster-General of the United States, containing likewise the recommendation of the Honourable George M. Bibb, Secretary of the Treasury of the US, who, along with the Hon. John C. Calhoun, Secretary of State, and the Hon. J. Y. Mason, Secretary of the Navy, were present at the President's mansion last evening, and who witnessed your delightful performance of the negro character.
>
> I am authorized by the President of the United States to inform you that both his lady and himself were highly pleased, and authorise you, when you arrive in England, to make mention of this fact, if you think it will aid you in forwarding your views as Ethiopian minstrels. The venerable Mrs. Madison, our late lamented President's widow, was likewise present, and expressed herself much amused. Permit me to hope your contemplated trip to England will prove one of profit, as well as of pleasure, and allow me, in conclusion, to wish you health and a speedy attainment of your desires.
>
> Very respectfully; I remain,
> Your obedient humble servant,
> (Signed) L. C. F. Fatio, Captain United States Marine.
> To Mr. Germon, for the Ethiopians[14]

The authenticity of this letter aside—there is some evidence for a presidential performance (for President Tyler)[15]—this testimonial serves several clear functions. It "authorises" the performance as suitable for an educated audience of mixed gender and mixed ages. It emphasizes the unusual character of the performance through the "unprecedented" nature of a letter of endorsement from the President of the United States. And finally, though less overtly, the letter endorses the uniquely American character of the performance by emphasizing both the specificity of the imitation ("your performance of the negro character"—meaning the plantation slave), and the sense of "mission" in a British tour ("forwarding your views as Ethiopian minstrels"). There is in this at least a hint that the letter views minstrelsy as a means to exhibit American culture abroad, in a similar manner to the exhibition of African, Asian, Middle Eastern, and South American culture and performance popular with the British middle classes at this time—a line of defense and promotion that was unquestionably used by minstrel performers in Britain. Their own concerns are also clearly, if indirectly, expressed in this letter—that a middle-class audience will not attend a stand-alone evening of their performances, even once, because of the potential for impropriety. The minstrel show as a separate business model could not surprise its audience at the saloon or as an entr'acte of a play; a testimonial such as this advocated for an initial trial, at which point the proof would have to be in the performance—whatever that performance may have become.

On the face of it, the Ethiopian Serenaders exhibited the basic traits of the genre. Songs were sung in dialect, imitations of the sounds of the city were created, sometimes with every instrument and a kind of whole-body playing and dancing at once. A popular feature was the "celebrated railroad overture" in which all instruments imitated what was then a new technology. G. W. Pell, in particular, the much-praised star of the troupe, embodied the popular traditions of minstrelsy as the (clearly) out-of-control clown, with a huge collar and bow, a frantic manner, bad jokes, and an extraordinary skill at percussion. But the changes from its working-class and street culture were apparent. Instead of a saloon, or as part of the bill of a theatre, the Serenaders booked the St James, a concert hall, where they played in repertory with a French-language theatre company, amateur theatricals, and classical concerts. By association, they were another alternative but respectable performance idiom, exotic but only slightly suspect. Instead of the ragged or garish costumes of other minstrel troupes, the Serenaders dressed in formal wear, apparently starting what became a standard feature of the genre, emblazoned with a bright yellow waistcoat for a neat, if sporting, appearance (Pell seems to have been the exception to this change, adapting his new apparel to the needs of his clowning). Most important, however, was the singing. Reviews of their first appearances, of course, mention their humor and discuss the relative authenticity of their "delineations" of plantation slaves, but the surprise to the critics was the high skill of the harmonies they presented at the St James.[16] This is not to say that other minstrels, performing for other types of audiences, did not sing in harmony; however, it seems clear that the Serenaders cast powerful voices in central roles, and highlighted multipart harmonies as a basic feature of the form. That this had not been a feature is evidenced by the fact that Pell—a child star of the minstrel stage, brother of one of the original Virginia Serenaders, and by this time an old hand (at twenty-one)—did not sing.[17] The troupe performed as a true concert, without burlesque afterpieces or other distractions. It was in some respects not like the minstrel troupes that came before or after; but this should not be surprising, considering its goal was to attract a new class of audience.

The Ethiopian Serenaders succeeded beyond their expectations. They remained in Britain, based at the St James, for nearly two years, playing a number of extended seasons for three nights each week, expanding their audience demographic the longer they stayed and the more familiar they became with the performance culture of the city. The clientele at their concerts included both women and men with social pretensions, but from a range of social positions. The Serenaders added weekly morning concerts for the benefit of children. They involved themselves with charitable fundraisers, exposing their work to the minor aristocracy, who paid attention; they subsequently performed at private functions (including a birthday celebration). Finally, in December of 1846, word having reached the Royal Court, they traveled to Arundel Castle outside of London for an evening's Royal Command Performance before Queen Victoria, Prince Albert, and the (now aged) Duke of Wellington; and they were subsequently invited in July of the following year to present a special concert to the Royal children at the St James.

This extraordinary achievement—for an entertainment that had only recently emerged out of American and British saloons and circuses—did not preclude performances further down the social scale. Although the Serenaders do not appear to have toured outside of London (itself an unusual decision, given touring practices of the time), they were not idle during their four dark nights each week; they traveled to the neighborhood theatres within easy striking distance, performing for audiences that no doubt could not have entered the St James.[18] Documentation is scarce, but I would argue that this troupe's conscious strategy was to perform for as many people in the city of London as was humanly possible. In an interview with journalist Henry Mayhew in the early 1850s, a lowly street minstrel born and bred in London emphasizes with pride that he learned his craft "from Pell at the St James."[19] It seems inconceivable that this individual would have entered that concert hall; I would instead argue that, as a matter of policy, Pell and his colleagues performed where such performers could see them, even in the local saloon (undocumented, of course). In effect, the tour established a pattern for the spectatorship of blackface minstrelsy as completely democratic, and therefore completely American. While this strategy may have had some nationalist ideology attached to it, as an entertainment for all people from a society that disdained class difference, the reasons were most likely economic. Having come from a society in which the populations were significantly smaller, there was a strong argument to be made not to specialize—American democratic taste was also good business. The net result, however, was to promulgate what was an entertainment that was clearly "set" in America and, through the character "delineation," the banjo, and the lyrics, establish an American "brand."

This first minstrel testimonial may have been most useful when the Ethiopian Serenaders first arrived in London; but it is striking that, otherwise, this and any other testimonials are absent from the promotional material. Certainly all submissions to the press—including copies of letters such as this one—constitute publicity, but in a broad survey of the advertisements for their appearance at the St James, which were repeated, regular, and ubiquitous, I have found only one paid advertisement where reference to this testimonial was included (in *John Bull*, January 17, 1846). It may be that a letter from America did not impress a British audience, even from the office of the President (whose celebrity status should not be assumed). It appears to have been valuable as leverage to convince this particular critic to attend a performance and to take it seriously; his subsequent review was glowing. It may also have been circulated privately, and even reached political and diplomatic circles, though this cannot be proven.

What is perhaps more surprising is that there is also no evidence that the Royal Command Performance, or other aristocratic appearances, were utilized in the troupe's advertising during this first, seminal run in London. The appeal of the Royal performance would seem to be obvious, certainly of greater value than a performance for the American President; the two made the same case for the appeal of minstrelsy across class, gender, and age—Pell famously made the dour Duke of Wellington laugh. There are a number of possible reasons for the absence of such a promotion. The most obvious is the general absence of testimonial advertising in London newspapers; it simply does not seem to have been a strategy at the time, perhaps for financial reasons.[20] But it is also pertinent that the troupe was not touring new cities and venues, had a long-standing performance commitment, and so perhaps did not need this kind of publicity. Perhaps a Royal Command performance, again because of the long-standing ties with the same urban culture over two years, was simply known by those who would be impressed and did not need to be broadcast. And, finally, perhaps such advertising would have had a negative effect on some portion of their intended, exceedingly broad audience. All of these are unproven, and the first explanation—that testimonials were not generally used for London newspaper advertising in 1846—seems the most credible. For whatever reasons, after the initial stimulus from America, the first Serenaders advertised (apparently) entirely through a constant round of performance, everywhere and to everyone.

Putting the "Boz" in "Juba": Testimonial Advertising and the Second London Appearance

The Ethiopian Serenaders returned to the United States late in 1847, appearing in the northeast briefly before disbanding.[21] G. W. Pell, however, reconstituted the troupe almost immediately, and returned to England in early June of 1848 with entirely different performers. Although it was in fact a new troupe, because all performers were in character and "blacked up" in any case, audiences would almost certainly have taken the appearance of the "Ethiopian Serenaders" as the return of a well-known fixture of the community, and not of a new commodity. In contrast to that first tour, testimonials were used in an aggressive publicity campaign in 1848; and although that campaign made regular reference to the popular run at the St James, and invoked the performances for Queen Victoria and other members of the aristocracy, its overwhelming focus was on the one performer who could be clearly distinguished from the troupe's previous incarnation, "Boz's Juba." He was distinguished in part because his dance was from every account extraordinary and certainly new to audiences in Britain. But he was also distinguished because he was a performer of color, and was not in blackface, appearing with a troupe of white men in blackface, and in an otherwise segregated form. Whoever devised the publicity campaign for Juba and the Ethiopian Serenaders—whether Pell or Juba himself—it effectively capitalized on both characteristics through the judicious appropriation of eyewitness description.

First and foremost, from the moment "Juba" arrived in London his character and performance was attached to the name Boz, Charles Dickens' early pen name, and more specifically to a passage from his book *American Notes*. Dickens had toured New York City late in 1841, and in his record of this journey (a book for which he was maligned in America), he visited a dance house in the notorious slum, Five Points. He described a young dancer there as follows:

> Suddenly the lively hero dashes in to the rescue. Instantly the fiddler grins, and goes at it tooth and nail; there is new energy in the tambourine; new laughter in the dancers; new brightness in the very candles. Single shuffle, double shuffle, cut and crosscut; snapping his fingers, rolling his eyes, turning in this knees, presenting the backs of his legs in front, spinning about on his toes and heels like nothing but the man's fingers on the tambourine; dancing with two left legs, two right legs—two wooden legs, and two wire legs, two spring legs—all sorts of legs and no legs, what is that to him? And in what walk of life or dance of life, does man ever get such stimulating applause as thunders about him when, having danced his partner off her feet, and himself too, he finishes by leaping gloriously on the bar-counter, and calling for something to drink, with a chuckle of a million of counterfeit Jim Crows in one inimitable sound![22]

This description is a richly poetic and sentimental evocation of a joyful moment (and movement) in an otherwise harrowing account of life in the slums. The surrounding description upset New Yorkers: gothic depictions of tenements overcrowded with sleeping black bodies in pitch-blackness, of the notorious Tombs prison, and of pigs wandering the streets with abandon. Dickens was so clearly despondent during his tour of Five Points that the vivaciousness of one dancer during a brief respite in a basement dance house became, in his memorial to the event, a cause for celebration.

From the outset, the Ethiopian Serenaders featured by name "Boz's Juba" along with this quotation (which became a ubiquitous part of any announcement or review for the rest of this performer's career). As a testimonial, it is in most respects at odds with the "presidential" offering for the Serenaders' first tour. That letter was offered—or solicited—with the conscious intent of authorizing both the skill of artifice and the trust that can be placed in specific performers to be circumspect in what they perform. The Dickens testimonial by contrast was appropriated from an existing text without permission (and without any subsequent reference by the author. Indeed, whether out of ignorance or a lack of interest, Dickens seems not to have mentioned this widespread exploitation of these words to such financial purpose. Neither explanation is convincing, and his silence remains a mystery). The resulting, constructed testimonial validates the wild abandon of the performer, as well as the exhibition of natural—and not artificial—skill. It is a picture of exotic being, not of instructive decorum. And it is, perhaps most important, a nonspecific reference to the exuberance of a race, not to a named individual. Of course, the individual that arrived in London in 1848 may have been the same individual Dickens saw and described late in 1841. A performer named "Juba" certainly lived and worked in New York City during that period, and in that area of the city. He had been a child performer (as "Master Juba") in New York with and for P. T. Barnum, a "champion" competitive and theatrical dancer in the northeastern United States, and a popular performer on working-class American saloon, variety, and minstrel stages. But for the record, there is no concrete contemporary evidence that the two "bodies" were the same, and there is no association of the names Boz and Juba until the June 1848 arrival in London.

Although the truth of this association is of interest, it is in fact significant that we cannot be certain of the performer's identity.[23] By historical tradition the performer who arrived in London as "Boz's Juba" in 1848, and who danced in New York prior to this, was a man named William Henry Lane. However, there is no mention of this name in any advertising, reviews, or broadsides related to this figure for the Serenaders' tour—only his stage name was used. This contrasts with all other (white) performers in the early minstrel show, who went to great lengths to advertise their individual names, and their race (that is, that they were in fact "white"). In this respect these performers were advertising their own skill at the "delineation" of an original American type, and their own control over that delineation. "Juba" in America was not separated from his stage character in any way, however highly praised for his distinct skills as a dancer, and for his skill at parodying other dancers. He was "being" and not acting; and as "Boz's Juba" in Britain, he was further cast as a representative of his race, performing "the National Songs and Dances of his country" and "the dances of his own simple people on festive occasions."[24] Boz's description, too, was representative, and in the absence of other evidence, any young dancer of color coming to Britain might have made use of this description—if he could.

A testimonial from the pen of Dickens—however it was constructed—provided the strongest endorsement possible in Britain at this time. His was a powerful voice that spoke across class lines; any association attracted just the broad-based attention the minstrel troupe was after. This populist appeal suited their primary London venue, Vauxhall Gardens, the nature of which stands in many respects in stark contrast to the St James. Vauxhall was south of the Thames, reached by foot, carriage, and the earliest of train travel.[25] It was a large outdoor venue, with extensive tree-lined walks past arbors and cafes, and instrumental and vocal concerts. The London darkness arrives late in the summer, but artificial light was still provided, and at dusk there was a fireworks display. Such gardens had been a feature of London summer life for many years, though they had fallen on hard times more recently; Dickens himself (as "Boz") had written about the prospective sadness of such a place, in the cold light of day, in one of his early sketches.[26] This particular year, however, the manager (Wardell) had made a widely praised effort to return Vauxhall to something like a commercial and critical success, and most especially to draw from the widest possible cross-section of society for his patronage. He did this through discounted tickets for the working classes, and specially organized events for the aristocracy; and he appears to have succeeded. To some extent he attracted different audiences on different nights and to different parts of the garden; but to some extent, as was the tradition of such gardens in the summer, Vauxhall in 1848 did seem to provide a space where cultures mixed.[27]

Rain or shine—unfortunately for Mr. Wardell, it was a rainy summer—there was an indoor establishment called the Rotunda open to all patrons, either standing or sitting in prebooked boxes. The entertainment varied from year to year, but during the second half of the 1840s Wardell successfully turned it into a circus, presented in the round. The bill, which was advertised with times for each participant, included among others: Van Amburgh, a lion-tamer; Barry, a clown and acrobat; Mlle. Marie Macarte with a troupe of Equestrians, in a display of acrobatic horsemanship; and the Ethiopian Serenaders. On the face of it, the context of performance appears to return Pell and his troupe to their roots in a rougher performance culture, the circus, just one of a number of acts on a bill rather than a stand-alone entertainment form, surrounded by the smells and other distractions that come from sharing a stage with animals. But, in fact, Vauxhall Gardens allowed the Serenaders to perform to a wide range of class cultures, from a working clientele with some leisure money, to the minor aristocracy, slumming though they might have been. It allowed for performances at special events for children, for dignitaries, and for women.[28] On the one hand, the roots of the Serenaders in American popular and folk forms would be exposed by the animals and acrobats that surrounded the Vauxhall performance; on the other hand, that context also reinforced the extent of the minstrel shows previous widespread exposure. It was now a distinct form, as well-known and popular as any other.

The description attached to Juba was so attractive to read, and to speak aloud, that it was reprinted repeatedly in newspapers across London, immediately extending the length of any press dedicated to Juba, and increasing his profile. The same was true in the simple listing of performers; since no such poetic evocation existed for Mr. Barry the clown (for example), his reference was slight compared with a performer who, while probably no more prominent on the bill, appeared to be the headliner by virtue of inches of copy.[29] Juba benefited greatly from this testimonial, and Pell benefited by association, for although Juba was frequently billed separately at Vauxhall, he was also clearly marked as part of the troupe.

The advertising campaign for this incarnation of the Serenaders did not end here, however. The quotation by Dickens appears to have been inspirational, and whether planned or not, reviews of Juba's dance themselves became uncommonly poetic. Some descriptions emphasized comparison with other dances, ranging from the Highland fling to Romantic ballet. Some emphasized a racialized national character. But overwhelmingly, descriptions emphasized the contradictory ideas that Juba's body was out of control (as noted, a common conceit of early minstrelsy), while his feet were nevertheless creating an entirely controlled percussion. One example follows:

> VAUXHALL GARDENS.—The instant focus of attraction is the Ethiopian Band of Serenaders, headed by the celebrated Pell, the Paganini of the bone castanets, who earned such loads of laurels at the St. James's Theatre, and a new comer who rejoices in the name of Juba, a genuine nigger. He is quite a youth, with a joyous expression of features, and sings the nigger songs with a rich gusto not to be imagined by those who have not heard him. His volubility is astounding, and his perfect enjoyment of his own efforts is quite delicious. He trills, he shakes, he screams, he laughs, as though by the very genius of African melody. He would be the Mario and Lablache of a negro opera-house at Timbuctoo. But his dancing cast into the shade all

> previous choreographic efforts. St. Vitus was a mere figurant compared to Juba. His limbs seems to be formed of catouchouc [*sic*] slightly diluted with gutta percha [note: caoutchouc and gutta percha are forms of rubber]—hence his elasticity and *aplomb*. Neither the great nor little Vestris, nor St. Leon, nor Perrot, may be compared with Juba. His pedal execution is a thing to wonder at, if his flexibility of muscle did not confound us. He jumps, he capers, he crosses his legs, he stamps his heels, he dances on his knees, on his ankles, he ties his limbs into double knots, and untwists them as one might a skein of silk, and all these marvels are done in strict time and appropriate rhythm—each note has its correspondent step and action. Now he languishes, now burns, now love seems to sway his motions, and anon rage seems to impel his steps. Juba's plantation dance is a sort of terpsichorean illustration of Collins's "Ode on the Passions." One feat which he achieves with his feet excites our especial wonder: he absolutely dances with one foot on the ground and the other never off it. Everybody should go and see Juba.[30]

Much has been made of such descriptions in recent years in an effort to argue that Juba's dance was so difficult to describe, and so seemingly exotic to these eyewitnesses, because it had deep roots in an African aesthetic.[31] That may be, but for this discussion it is more important that the conceit of these writers—following closely that of Dickens—portrayed a dance both indescribable and inspirational. The use of the Dickens quotation stimulated what was, in effect if not in intent, a creative writing contest among critics, multiplying the number of descriptions that the troupe might appropriate as endorsements. This is the source for the souvenir Silk that, I suggest, is an early version of the press kit, and an early appropriation of the review-as-testimonial.

TESTIMONIAL *IN EXTREMIS*: THE NORTHERN TOUR

Pell, Juba, and the Ethiopian Serenaders left London in the Fall of 1848 for a tour that took them to many large- and medium-sized urban centers in the Midlands, the northern industrial regions around Sheffield and Manchester, and into Scotland; with a brief return to London, they were on the road until the summer of 1850. A review of the periodicals in a number of these cities shows quite clearly that the troupe not only continued their testimonial advertising campaign, but also intensified it. Their appearance in Stirling, Scotland, can serve as an example. The *Stirling Observer*'s anticipatory article about their appearance (August 30, 1849) quotes the Dickens description in full. In addition, the paid advertisement in the same issue invokes the Royal Command Performance of the previous tour, promising "several celebrated pieces, as sung before her Majesty Queen Victoria, Prince

Albert, and Suite, at Arundel Castle." The same advertisement includes the following:

> The following Note has been sent by order of his Grace the Duke of Devonshire, to G. W. Pell, (the original bones) from America:—
>
> Devonshire-house, Piccadilly, London, December 22, 1848.
>
> Dear Sir,—I am directed by his Grace the Duke of Devonshire to inform you how much pleased himself and Friends were by the performance of yourself and Company at his House, and also at your public concert. I am glad, also, of this opportunity to add my testimony to the excellence of your amusing and harmonious entertainment. Wishing you success in your tour, dear Sir, yours very faithfully,
>
> Charles Coote, Pianist to his Grace.

These testimonials span two tours and an almost complete change of personnel, and represent a departure from the London appearance, which seldom distracted attention from the description by Dickens. Attracting an audience on the road requires greater effort, however; if one testimonial fails, another might succeed. In addition, a writer in the *Sterling Journal and Advertiser* (August 31, 1849), reviewing what seems to have been a press performance, includes the following:

> Do you wish to be brought into a merry mood, to riot in fun and laughter? Then go and see Juba. Do you love to indulge in a melancholy train of thought? Then place fifty miles between you and Juba—for even the most excruciating twinge of demoniac gout itself could not raise upon the face of one of its greatest and most irritable martyrs the slightest symptom of a painful contortion, while he remained within the sphere of the laughter-laden atmosphere with which Juba surrounds himself. The *Morning Post* says of him....

The writer then prints—in full, at length, in a smaller font than his own words—the description quoted above from the London newspaper. This raises the number of testimonials to members of the Ethiopian Serenaders in Stirling to five, prior to the run. It also continues what now clearly appears to have been a deliberate campaign to encourage writers to out-Dickens Dickens, by providing the local press with the London reviews. In general the local reviewers did not acknowledge this provision, but (by way of corroboration) the *Perthshire Constitutional* (September 12, 1849) quotes a different London paper with this admonition: "...we candidly assure our readers we have selected it as being the least rapturous in its admiration...." He had a selection from which to choose, which could only have come from the minstrels themselves. The evidence suggests, then, that the Ethiopian

Serenaders aggressively distributed press clippings as they traveled, and that these clippings continued what had become a campaign inviting people to attempt to describe the indescribable Juba. This provided more press devoted to this tour than is evident in other touring variety performers during the same period, certainly far more than for any other minstrel performers of the time. It also provided, not only from London but from Sheffield, Manchester, Liverpool, and elsewhere, an extraordinary body of writing about dance.

Unpacking the Silk: Middle-Class Decorum and the Suppression of Playful Typography

First of all, based on the documentation presented here, I suggest that what is printed on the silk souvenir is a one-page compilation of reviews created by the Ethiopian Serenaders as part of their testimonial-based British advertising campaign. It includes all London reviews later mentioned in provincial papers, and many more besides. If printed on paper, a page of this size could easily be carried in bulk for distribution to local reviewers. Alternatively, a silk souvenir itself might have been the means by which the reviews were distributed to the press; there is no way of knowing, though the greater expense of the silk argues against the prospect. Either way, the production of a silk version of these reviews for distribution to spectators at Vauxhall is not unreasonable, if we consider the spectator as another participant in this campaign. The reviewers, in their poetic incapacity to describe the dance adequately, repeatedly admonish spectators to see for themselves and, by extension, attempt the description. In effect, so does the silk.

This does not, however, entirely explain the appearance of the silk, but only the content. For reviewers, it would be of no consequence how the page was constructed visually; economy of production and a desire to ensure a maximum number of reviews on one page would be the sole criteria. It may be that, with a page already composed in this way, it was simply an inexpensive way to produce a souvenir, its dull appearance only a byproduct of its original purpose. It might also be argued that its visual presentation is both deliberate and persuasive; it impresses upon anyone who views it—whether on silk or paper—the number and range of positive responses to Juba's dance (it even includes a review in German). It thus attests to the broad popularity of minstrel performance. But I believe there is more to its design.

Although newspapers in Britain at this time still generally printed as many words to a page as possible, in a six- or seven-column structure, there were alternatives. If a press sheet, or a hastily produced printed newspaper, required a uniform and efficient presentation, a silk souvenir had other models in the popular print and playbill, both of which were well established

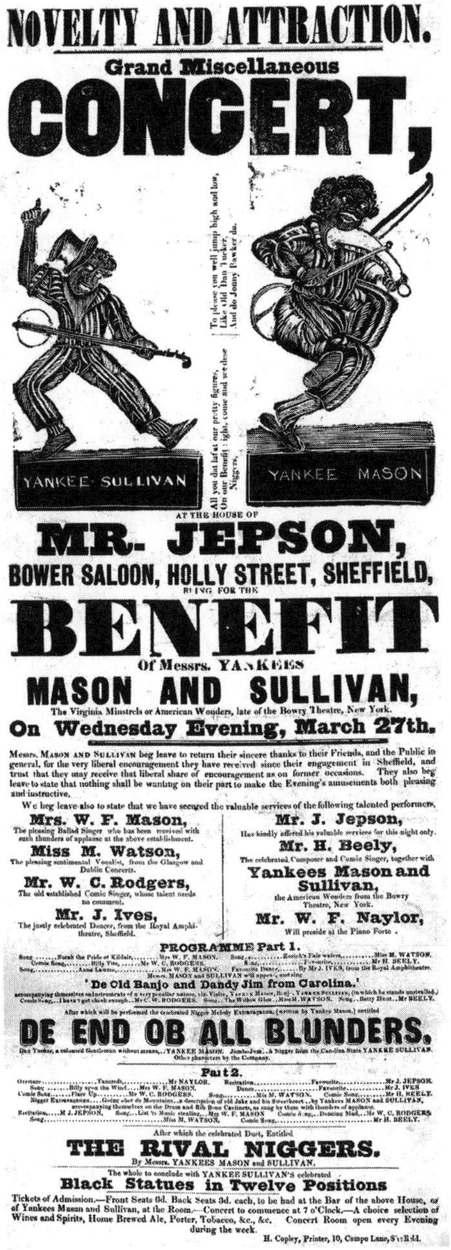

NOVELTY AND ATTRACTION.

Grand Miscellaneous

CONCERT,

All you dat lafat our pretty figures,
On our Benefit night, come and we dese
Niggers,
To please you well jump high and low,
Like old Dan Tucker,
And do Jonny Fawker do.

YANKEE SULLIVAN

YANKEE MASON

AT THE HOUSE OF

MR. JEPSON,

BOWER SALOON, HOLLY STREET, SHEFFIELD,

BEING FOR THE

BENEFIT

Of Messrs. YANKEES

MASON AND SULLIVAN,

The Virginia Minstrels or American Wonders, late of the Bowry Theatre, New York.

On Wednesday Evening, March 27th.

Messrs. MASON AND SULLIVAN beg leave to return their sincere thanks to their Friends, and the Public in general, for the very liberal encouragement they have received since their engagement in Sheffield, and trust that they may receive that liberal share of encouragement as on former occasions. They also beg leave to state that nothing shall be wanting on their part to make the Evening's amusements both pleasing and instructive.

We beg leave also to state that we have secured the valuable services of the following talented performers,

Mrs. W. F. Mason,
The pleasing Ballad Singer who has been received with such thunders of applause at the above establishment.

Miss M. Watson,
The pleasing sentimental Vocalist, from the Glasgow and Dublin Concerts.

Mr. W. C. Rodgers,
The old established Comic Singer, whose talent needs no comment.

Mr. J. Ives,
The justly celebrated Dancer, from the Royal Amphitheatre, Sheffield.

Mr. J. Jepson,
Has kindly offered his valuable services for this night only.

Mr. H. Beely,
The celebrated Composer and Comic Singer, together with

Yankees Mason and Sullivan,
the American Wonders from the Bowry Theatre, New York.

Mr. W. F. Naylor,
Will preside at the Piano Forte.

PROGRAMME Part 1.

Song........Norah the Pride of Kildair,..........Mrs W. F. MASON. Song..........Zorick's Fair waters,..........Miss M. WATSON.
Comic Song,..........Billy Vite,.......Mr W. C. RODGERS. Song..........Favourite,..........Mr H. BEELY.
Song,..........Anne Lawrie,..........Mrs W. F. MASON. Favourite Dance,......By Mr J. IVES, from the Royal Amphitheatre.
Messrs. MASON and SULLIVAN will appear, and sing

'De Old Banjo and Dandy Jim from Carolina.'

accompanying themselves on instruments of a very peculiar nature, viz. Violin, YANKEE MASON, Banjo, YANKEE SULLIVAN, (in which he stands unrivalled.)
Comic Song,..I havn't got cheek enough..Mr C. W. RODGERS. Song..The Willow Glen..Miss M. WATSON. Song..Betty Hunt..Mr BEELY.

After which will be performed the celebrated Nigger Melody Extravaganza, (written by Yankee Mason,) entitled

DE END OB ALL BLUNDERS.

Dan Tucker, a coloured Gentleman without means,..YANKEE MASON. Jumbo Jum..A Nigger from the Carolina State YANKEE SULLIVAN.
Other characters by the Company.

Part 2.

Overture..........Tancredi,..........Mr NAYLOR. Recitation..........Favourite,..........Mr J. JEPSON.
Song........Billy upon the Wind....Mrs W. F. MASON. Dance..........Favourite..........Mr J. IVES
Comic Song......Flare Up..........Mr W. C. RODGERS. Song..........Miss M. WATSON. Comic Song..........Mr H. BEELY.
Nigger Extravaganza....Going ober de Mountains,..a description of old Jake and his Sweetheart,..by Yankees MASON and SULLIVAN, accompanying themselves on the Drum and Rib Bone Castinets, as sung by them with thunders of applause.
Recitation,....M J. JEPSON, Song...List 'n Music stealing,..Mrs W. F. MASON Comic Song,..Dancing Mad,..Mr W. C. RODGERS
Song..........Miss M. WATSON, Comic Song,..........Mr H. BEELY.

After which the celebrated Duet, Entitled

THE RIVAL NIGGERS.

By Messrs. YANKEES MASON and SULLIVAN.

The whole to conclude with YANKEE SULLIVAN'S celebrated

Black Statues in Twelve Positions

Tickets of Admission.—Front Seats 6d. Back Seats 3d. each, to be had at the Bar of the above House, or of Yankees Mason and Sullivan, at the Room.—Concert to commence at 7 o'Clock.—A choice selection of Wines and Spirits, Home Brewed Ale, Porter, Tobacco, &c., &c. Concert Room open every Evening during the week.

H. Copley, Printer, 10, Campo Lane, Sheffield.

Figure 1.2 A playbill printed in Sheffield in the mid-1840s for a performance by a minstrel troupe at a saloon.

Source: Courtesy Central Reference Library, Sheffield, UK.

by the late 1840s.[32] The choice that had to be made, whether deliberate or not, can be best illustrated by two contrasting documents.

The first document is a playbill printed in Sheffield in the mid-1840s, prior to the appearance of the Ethiopian Serenaders, for a performance by a minstrel troupe at a saloon (figure 1.2). Its visual appearance, in my opinion, reflects the chaos of working-class minstrelsy. I count at least ten different kinds of type; some of the print runs vertically, and the line width is only occasionally justified. The imagery consists of crude woodcuts, which evoke movement surprisingly well, particularly in the twisted body of the right-hand figure. The clown-like costuming and primitive instruments (including an actual jawbone) are more prominent than the racial imperative of the blackface makeup. While certainly present in the print, race is depicted in the same way as the crosshatching of the costume and the soles of the feet, emphasizing its artificiality. The print emphasizes the ongoing relationship between performers and spectators based on past performances in Sheffield, as well as the twin sources of their appeal, hard work and an American culture. The bill explodes with the promise of entertainment. It is busy, playful, overloaded with information, with a view toward eye-catching display, and possibly appealing as a souvenir.

Many playbills from this period are similarly chaotic, and minstrelsy in particular, with its roots in that most itinerant of entertainments, the circus, pioneered the aggressive use of the street poster to create suspense.[33] There is some indication that the Ethiopian Serenaders did not abandon this tradition as they toured. The reviewer from Stirling seemed genuinely impressed with this additional arm of the advertising campaign, as well as surprised:

> WHO IS JUBA?—On Tuesday morning many of the inhabitants were not a little surprised to see huge placards upon the walls, with the mysterious announcement—"Juba, the world's wonder, will shortly arrive in town." Immediately the question arose, "Who is Juba?" No one could tell; there was the monster placard, but who or what the cabalistic letters "JUBA" signified all were alike ignorant. Was Juba a man or a woman, a beast or a bird, a fish or a reptile; or had some mischievous "printer's de'il" invented the words merely to terrify the inhabitants by the anticipation of some coming evil? No one could say. (*Stirling Observer* August 30, 1849)

The poster is consistent with the traditions of the show business already associated with Barnum, who, as noted, had only recently toured in Britain. There are hints of its possibly garish, chaotic visual appearance embedded in the description above, as well as in other provincial reviews:

> BOZ'S JUBA. JUBA, the inimitable Juba!—JUBA immortalized by Boz!—JUBA, the best Dancer living!—JUBA, the greatest wonder in the

> world!—JUBA as "Miss Lucy Long," (Original-in Character.)—JUBA in "Jenny, put the Kittle on"—JUBA in "Way down South"—JUBA in "Marriage Festival Dance"—JUBA in "Plantation Dance" [pointing finger] Juba is a perfect phenomenon, a genuine Son of the Southern clime, who will introduce the NATIONAL SONGS and DANCES of his country. . . . (*Sheffield and Rotherham Independent* October 28, 1848)

It is possible to imagine this text laid out in the manner of the Sheffield playbill. It is an appeal to an audience that did not read newspapers, consistent with early minstrelsy's attempt to attract the full range of patrons. It is also consistent with the other advertising strategies for this tour; indeed, the mystery promoted by the Stirling poster complements the testimonials, which are generally beside themselves with their delight in the mystery of the performance. This was an alternative model the Serenaders could, and to some extent did, use in their search for patronage. But it does not appear to have been their dominant strategy.

The second document is an image of the first Ethiopian Serenaders, taken from a sheet music cover, but reproduced in a number of contexts. I find three elements striking, in contrast to the Sheffield playbill. First of all, the costuming has been normalized and naturalized, to the point where the performers might walk out of the theatre and onto the street (or more likely, into a parlor as a house servant). The faces have likewise been naturalized, which means they have been racialized, so that there is no question of considering the artificiality of the performance. And finally—the slightly melancholic poses of the endmen notwithstanding—almost all sense of movement has been eliminated from the image. These are in no way bodies out of control, nor are they indescribable. This image might easily be paired with an extant playbill from their appearance at the St James, which uses no more than three styles of font, is completely formal and symmetrical in composition, has no sense of playfulness, and no imagery. Such documents are not designed to encourage a roving eye, or reexamination. They are designed to emphasize impersonation and decorum. Implicit in this image is the effort by minstrelsy to pitch itself to a sentimental, respectable patron, not as a troupe of wild circus clowns but as an authentic re-creation of an exotic culture. As such, minstrelsy was no different in its pedagogical efforts from the exhibitions of other cultures previously mentioned—Bedouin Arabs, Kaffir Zulus, Bushmen, Maori, among others—with which it so often shared advertising space in the newspapers.[34] However much middle-class audiences laughed once they were in the theatre, it was not laughter that justified their attendance. Curiosity fuelled their visits, of course, but this was justified by the promise of self-improvement and moral uplift.[35]

Conclusion: Writing as Seeing

Testimonials might be used as the authorization to attend a performance, and as the validation for that performance; they can excite potential patrons by passionate admonition, and they can calm moral and emotional fears with the promise that the performance will not offend or hurt.[36] In this case, I can draw a complex set of conclusions, fitting for a complex form of entertainment. The testimonials respecting Juba based on the Dickens description created a kind of contest among critics to match the description; the silk in effect invites the reader to attend the performance and do the same. This is an inclusive, antiauthoritarian use of the testimonial. It is even possible to argue, beyond this invitation, that there is an irony in the invitation, since the descriptions conspire against the very possibility of accurate description. Advertisements are, after all, not records of reception; it may be that audiences attended a minstrel performance, watched Juba, and felt either cheated or, more likely, contentedly entertained but not in the way they had thought (*pace* Barnum).

Writing, however, is a way of thinking, and the emphasis on print in this case focuses attention on the potential, at least, of accurate description. The frequent admonition of the failure of language in these reviews may be subversive, in a way; but the reviews themselves by their number advocate writing, and the description of performance through words, as a way of seeing performance. A potential spectator attends the performance, review in hand, in order to attempt a description. It is a rational and controlled response that fits well with the pedagogical imperative of the middle class, the interest in the exotic exhibition, and the categorizations of Victorian ethnography. The formal visual structure and the emphasis on text in the advertisements for these patrons argue more for this un-ironic, un-playful response. There is no wild abandon here, though there is, for the historian, a welcome increase in the number of valuable documents that make the attempt to capture the event.[37]

Two brief responses to the Ethiopian Serenaders reinforce the complex field of audience responses with which the minstrel men had to contend. The first is from the industrial town of Huddersfield: "The performances of Boz's Juba have created quite a sensation in the gallery, who greeted his marvellous feats of dancing with thunders of applause and a standing encore."[38] The second is from a performance for a middle-class audience in Manchester: "many were the handkerchiefs employed to conceal the smothered laughter of their fair owners."[39] The "gallery crowd" of Huddersfield responded to the minstrel performance with a whole-body percussive participation. The "fair" spectators of the middle-class venue required an intermediary between themselves and the minstrels.

It was a handkerchief, perhaps made of silk.

NOTES

1. Crucial research for this project was conducted by Diana Manole and Birgit Schreyer. For further information on early blackface minstrelsy in Britain, and the documentation and results of a research project on the subject, see The Juba Project at www.utm.utoronto.ca/~w3minstr/
2. The Vauxhall Silk was purchased for the New York Public Library's Dance Collection in 1991. It is 18.5 inches across and 24.4 inches tall, mounted on an acid-free board with an additional 0.5 to 0.75 inches attached to the verso. Traces of fringe can be seen on the verso top and bottom. There are water stains on the front lower right and left, a brown stain (paint?) in the lower middle. The four corners have a floral filigree with traces of gold-leaf, and in the middle of the two side borders are small portraits of Queen Victoria and Prince Albert. The top and bottom middle borders have royal symbols (lion and unicorn, crown), as befits the venue, the "Royal" Vauxhall Gardens, though this designation was as spurious then as it is now. The printing on the silk is in columns 3.5 inches wide and 18 inches in length. The print appears to be from a press, but individual letters are surprisingly well defined under magnification.
3. The Billy Rose Theatre Collection in the New York Public Library has a good collection of silk programs and broadsides. I examined an array of examples from 1811 (a private theatrical by the Marquis of Bradford) to 1971 (for *Fiddler on the Roof*). Most celebrate a specific number of performances (100), a singular performance, a charity benefit, or a benefit for an individual performer. Among the differences between these examples and the Vauxhall Silk is that it appears not to refer to a specific date. Silk programs can be found in most theatre collections, though not typically in large numbers.
4. For information on the use of type during this period, see Patricia Anderson, *The Printed Image and the Transformation of Popular Culture, 1790–1860* (Oxford: Clarendon Press, 1991). Although a playfulness in typesetting and use of illustration was not widespread in newspaper culture, it was available. Both were standard in posted performance bills and can be found in other extant silk souvenirs in the Billy Rose Theatre Collection, and in the Museum of the City of New York, for example.
5. See, for example, Giovanni Levi, "On Microhistory," in *New Perspectives on Historical Writing*, ed. Peter Burke (Cambridge: Polity, 1991), 93–113; and Carlo Ginzburg, "Microhistory: Two or Three Things That I Know About It," *Critical Inquiry* 20, 1 (Autumn, 1993): 10–35.
6. Blackface as a theatrical convention was still in use on American and British television in the 1960s. From personal experience, I know that service clubs in North America still used the form as a feature of fund-raising events in the 1980s.
7. The Hutchinson Family was an American concert troupe that, while advertising its cultural origins, performed a range of skilled vocal harmonies. The *Court Gazette and Fashionable Guide*, February 14, 1846, advertises the Hutchinsons and the Ethiopian Serenaders contiguously, clearly meant as comparative American performances.

The history of early minstrelsy has been written with enthusiasm almost from its inception. T. Allston Brown published what amounts to a (surprisingly accurate) documentary history in the *New York Clipper* in an 1876 series, revised and expanded in 1912. An abundance of newspaper articles can be found in files and scrapbooks in the New York Public Library and the Harvard Theatre Collection, among other archives; by their existence and content, it appears that minstrelsy had a strongly loyal and long-lived fan base, which was keenly interested in the origin of the genre, and its change over time. For later narrative histories, see Carl Wittke, *Tambo and Bones: A History of the American Minstrel Stage* (Durham: Duke University Press, 1930); Harry Reynolds, *Minstrel Memories: The Story of Burnt Cork Minstrelsy in Great Britain from 1836 to 1927* (London: A. Rivers, 1928); Edward Leroy Rice, *Monarchs of Minstrelsy, from "Daddy" Rice to Date* (New York: Kenny Pub. Co. [c1911]); and especially Hans Nathan, *Dan Emmett and the Rise of Early Negro Minstrelsy* (Norman, OK: University of Oklahoma Press, 1962); and Robert C. Toll, *Blacking Up: The Minstrel Show in Nineteenth Century America* (New York: Oxford University Press, 1974).

8. Eric Lott's *Love and Theft : Blackface Minstrelsy and the American Working Class* (New York: Oxford University Press, 1993) examines the complex psychology and politics of that first, working-class audience; Dale Cockrell's *Demons of Disorder: Early Blackface Minstrels and their World* (New York: Cambridge University Press, 1997) and William Mahar's *Behind the Burnt Cork Mask: Early Blackface Minstrelsy and Antebellum American Popular Culture* (Urbana: University of Illinois Press, 1999) examine its roots in folk and popular tradition, and its transition into a commercial form; W. T. Lhamon's *Raising Cain: Blackface Performance from Jim Crow to Hip Hop* (Cambridge, MA: Harvard University Press, 1998) explores the genre's long-term legacy. A range of periodical literature also exists in what has been a rich field of research over the past fifteen years.
9. Aside from the works already noted, Robert B. Winans' work particularly explores the shift in audience through the corresponding shift in song repertory during this crucial first ten years. See Winans, "Early Minstrel Show Music, 1843–1852," in *Inside the Minstrel Mask: Readings in Nineteenth-Century Blackface Minstrelsy*, ed. Bean, Annemarie, James V. Hatch, and Brooks McNamara (Hanover, NH: Wesleyan University Press, 1996).

I use the plural of class in all instances, in an effort to avoid the tendency to simplify this complex word, as if easily defined, monolithic, homogeneous, and discrete. Individuals are members of a range of cultures and subcultures, some of which may be defined through class. See, with respect to this study: Hugh Cunningham's *Leisure in the Industrial Revolution, c. 1780– c. 1880* (London: Croom Helm, 1980), which outlines three popular cultures expressing hedonism, methodism, and radicalism, 37–41; Bluford Adams' *E Pluribus Barnum: The Great Showman and the Making of U.S. Popular Culture* (Minneapolis: U of Minnesota Press, 1997), which follows Barnum's tactics for appealing to and manipulating a cross-class culture of "respectability"; and Karen Halttunen's *Confidence Men and Painted Women: A Study of*

Middle-class Culture in America (New Haven: Yale University Press, 1982), which explores with elegance the phenomenon of the middle classes as a culture "in social motion" (29). These arguments inform this study.

10. I am indebted specifically to Michael Sappol's work on the nineteenth-century anatomical museum for the idea of the minstrel as a body out of control in a society for which this was both captivating and troublesome. He in turn cites Eric Lott's work. See Sappol, *A Traffic in Dead Bodies: Anatomy and Embodied Social Identity in Nineteenth-Century America* (Princeton: Princeton University Press, 2002).
11. Adams assesses Barnum's rise through the "classes" of America through his writing. See Adams, *E Pluribus Barnum,* esp. xiii, 11 (on his letters from Britain to the *New York Atlas*); 16 (on his own increased "respectability" in New York society after his British tour); 76 (on a "respectable" culture that crossed class lines); and 94 (on the sometimes vulgar tastes of the so-called middle class). Bruce McConachie also discusses Barnum's relationship with class and audience in "Pacifying American Theatrical Audiences, 1820–1900," in *For Fun and Profit: The Transformation of Leisure into Consumption*, ed. Richard Butsch (Philadelphia: Temple University Press, 1990), 47–70. The idea that audiences in America moved from integrated to segregated during the nineteenth century is argued in Lawrence W. Levine's perhaps too-simple, but still strong, argument in *Highbrow/Lowbrow: The emergence of cultural hierarchy in America* (Cambridge, MA: Harvard University Press, 1988).
12. See Nathan, *Dan Emmett and the Rise of Early Negro Minstrelsy* on Emmett, one of the original Virginia Serenaders. This information exists as well in a range of fugitive clippings in the New York Public Library and the Harvard Theatre Collection. For an example of the reference to a "glut" of minstrels, see *John Bull* (October 24, 1846): "So many things of this kind have been brought forward lately, by Henry Russell, the Hutchinson Family, the Ethiopean Serenaders, and we do not know how many others, that they are getting quite stale; and any further attempt of the sort must have some wholly new features in order to become attractive."
13. The members of the first Ethiopian Serenaders were Frank Germon, Moody Stanwood, George Harrington, Gilbert Pell, and William White. James A. Dumbolton was the "agent," though his relationship with the troupe is unclear, since Pell was clearly the most prominent member, and Germon seemed to handle the press. See *New York Clipper* (March 30, 1912).
14. *Morning Chronicle* (January 20, 1846).
15. See T. Allston Brown's "Early History of Negro Minstrelsy: It's Rise and Progress in the United States," in the *New York Clipper*, March 30, 1912, reporting that a group called "The Original Boston Serenaders," including some of the troupe later making their way to England as the Ethiopian Serenaders—George Harrington, Gilbert Ward Pell, Moody Stanwood, Frank Germon—performed for President Tyler early in 1844 as the "American Ethiopian Serenaders."
16. As examples: *The Court Gazette and Fashionable Times* (February 14, 1848), "In addition to their drolleries, they are vocalists of a very superior class,

and their sentimental effusions are given with the most delicate accuracy of expression—and the most perfect finish and effect…"; and *John Bull* (January 24, 1846), "We must confess, that we were by no means prepared for so rich and varied a musical treat; as we did not suppose the vocalists, or the instruments they employed, could have discoursed such eloquent music…."

17. See T. Allston Brown's "Early History of Negro Minstrelsy" series in the *New York Clipper*, especially (March 30, 1912). A full description of the talents of the original Ethiopian Serenaders exists in a fugitive clipping in the Harvard Theatre Collection, including the program for a performance for the Duke of Cambridge on February 24, 1846, as well as the statement that "Pelham, subsequently known as Pell, did not sing…."
18. A number of London newspapers were surveyed for this information, including the *Observer* and *John Bull*. See, for example, the *Observer* (May 16, 1847) for reference to regular morning concerts, to private performances, and a more self-serving reference to the "vulgar imitations" of other blackface minstrels. See the *New York Clipper* (October 7, 1876) for a reprinted program of a performance by the Serenaders at the Duke of Devonshire's birthday party (May 30, 1846). See the *Observer* (June 27, 1846) for a review of the performance for the Royal children; and the same newspaper for (June 7, 1846) for their appearance at "The Horns, Kennington" on a dark night at the St James. Particularly telling is this report from *John Bull* (April 11, 1846) describing their appearance at a Covent Garden fundraiser: "…the royal Duke was so much pleased with them, that he sent to request them to repeat one of their pieces; and afterwards permitted them to sing in the more immediate presence of the ladies, where they were again encored." Their appearance at Arundel Castle for the Royal Family was in early December 1846.
19. From Henry Mayhew's *London Labour and the London Poor* v. 3 (London: Griffin, Bohn, 1862), 191: "I used to wear the yellow waistcoat, in imitation of them at the St. James's Theatre.… They first came out at the St. James's Theatre and they made a deal of money.… Pell's gang was at the top of the tree."
20. See Pamela Walker Laird, *Advertising Progress: American Business and the Rise of Consumer Marketing* (Baltimore and London: The Johns Hopkins University Press, 1998), 42–48, for reference to a dynamic print culture during these years; but it must be remembered that paper was expensive, the selling of advertising space relatively new, and newspaper printing formally conservative. See also Anderson, *The Printed Image and the Transformation of Popular Culture.*
21. When the original Ethiopian Serenaders returned to the United States, playbills trumpeted their performance for the Queen and their other successes. From the scant evidence, they were not financially successful, which must have been a great disappointment after their extraordinary popularity in Britain. There is no evidence as to why this happened, though there may have been a backlash against their more "polite" entertainment by working-class

audiences. In any event, dissension seems to have entered the troupe, which quickly split into two, identically named. One, with Dumbolton and Stanwood, continued in America, returning to England in 1849 (this tour will not be treated in this study).

22. This is the full quotation used in numerous publications, and can be found in Charles Dickens, *American Notes for General Circulation* (London; New York: Penguin, 2000), 91.
23. For the record, many other writers are convinced of this association, though in my opinion this results from reliance on a desire for a stronger biographical narrative by earlier historians. The most influential article about Juba's life is by Marian Hannah Winter, "Juba and American Minstrelsy," *Dance Index* 6, 2 (February 1947): 28–47, but this is based on a very few documents. Many more are now available for study. See www.utm.utoronto.ca/~w3minstr/
24. These quotations are indicative of a general tone, though from later in the tour: *Sheffield and Rotherham Independent* (October 28, 1848); *Manchester Guardian* (October 18, 1848).
25. It was only six minutes from Waterloo Station, according to the advertisement in the *Morning Chronicle* (July 17, 1848).
26. Charles Dickens, "Chapter XIV—Vauxhall Gardens by Day," in *Sketches by Boz and other early papers, 1833–1839*, ed. Michael Slater (Columbus: Ohio State University Press, 1994), 127–132.
27. Information on Vauxhall Gardens in the 1840s comes from a survey of London newspapers. See, particularly, the *Globe and Traveler* (June 2, 1846), and the *Morning Advertiser* (June 13 and 20, 1848), for descriptions. The *Morning Chronicle* (July 8, 1848) describes a fundraiser for the Distressed Needlewomen's Society, attended by the Lord Mayor and other dignitaries and aristocrats. The same paper reported, August 30, 1848 and September 4, 1848, discounted tickets and large attendance figures (6,000 and 20,000 respectively, though these cannot be trusted). Other information may be found in a dedicated file on the Vauxhall in the Harvard Theatre Collection. See also Warwick Wroth, *The London Pleasure Gardens of the Eighteenth Century* (New York: Macmillan, 1979 [London 1896]), and Jonathan Conlin, "Vauxhall Revisited: The Afterlife of a London Pleasure Garden, 1770–1859," *Journal of British Studies* 45 (October 2006): 718–743.
28. See the *Observer*, July 31, 1848, for an advertisement by the Vauxhall listing the range of Dukes, Lords, Marquises, and Viscounts who had visited that summer. The Garden was a mixed-gender venue, and although difficult to document, the popularity of minstrel sheet music in the middle-class British parlor suggests a sizable (and commercially significant) female audience for blackface minstrelsy. It is perhaps most telling that a print of Juba dancing in the *Illustrated London News* (August 5, 1848) includes a sketch portrait of his audience, and all of them are women.
29. An attempt is made in the *Observer* (August 6, 1848) to provide the same profile for Mlle Marie Macarte with a quotation from the American Press (the *Boston Democrat*), but it is a prosaic description of her career.

30. *Morning Post* (June 21, 1848).
31. See Robert Farris Thompson, "An Aesthetic of the Cool: West African Dance," in *The Theatre of Black Americans: A Collection of Critical Essays*, ed. Errol Hill (New York: Applause, 1980/1987), 99–111. Originally published in *African Forum*, 2, 2 (Fall 1966): 85–102. See also Brenda Dixon Gottschild, "First Premises of an Africanist Aesthetic," in *Digging the Africanist Presence in American Performance: Dance and Other Contexts* (Westport, CT: Greenwood Press, 1996).
32. See Anderson, *The Printed Image and the Transformation of Popular Culture*, on the illustrated playbill as "itself a minor form of entertainment." Other extant silk souvenirs replicate this kind of popular playbill.
33. T. Allston Brown in the *New York Clipper* (May 18, 1912): "From the days of Edwin P. Christy down to date the minstrel managers have been good advertisers. Christy, like some of the ambitious politicians, 'claimed everything in sight'; very naturally the early minstrel managers, shrewd and observant, patterned after the circus in the method of advertising, especially in poster billing and press work, and later on as to the street parade. To begin with, the pioneers of minstrelsy did not employ the posters to any great extent, for the reason that the placing of the pictures on the walls was limited, the billposting business still being in its infancy. The billposter was in most instances the janitor of the hall, and 'the hall' was bare of scene and the stage but little more than a platform."
34. For documentation on the exhibition of race and the exotic in this period, see Richard Altick, *The Shows of London* (London: Belknap Press, 1978). See also Edward Ziter, *The Orient on the Victorian Stage* (Cambridge: Cambridge University Press, 2003); and Hazel Waters, *Racism on the Victorian Stage* (Cambridge: Cambridge University Press, 2007), among a range of recent writing. More specifically, the *Morning Chronicle* (May 27, 1846) advertises the Ethiopian Serenaders in the same column as the exhibition of a Maori chieftain, and Scottish dwarves. The *Observer* (May 2, 1847) advertises the exhibition of South African Aborigines, or Bushmen. Such displays were numerous, and included, at least as advertised, a group of African Americans.
35. See Halttunen, *Confidence Men and Painted Women*, 101, concerning the need for a sentimental culture to control its own character, and emotion. Both Juba's exhibition of "being" and minstrelsy's (advertised) exceptional accuracy of imitation reinforced the possibility of authenticity.
36. See Roland Marchand *Advertising the American Dream: Making Way for Modernity, 1920–1940* (Berkeley, Los Angeles, and London: University of California Press, 1985), 96–99 on the uses and pitfalls of the testimonial.
37. For discussion of the ways in which print changes experience, see Michael Schudson, *Advertising: The Uneasy Persuasion: Its Dubious Impact on America Society* (New York: Basic Books, 1984), esp. 209; and Chandra Mukerji and Michael Schudson, eds., *Rethinking Popular Culture: Contemporary Perspectives in Cultural Studies* (Berkeley: U of California Press, 1991), 10. See, in particular, the work of Jack Goody, in *The Interface between the*

Written and the Oral (Cambridge: Cambridge University Press, 1987); also the work of Carlo Ginzberg, *The Cheese and the Worms: The Cosmos of a Sixteenth Century Miller* (Baltimore: Johns Hopkins University Press, 1980); and Peter Burke, *Popular Culture in Early Modern Europe* (New York: Harper and Row, 1978).

38. *Huddersfield Chronicle and West Yorkshire Advertiser* (November 30, 1850).
39. *Manchester Guardian* (October 18, 1848).

CHAPTER 2

THE TESTIFYING SUBJECT: RELIABILITY IN MARKETING, SCIENCE, AND LAW AT THE END OF THE AGE OF BARNUM

MICHAEL PETTIT

In his exposé of popular hoaxes and delusions, *Humbugs of the World* (1866), the showman P. T. Barnum related an incident that took place late into his tenure as owner of the American Museum. Barnum had acquired a white whale off the coast of Labrador and kept it in an immense water tank in the basement of his New York City museum. A "Yankee" woman, whom he suggested was a fairly typical attendee, simply refused to believe that the whale was real. Having heard of Barnum's reputation for humbuggery, she would not concede that the creature was a living organism, insisting instead that it was yet another mechanical contraption designed to deceive her. To give the woman satisfaction and a sense that she had gotten her money's worth, Barnum falsely admitted that the beast was in reality a machine; the woman left that day content with her superior abilities to detect deception. While recounting this event, Barnum speculated that one problem America faced was that its citizens were becoming too incredulous, too cynical. From Barnum's perspective, they succeeded in fooling themselves by believing in too little rather than accepting too much.[1]

Throughout the middle decades of the nineteenth century, Barnum had fashioned a public persona for himself as the prince of humbugs. He began his career in 1834 by exhibiting a woman named Joice Heth who regaled her audiences with fictitious recollections of having served as a young George Washington's enslaved nanny. In the following decades, Barnum made his fortune displaying such dubious objects as the Feejee Mermaid, in fact a monkey's torso carefully stitched onto the body of a fish, and the What Is It?, an African-American man cloaked in furs and presented as a potential missing link between humans and animals. Each of these "humbugs" called upon the audience members to decide the true nature of what was on display for themselves. Through these "struggles and triumphs," Barnum ultimately became a rich man by deferring epistemological authority, the right to judge and decide upon an object's true nature, onto his audience. The success of his amusements was contingent upon a vision of ordinary consumers as capable of assessing conflicting evidence and formulating true beliefs for themselves. During this "Age of Barnum," the consumer was conceptualized as a rather robust individual, in possession of keen sense perception that could successfully navigate the deceptive terrain of the marketplace.[2]

This essay examines if and how this Age of Barnum came to an end. It will trace changing notions of testimony in the arenas of marketing, the law, and the sciences to determine how these reflected a growing uneasiness with this understanding of a self-reliant commercial subject.[3] The rather uncommon dilemma of whether or not to believe that a white whale resided in a basement of a New York City museum during the mid-nineteenth century provides an entry point to consider the divergent ways that trust, certainty, and reliability are generated in American commercial culture. How can consumers be certain of the evidence and information provided to them by marketers and entrepreneurs? While puffery, imitation, and other forms of deception have been essential to the practice of marketing, they have had to be executed in a way that does not totally undermine the consumer's trust. Barnum's audience had been exposed to conflicting testimonials concerning his potentially deceptive exhibits for decades. Testimonial advertising came of age in an era when the credibility of eyewitness accounts was being questioned, not only in the realm of marketing but also in other areas where testimonials played a crucial role, namely, the courtroom and the laboratory. While a number of strategies were deployed to bolster the credibility of the testifying subject in each of these realms during the nineteenth century, such authority was constantly at risk of being dismissed, much like Barnum's sickly white whale.

To make better sense of the ways in which personal experience became a kind of evidence in advertising, it is helpful to contextualize this development within the wider framework of the history of testimony. While the testifying subject of advertising differed from those in the domains of science and law, they shared certain common features. One can see the Gilded Age and Progressive Era as periods acutely concerned with credulity.[4] In a number of areas of social life, people became acutely aware of humanity's potential both to deceive and be deceived. The new scientific discipline of psychology was largely built on the claim to be able to map and make legible these subjective aspects of human nature.[5] The vision of a subjective, unreliable self produced in psychology was reinforced by the omnipresence of various forms of deceptive and fraudulent practices in the commercial realm. This cultural concern with deception allows the historian to explore the negotiations that go into making and unmaking an authoritative, reliable witness.

SCIENCE, OBJECTIVITY, AND RELIABLE WITNESSES

A concern with the production of trust and the construction of authority within and across socio-professional boundaries has been at the heart of an important tradition in the sociology of knowledge. Although employing a wide range of case studies and methodological approaches, much of the research within science studies has focused on mechanisms for authenticating the reliability of the scientific observer's testimony. While the received view of science stresses its objectivity due to its universal methodology, scholars working in the sociology of knowledge have analyzed how the reception of scientific knowledge is frequently tied to subjective factors linked to its author's authority: the individual scientist's social and professional standing, the use of persuasive rhetoric, and strategies for enrolling other actors' knowledge or practices into endorsing one's claims.[6]

To be a credible scientific observer required certain forms of self-discipline and self-fashioning. Historians of science tend to locate the origins of the modern model of reliability in the natural philosopher Robert Boyle (1627–1691). Boyle was one of England's leading experimental philosophers during the Restoration and the most celebrated figure in the new Royal Society of the seventeenth century. Boyle faced the problem of how to communicate his knowledge across distances and convincing skeptical contemporaries that his experimental method was the proper way to extract the truth about nature. To do so required reproducing the experience of witnessing a specific experiment for those who could not be present, thus enabling them to replicate and authenticate his results while at the same time playing down the experimenter's agency in producing such results. Boyle encouraged advocates of the new natural philosophy to embrace the virtue of modesty in their writing and social interactions. As Steve Shapin and Simon Schaffer have argued, Boyle fashioned himself as "a moral model for experimental philosophers" through a prose style that was ascetic, flourish-free, and functional. Modesty was a necessary virtue in the new natural philosophy since it signaled to the audience that the experimentalist intended to let nature speak for itself in spite of his technological manipulations of it. Furthermore, modesty was to efface the particular circumstance of the experimentalist from the truth of nature contained in his report.[7] This gesture meant the reinscription of the traditionally female virtue of modesty onto the character of the masculine gentlemen of science. It was also to reinforce class distinctions, as the laboratory assistants who frequently performed the experiments, Boyle's servants, were erased from the text.[8] These strategies were employed to assure Boyle's readers that he was a gentleman of character whose words were to be trusted.

The sciences of the nineteenth century became increasingly uneasy with the testimony of lone, charismatic individuals. Quantification emerged as a powerful technology of trust since numbers were seen as interchangeable and could travel across political, institutional, and disciplinary boundaries. As Theodore Porter has argued, quantification has been adopted in professions that face opposition from powerful outsiders, as a means of abandoning an overreliance of expert judgment in the name of public standards.[9] Similarly, from the 1820s onward, the ideal of "mechanical objectivity" governed much scientific practice—investigators were to keep their individualized, idiosyncratic qualities in check, modeling their behavior on the regular rhythm of the machine. The lone romantic genius with his flashes of insight had no place in a scientific enterprise that linked a wide array of actors and objects in common projects.[10]

In sciences that rested on empirical fieldwork such as geology, natural history, and anthropology, the problem of reliable testimony was particularly acute. Unlike laboratory-based science where the environment could be largely controlled and experiments replicated, field sciences required close, detailed observation of distant places. The very empirical basis for these sciences depended upon the accuracy of these descriptions. These sciences frequently relied upon the knowledge, skills, and information of locals who did not possess the same technical expertise or social standing as esteemed, metropolitan scientists. In such instances, other means of ascertaining reliability were used. The witness's race was usually critically important, as was the appearance of not engaging in commerce. Once again, the virtue of modesty was highly valued; a reliable witness was someone who respected the research of others by not making claims within another's realm of specialty.[11]

While we have a rather detailed understanding of the evolution of the idealized scientific observer from the seventeenth century to the present day, the norms, values, and emotions linked to witnesses in other social arenas have yet to be fully examined.[12] Although rarely placed in dialogue, the work of historians of American consumer culture and advertising and scholars concerned with the historical epistemology of the sciences would benefit from examining each other's methods and findings. By studying the history of advertising and promotion, we can further broaden our perspective on the kinds of reliable witnesses that operate in the modern world.[13] By examining the history of marketing with the questions raised by these social studies of science, I will trace some of the alternative ways that trust has been constituted in the form of testimony. In contrast to the sciences, which increasingly turned toward mechanized means of securing reliability, in the commercial realm of testimonial advertising, personal judgment remained an important imperative. In spite of the rise of consumer research and product testing, the world of buying and spending demanded that consumers constantly evaluate and judge the competing claims of entrepreneurs.[14] By keeping in mind other endeavors, historians of science can rethink the narratives about their own particular testifying subjects.

Testimony of the Earth and of Men: The Cardiff Giant Hoax

A helpful starting point for thinking through the testifying subject that operated in the American marketplace is the important historiography of "character" and "personality." Following the lead of Warren Susman, historians have argued that selfhood in the twentieth century's consumption regime has been organized around the ideal of a dynamic, fluid personality. In contrast, "character" represents the kind of personhood embodied in the nineteenth-century world of Protestant thrift, industry, and temperance.[15] The testifying subjects examined in this section highlight some of the difficulties in understanding character and personality as strictly dichotomous. By investing authority in the words of a recognizable individual, testimonial advertising played an important role in the formation of the culture of personality; by emulating the fashion, one could remake oneself. While certainly those who proffered testimonials frequently were seen as morally dubious, for the advertisement to be successful their word had to be trusted. The very authority that their mere words carried was bolstered by the reliability proven by established moral character. In addition to a recognizable and charismatic personality, moral qualities such as modesty and decorum were key assets in marketing, science and the law in the guaranteeing of reliability. After all, salesmanship as a profession in the United States originated not only among traveling peddlers but also in the social world of evangelical revivals of the 1830s and their circulation and selling of printed Bibles. In such settings, selling functioned as a form a conversion where convincing others of one's personal character was paramount.[16]

Despite the fact that every audience member was supposed to decide the nature of the exhibit for themselves in Barnum's world, showmen would cultivate and circulate testimony clearly identified with notable individuals in order to frame the audience's debate by suggesting avenues for arguments. Among these authoritative witnesses, expertise was certainly an important criterion, but so was their locally determined character and celebrity. A readily recognizable person with an established reputation could do much to dissipate the connotations of fraud surrounding such spectacles and convince potential audience members that the exhibit was worth the price of admission.

How celebrity, expertise, and character went into the making of a reliable commercial witness can seen in an analysis of the promotional materials produced for the Cardiff Giant, a hoax exhibited toward the end of "the Age of Barnum." In October 1869, while supposedly digging for a well on his property, a farmer outside of Syracuse, New York, William "Stubbs" Newell, uncovered the remains of what appeared to be a ten-and-a-half-foot tall, petrified man. The giant was in fact a gypsum statue commissioned by Newell's brother-in-law, George Hull, in the hopes of making a profit while simultaneously exposing religious credulity. Hull's scheme succeeded as thousands of visitors swarmed to the farm, paying the fifty-cent viewing fee despite the protestations by certain skeptics that the object was a recent statue and hoax. Certain observers came to view the giant because of their conviction that it embodied physical evidence of the literal truth of biblical revelation, archaeological evidence of the giants who once roamed the earth. Some viewers thought it was a wholly natural curiosity or wonder. Some claimed it was an example of early Native American artwork. Others came to visit in order to figure out the trick behind the hoax for themselves. The spectatorship of the giant was a form of nineteenth-century consumption that combined religious experience and commercial tourism.[17]

Drawing on techniques mastered by Barnum, local promoters of the Cardiff Giant used testimonials from respectable and reliable local witnesses to advertise a natural wonder while rumors that it was a crude hoax continued to circulate around it. Publicity pamphlets such as *The American Goliah* (1869) [*sic*] and *The Onondaga Giant* (1869) offered a collage of eyewitness accounts cobbled together from newspaper reports and open letters to the public (figure 2.1).[18] Although the promoters emphasized that the exhibit was targeted toward a wide audience and that final judgments about the object needed to be suspended, not all testimony bore equal weight. Yet authority did not derive from scientific expertise or knowledge about natural history or geology but rather from the established character and reputation of locally recognizable personalities. Visitors could be assured that the body was worth visiting because William Newell, the local man who discovered

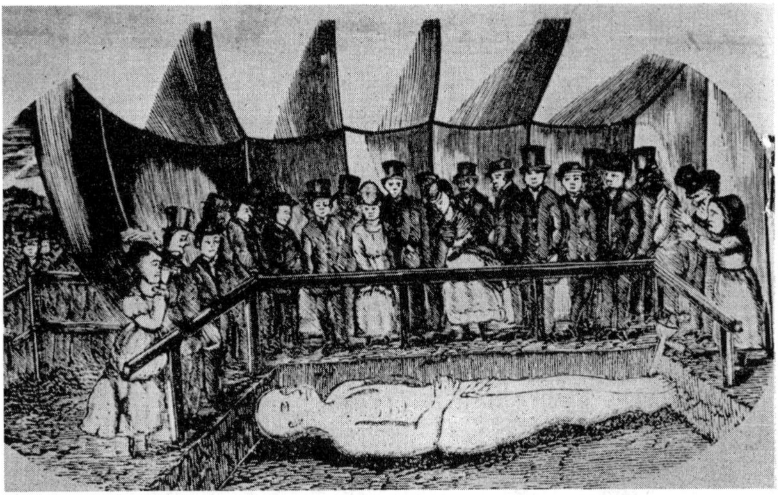

Figure 2.1 Woodcut from *The American Goliah: A Wonderful Geological Discovery*, 2nd edition (Syracuse: Redington and Howe, 1869). The image captures both the giant, fenced in and under a tent, and the audience that attended the exhibit. Present were women, children, men, gentlemen from the city, and local farmers. Many watch attentively while others seem to be more interested in discussing the wonder with others.

it, was known to be "a sober, industrious and worthy citizen," possessed of a strong character.[19] Such characteristics carried over to individuals initially asked to visit the giant, such as local temperance lecturer, John Clarke.[20] Their words could be trusted, not because they were members of an intellectual or aristocratic elite, but because they embodied good, republican virtues.

As these examples suggest, amusements like the Cardiff Giant operated within definitively policed moral boundaries and reinforced the middle-class culture of respectability. In his autobiographical writings, Barnum framed his life in the humbug trade with his commitment to temperance where he publicly testified to giving up the drink. Barnum scholars, like Steven Belletto, have highlighted the importance of various forms of contracts, from the temperance pledge to financial agreements to written contracts that aimed at convincing the reader that his life did not constitute risky speculation, but industrious work.[21]

The testimony of George Geddes highlights how individuals negotiated the difference between providing scientific evidence for and commercially endorsing the Cardiff Giant. The local press had cited Geddes, an expert in geology and agricultural science, as an early exponent of the theory that the giant was an ancient petrification. As a scientist, he was unwilling to publicly authenticate the object and took refuge in the mode of science's modest witness. He stated that he could not be certain of the object's true nature due to the fact that he was prevented from close inspection by a gate, the tent covering the body, and the surrounding audience. As a commercial spectator, he offered an entirely different evaluation. He stressed how the proprietors politely answered his inquiries and exuded a sense of transparency and trustworthiness. Geddes provided a hearty endorsement of the value of the ticket price: "I have traveled far and spent much money to see things of not one-tenth the interest that this stone giant was to me, and thought I made good use of time and money." Geddes remained unsure of the giant's natural status but he was convinced that the price of admission was well-spent and encouraged others to attend.[22]

To provide such commercial testimonials on the giant's behalf, the proprietors did not simply rely on the word of scientific experts. For example, in promotional materials, Elias Leavenworth, formerly the mayor of Syracuse and then Secretary of State for New York, also endorsed the object's value to potential visitors. At the point in *American Goliah* where the anonymous editor raises the specter of "is there any fraud or deception," Leavenworth's verdict is cited. The local politician is the person who reassures the reader and potential visitor that no one sincerely doubts the object's antiquity, despite considerable debate over its true nature.[23]

Although nineteenth-century spectacles allowed audience members to decide the truth of the matter for themselves in a supposedly open manner, those witnesses whose authority was cited by name adhered to a certain profile. They were prominent local men of some social standing whose words were bolstered either through professional status or public service. While publicity materials emphasized the number of women and children who attended the spectacle, testimonies from these audience members do not seem to have been solicited. When men such as Geddes or Leavenworth did speak on the giant's behalf, their testimony adhered to the norm of modesty closely bound to their moral character. Although reluctant to speak definitively on the giant's status as a natural object, these recognizable gentlemen could reassure the skeptical that, if nothing else, a visit to the exhibit was worth the cost of admission. By reserving judgment and avoiding grandiose claims, in fact, they bolstered their reliability as witnesses.

Less restrained local merchants used the "celebrity" generated around the Cardiff Giant to utilize the silent stone statue as a kind of testimonial for their own goods. The Syracuse Boot and Shoe Store claimed to display "the identical shoe and glove worn by his majesty long before the flood" and offered free admission to see such artifacts in an attempt to use the novelty of the giant to bolster their own sales.[24] Similarly, the proprietor of the giant "Baltimore Oysters" reminded readers that although scientists had yet to definitively authenticate the giant, his own museum artifacts were the genuine thing and available to see daily except Sundays. To attract the reader's eye, the advertisement was simply titled "The Onondaga Giant."[25] E. McDougall compared "the immense crowds that daily throng" to his shoe and boot emporium to the numbers attending the spectacle of the giant.[26] The increasingly regional and national celebrity of the giant offered an array of commercial opportunities for local residents who offered horse and carriage rides from the railway line to the site of the excavation for a dollar, and others who built restaurants there to cater to the needs of visitors.

By mid-December, after two months of avid public speculation and a series of scientific examinations by leading geologists and paleontologists, the giant's designer George Hull publicly confirmed that it was hoax. This exposure raised concerns about a commercial culture where reliability was grounded in character and reputation. The social standing of men such as Newell, Leavenforth, and Geddes proved to be no guarantee that they could serve as reliable witnesses. In the following decades, as the controversy was restaged in middle-class periodicals, numerous commentators used the episode as a cautionary tale, warning of the limits of individual observational skills and the threat of popular enthusiasm and credulity.[27] Although the concern of elites over excitement among the lower orders has a long history, it took particularly modern forms in late nineteenth-century America. To a large degree, there was a democratization of human credulity and error; it was no longer seen as the exclusive domain of the working classes, "primitive" peoples, or women, but came to be seen as an undeniable element of the human condition.[28]

Trusting Testimonials: Questions of Truth and Reliability

Although Barnum built a successful career, a financial fortune, and national celebrity through his calculating use of testimonies, the showman's trade was not the only industry that used the technique. During the Gilded Age, testimonial advertising was most closely associated with the trade in patent medicines. Patent medicines held wide appeal in a society that was largely skeptical toward the expertise of professionals.[29] Instead of relying solely on the advice and prescriptions of professionals, Americans embraced these readily available medicines. Although the specific contents of these unregulated tonics were largely kept secret, they were accessible without a doctor's authorization, claimed to cure a wide array of ailments, and sold incredibly well throughout the nineteenth century.[30] This industry produced one of the most widely recognized testifying subjects of the late nineteenth century: Lydia E. Pinkham, the supposed proprietor of the

Vegetable Remedy. The original Pinkham had established this family business in 1875, but her descendents kept her image and persona alive long after her 1883 death. As a woman selling a remedy for a variety of female complaints, the success of the brand was intimately tied to the networks of trust that Pinkham had initially built with consumers through testimonials, personal correspondence, and recommendations. As historians Sarah Stage and Elysa Engelman have argued, Pinkham's heirs intentionally resurrected the image of a female entrepreneur in the 1890s to maintain the product's goodwill with female purchasers. Women had come to build a personal relationship with the image of Pinkham, for she was a persona whose word could be trusted.[31]

Although successful, the testimonial's association with morally dubious goods like Barnum's humbugs and patent medicines harmed the public image of this advertising style. Even Barnum sought to distance himself from the testimonials for commercial medicines. In *Humbugs of the World*, he made a clear distinction between his kind of entertaining deceptions and far more dangerous ones. He especially targeted as harmful those deceptions that were linked to the care of one's body. Patent medicines, false tonics, and other remedies that promised good health but had no actual therapeutic value deserved particular condemnation.[32] In the 1890s, these forms of testimonial advertising came under further attack due to the disreputable nature of early campaigns centering on the recommendations of actresses. The controversy surrounded the belief that the same individuals were offering similar testimonials for goods competing against one another.[33] With celebrated individuals endorsing so many different, frequently competing, goods, how could their word be trusted? This early crisis of testimonial advertising revolved around a failure to adhere to a sense of modesty, with those providing testimonials voraciously backing numerous goods.

Building consumer trust through personalized, written communication, another of Pinkham's favored techniques, became a particularly contested site during the Gilded Age. This technique raised concerns about these industries' fraudulent use of the mail to promote their products. The moral reformer and special postal inspector Anthony Comstock waged a decades-long battle against what he perceived as the perversion of this federal government service in order to circulate obscene materials such as erotica and information about contraception. Historians have insightfully probed how Comstock both emerged from but also profoundly shaped Americans' understanding of their sexual selves.[34] Building on such insights, one can see how Comstock conceptualized the purchasing public. Although concentrating on the regulation of public sexual vice, Comstock grounded his campaigns in the language of eliminating fraud. He understood individuals as weak and open to undue influence; for Comstock the ordinary purchaser was "unwary and credulous."[35]

Although Comstock's moral crusades seem overwrought in retrospect, he was responding in part to a real phenomenon, to new forms of swindling that preyed upon the anonymous nature of the marketplace.[36] Social commentators frequently warned of the dangers of believing the testimony of strangers when approached through the post. In his 1892 exposé, David Leeper noted how these strategies worked by flattering the potential mark: "Some men who receive a well worded and very flattering circular letter from New York or some other eastern city, feel very highly complimented. Especially when the one sending it pretends to have selected them upon the recommendation of their neighbors and friends as being eminently fitted to attend to their business in that country."[37] The only reliable means of avoiding being taken in by such words was to seek refuge in one's personal modesty, to ignore the enticing, flattering words.

Self-proclaimed grafter Ben Kerns prided himself on his ability to fabricate a persona for himself that would entice people to give him money. In Gilded Age Saint Louis, he set himself up as a real estate agent who offered to advertise property in a variety of national newspapers for a ten-dollar fee. Secretly, the running of the advertisements cost him fifty cents and he had no intention of ever moving the property although he persistently solicited clients through the mail. According to Kerns, a major strategy "in bringing in the money and winning the confidence of the people was a little booklet I wrote up containing many spurious testimonials and letters of recommendation, all of which were alluring, by the pen of some well-satisfied client."[38] Claiming to ground his fraudulent trade in his superior knowledge of human psychology, Kerns held that the key to crafting a successful career in fraudulent advertising schemes was appealing to people's wants and desires. Kerns prided himself on his own mastery in designing deceptive words that enticed people's secret wishes.

By the turn of the century, the gradual eclipse of the notion of moral character as the dominant way of understanding the self had significant repercussions for testimony in a number of arenas. For much of the nineteenth century, reliability in the commercial sphere revolved around the question of whether one could trust the words of others. The confidence man exemplified how those of bad character could use testimony to manipulate and defraud others. At the time that commercial swindlers were demonstrating how the word of the stranger could not be trusted, experimental psychologists were advancing a view of human nature that held that one should not even be confident in the reliability of one's own senses.[39] Although disagreeing with the method of the experimentalists, jurists were simultaneously developing a similar understanding of human subjectivity while arbitrating trademark infringement. To protect the marketplace rights of established merchants, Gilded Age judges constituted the legal notion of an unwary purchaser.

Psychologists Witnessing on and off the Stand

Despite psychologists' attempts to portray themselves as being apart from the marketplace, their knowledge was intimately bound to it. Optical illusions, for example, created a bridge between the leisurely commercial culture advertising and the psychological thinking of the late nineteenth century. Illusions featured prominently in amusing optical toys, amusement parks, and middlebrow periodicals. These objects, which began in the commercial sphere, were developed into psychological tools that were in turn used to explain consumer behavior.[40] Psychologists argued that illusions were not merely confined to the realm of physiology and sense perception, but were located in how the mind orders sensory data.[41] For example, when applied psychologist Walter Dill Scott wanted to explain human nature and perception to advertising professionals in the first decade of the twentieth century, he frequently used optical illusions to visualize these principles.[42] Scott, a German-trained experimental psychologist, received an invitation from advertising executives to present the insights from his science to the Agate Club a year after his appointment at Northwestern University in 1900. Through this venture and the resulting series of articles in John Lee Mahin's magazine, he was among an early advocate of impressionist rather than rationalist styles of advertising. In the various editions of his *Theory and Practice of Advertising* (1903), Scott used an array of optical illusions to explicate how the mind of the consumer was likely to function. For example, he used the famed duck-rabbit, first introduced into the technical literature by University of Wisconsin psychologist Joseph Jastrow in 1899, after having seen the amusing figure in an issue of *Harper's*. For him, among of the most pressing psychological problems facing advertisers were "errors of expectancy."[43]

According to Scott, poorly crafted advertisements function as a kind of visual deception within the purchasing public. In discussing "illusions of apperception," Scott initially analyzed through anecdotal evidence the graphic organization of a series of unsuccessful advertisements. For example, he describes two competing groceries in the Chicago area, Winter's Grocery and Robinson Brothers, whose inserts into the morning paper were virtually indistinguishable. Scott relates the experience of an acquaintance whose wife asked him to purchase a large order from one of the outlets that was having a sale one particular week. Not realizing the difference, the man purchased the goods from the wrong grocery, and when scolded by his wife he produced what he sincerely believed to be the advertisement for the correct store but which of course was not.[44] Scott's other examples of misleading advertising were even more visual in orientation, and he gives examples of distinct manufacturers sharing advertising space on the same page of a newspaper and magazine, resulting in customers soliciting business from the wrong one.[45] From these examples, Scott reproduces a series of ambiguous images from the psychologist's repertoire, each illustrating how one's preconceptions affect what one perceives.

Scott's use of optical illusions to explain psychological principles to advertisers completes the circle that links experimental psychology and commercial culture. Objects that originated as visual images meant to entertain the purchasers of mass circulation periodicals came in time to provide a much clearer conception of how consumer minds operated. The mechanism through which advertisements misled and inadvertently deceived readers was filtered through these visual tools, such as the duck-rabbit. These images "illustrate the same principles of illusions of apperception, but they make it clearer than any confusion of concrete advertisements can possibly do."[46]

In the United States, the most vocal advocate of the belief in the inherent unreliability of humans as observers was the German émigré, Hugo Münsterberg. Initially trained as an experimentalist in Wilhelm Wundt's pioneering laboratory at Leipzig, Münsterberg focused his energies on applied psychology during his tenure at Harvard (1892–1916). As a popularizer of the new experimental psychology during the Progressive Era, Münsterberg was rarely, if ever, a modest witness. He soon abandoned the cautiously crafted report for psychology periodicals in favor of polemical articles and spectacular demonstrations in the public sphere. His primary aim became not to refine experimental technique but to embed his science into social institutions.

One of his favorite targets was the legal profession. Münsterberg undertook a considerable campaign to transform the application of the law through psychological insights. In a series of popular essays, initially published in mass circulation magazines and later collected as *On the Witness Stand* (1908), he sought to reform the norms of testimony and judgment by replacing the evaluation of a person's social character with the measurable study of human behavior grounded in specific experimental tests. Two themes predominate the essays: that character alone is an insufficient guarantor of reliability, and that common sense is an insufficient guide in evaluating testimony.[47] In an early chapter on "Illusions," he sets out his position with an anecdote. He asks the reader to picture a courtroom situation concerning a car accident. Fortunately, there are two independent witnesses to give firsthand testimony; unfortunately, they cannot agree upon what they saw. One claims that the road was wet while the other insists it was dry. One claims that the offending driver had sufficient time to brake while the other heartily disagrees. Münsterberg stresses that the witnesses' differences of opinion are not due to personal interest or intentional deceit, for both are testifying honestly based upon their own abilities: "Both witnesses were highly respectable gentlemen, neither of whom had the slightest interest in changing the facts as he remembered them." The problem, according to Münsterberg, is with testimony itself: an individual's unmediated observation is simply not a reliable kind of evidence, regardless of the person's moral character. Thus one would never be able to arrive at the truth merely through a commonsense evaluation of their respective testimonies.[48] To strengthen his argument, Münsterberg notes that he himself, outside of the exacting environment of the laboratory, is equally prone to such errors of perception.[49]

An essential tension operated within Münsterberg's presentations on the eyewitness testimony. His stated goal was the replacement of the jurist's common sense about human subjectivity with the precise measurements of the experimental psychologist. In making his case to a popular audience and to professionals outside of his own discipline, Münsterberg needed to draw upon ordinary examples that were relatable to the experiences of the reader. Despite his claims to ground the courtroom testimony in the mechanical objectivity of psychological instruments, Münsterberg himself was forced to call upon the resources of everyday life. He frequently drew upon a commonsense understanding of human nature, such as the visible traces of emotion in a person's face, despite his claims to ground his knowledge purely in experiments. Rather than clearly laying out his procedure, as had been a normative practice of the reliable witness since the time of Boyle, Münsterberg's public advocacy of psychology as a science and a solution to social problems required that the audience place their trust in his expertise, reliability, and authority. These problems with his style of presentation were also mirrored by the decision to publish his early essays in mass circulation periodicals like *McClure's Magazine*, rather than in scholarly journals.[50]

Münsterberg attracted a host of critics owing to his lack of humility and modesty in his public pontifications on subjects outside of the already established domain of experimental psychology. Lightner Witmer, professor of psychology at the University of Pennsylvania, was highly critical of what he perceived as Münsterberg's crass commercialism. He condemned his Harvard colleague for "crying his psychological wares in the marketplace."[51] Münsterberg would use sensational episodes that attracted the public's attention and offered dramatic solutions. The cautious, disinterested prose style was frequently abandoned, although he would occasionally include sufficient technical details in order to replicate his apparatus. While Münsterberg crafted both a career and a public persona for himself as an expert in the unreliability of human observation, he did so in a manner that undermined many people's willingness to believe his own claims.[52]

Probably the most notorious attempt by Münsterberg to subject legal testimony to his psychological tests centered on the 1907 trial of "Big Bill" Haywood, famed head of the International Workers of the World.[53] Haywood was placed on trial in Idaho after convicted murderer, Harry Orchard, claimed that he was an agent of western mining unions, and was ordered to sabotage the mine works and assassinate officials on their behalf. With a commission from *McClure's Magazine* to write up his experience in an article, Münsterberg left for Boise hoping to subject Orchard to a series of experiments to determine whether he was truthful about implicating Haywood. Receiving the state's permission to interview Orchard, Münsterberg claimed to have subjected the man to a barrage of tests over the course of seven hours. In all likelihood, the socially conservative Münsterberg played up his earlier admiration of Haywood to make the revelation more dramatic. He insisted "that I changed my personal feelings resulted from our conversations, but that I changed my conviction as to the truthfulness of his words has been entirely the result of my psychological experiments." Münsterberg claimed that his psychological tests affirmed Orchard's story and the state's case against Haywood. He stressed that physiogamy, the ancient practice of assessing an individual's character from their physical appearance, especially facial features, was an unreliable indicator of reliability in this instance; while Orchard possessed a "brutal" and "vulgar" profile, his ear was deformed, his eyes shifted irregularly, and his lower lip was abnormal, Haywood, in contrast, despite a missing eye, radiated honesty from his face. Physiogamy had been revived as a popular science at the end of the eighteenth century, thanks to the influence of scientists such as Johann Kaspar Lavater, and had flourished during the nineteenth century, offering urban dwellers a commonsense technology for assessing strangers while also dovetailing with the scientific racism grounded in physical differences encouraged by slavery and colonialism. By the early twentieth century, however, academic psychologists such as Münsterberg sought to displace popular science in favor of their own attempt to map inner traits and abilities through mental testing.[54] Yet Münsterberg never made clear precisely which psychological tests he applied to Orchard. Against standard procedure for reporting scientific results, he did not detail his apparatus or procedure, insisting that others must rely upon his own word and reputation. For a man who claimed that such qualities were no guarantee of reliability, Münsterberg was placed in at best a paradoxical, if not hypocritical position. Certainly this is how Haywood's attorneys felt.[55]

The problem facing Münsterberg was that the jury possessed a very different evaluation of the testimony, finding Haywood innocent of the state's charges. Despite the barrage of tests to which Münsterberg claimed Orchard had been subjected, he felt sufficiently unnerved by the verdict that he did not want his scientific expertise to be seen as publicly contradicting it. He wrote a quick note to the *McClure's* office asking that the article be scrapped and then penned another to Haywood's attorney, Clarence Darrow, insisting that he had no wish to continue their quarrel over the case.[56] The verdict in the Haywood trial was not an isolated incident, and when Münsterberg's essays were collected in book form, despite his publisher's attempts to market the book to lawyers, the reception among the legal community was hostile. John Wigmore, dean of Northwestern University's law school and the leading authority on the nature of legal evidence, exemplified this reaction and penned a hostile review of the book.[57]

Despite his reservations about Münsterberg's specific approach, Wigmore himself was well aware of the potential unreliability of eyewitness accounts. Instead of drawing upon experimental psychology, Wigmore recommended that jurists pay careful attention to the demeanor and behavior of witnesses while testifying. For Wigmore, the study of witness behavior ought to be grounded in judicial experience rather than experimental tests, and he reminded jurists to be wary of witnesses who were overly confident in their recollections and observations: "It is a commonplace of judicial experience that testimony most glibly delivered and most positively affirmed is not always the most trustworthy. The honest witness who will not exaggerate the strength of his recollection is well worth listening to because of this very caution." Similarly, when attorney Francis Wellman gave advice on handling witnesses, he noted that if your own witness is too bold "and may injure your case by pertness or forwardness, observe a gravity and ceremony of manner toward them which may be calculated to repress their assurance." A reliable witness was a modest one who recognized and acknowledged the limits of his or her abilities.[58]

Although the majority of American jurists echoed Wigmore's skepticism toward the psychological reform of the law, ironically many judges were simultaneously constructing a legal knowledge grounded in similar discomfort with the nature of observation. In doing so, they drew upon the epistemology of the "buckram-bound volumes of old decisions," of which Münsterberg was so critical.[59] When it came to cases concerning trademark infringement and deceptive advertising in the late nineteenth century, American judges tended to assume the careless and frivolous nature of the consumer's behavior. In doing so, presiding judges drew upon legal precedent, what they viewed as common knowledge, and their own senses to derive their decisions rather than having to rely on the testimony of actual customers or experimental psychologists. That the average observing subject was prone to deception and not to be trusted was reinforced in two ways in these cases. First, the individual eyewitness accounts from potential customers were deemed to be neither reliable nor particularly useful.

More importantly though, the logic behind these decisions centered upon the presumed psychology of the "ordinary purchaser": carelessness, inattention, and unwariness. At a time when advertisers continued organizing their trade around transparent appeals to "rational," male breadwinners, the legal construction of the purchasing subject anticipated early twentieth-century advocacy of a frivolous, emotional, and female consuming public.[60]

Cases grounded in this commonsense psychology of the unwary purchaser began proliferating in the 1870s. The logic was set out in the frequently cited case, *McLean v. Fleming*, argued before the Supreme Court in 1878. The question at stake was whether the trade of one merchant in liver pills unfairly infringed upon the rights of a competitor because their labels were too similar. In the deciding opinion it was argued that "[w]hat degree of resemblance is necessary to constitute an infringement is incapable of exact definition, as applicable to all cases. All that courts of justice can do, in that regard, is to say that no trader can adopt a trade-mark, so resembling that of another trader, as that ordinary purchasers, buying with ordinary caution, are likely to be misled."[61] This decision came to imply that the legal standard for infringement was to be grounded in the perceived mental capabilities of the ordinary consumer. To determine whether one trader's packaging, labels, or advertisements infringed upon the rights of his or her competitors, the presiding judge had to contemplate whether it was likely that the average purchaser would be deceived by the imitation during the course of shopping. Exact similitude between the two goods was not required, since it was held that the ordinary purchaser tended to act quickly, in the moment, and without making comparisons, and was therefore most likely to be deceived.[62]

Petitioners did not have to provide actual customers to testify that they had been deceived by the imitator. While reaffirming their own abilities to detect visual deceptions, these judges downplayed the role of consumer testimony in these cases. Rather the application of the law centered on how the judge determined the probability that a customer may be deceived; even when the testimony of deceived purchasers was available, the courts did not place great weight upon it. For example, in *McCann v. Anthony* (1886), a case where the plaintiff could provide two customers who swore they had been deceived by the competitor's similar packaging, the court did not find their testimony to be evidence of critical importance. Instead, Justice Thompson relied upon his own judgment to observe the competitors' labels to determine whether it was probable that the purchasing public would be misled.[63] In such cases, the judges held that in all probability the competitor could provide alternative testimony. Similarly in *Britton v. White Manufacturing* (1894), in a case over the design of lamps, the Connecticut judge dismissed the evidence of designers, arguing that their expertise was irrelevant since it lay in the domain of the production of the goods and not in how the ordinary purchaser was likely to perceive them.[64] In the place of eyewitness accounts, judges substituted their own evaluation of the brands and marks to determine whether deception was likely to occur. In the space of the courtroom, the judge had the ability to carefully assess the similarities between goods, a luxury not available in the marketplace. They did not require a laboratory or an experimental test to assess these claims, only time and common sense.[65]

CONCLUSION

Each of the realms discussed in this article—science, the law, and advertising—faced a broad questioning of the reliability of eyewitness testimony. Despite this common experience, each of these arenas had particular demands and expectations of their witnesses. For example, when jurists rejected Hugo Münsterberg's psychological reforms, they reaffirmed their own ability to determine the criterion for a good, reliable witness. The law had its own style of knowing and along with it a particular understanding of such concepts as observation and evidence. It is important to recognize that knowledge is constituted differently in the field of advertising, as distinct from science and the law, and the ways in which celebrity remained an important resource when configuring testimonials despite the broader cultural critique of this category of evidence. Just as the law only occasionally embraced the psychologist's vision of human subjectivity, so advertisers managed to rehabilitate the testifying subject.

Did the developments outlined in this essay constitute an end to the age of Barnum? Certainly the turn of the twentieth century saw the proliferation of scientific and legal technologies for promoting public incredulity. Especially in the realm of pharmaceuticals, reformers sought to limit the influence of individualized testimonials on a product's behalf in favor of standardized testing and measurement.[66] In tandem, a cohort of advertisers, self-conscious about their newly achieved professional status and inspired by the possibility of Scott's science of selling, rejected the testimonial as an unfortunate legacy of the industry's origins in hucksterism and puffery. Of particular prominence was the "Truth in Advertising" campaign championed by the industry's leading trade journal, *Printers' Ink*. Established by New York City advertisers in 1888 primarily to promote more effective techniques to sell goods, in the early twentieth century the journal embraced the language of reform so prominent in the wider culture. Commencing in 1911, the journal's publisher, John Irving Romer, began a formal campaign of lobbying state legislatures to pass a bill that would intently police merchants about misleading the public about their wares. He sought to reinstitute rational and transparent lines of communication between industry and consumers.[67]

Yet there were deep tensions within the industry's self-styling as an arbiter of sincerity and transparency. During the same period that "Truth in Advertising" and the new laws it hoped to engender became its mantra, *Printers' Ink* also served as a leading organ for reports about the efficacy of introducing psychological knowledge into the craft of designing advertisements. Expanding upon the early work of Walter Dill Scott and Hugo Münsterberg, during the 1910s and 1920s *Printers' Ink* regularly featured articles detailing how to make advertising copy function psychologically. Calls for greater transparency in advertising were accompanied by practices that placed a new emphasis on emotions and feelings, entities understood as moving the consumer to immediate action.[68] For example, in the very same issue that declared an initial legal victory for the truth in advertising statute also featured an article encouraging authors of copy to deploy more subtle psychological techniques to appeal to the reader.[69]

Psychology was trumpeted as a means of making advertising more effective by basing the communication of information on principles of perception and emotional associations. Psychologically oriented advertising was also meant to appeal to desires and beliefs not fully articulated, thus manipulating the behavior of the consuming public. In other words, the call for truth in advertising occurred at precisely the same moment and in the very same spaces where the psychologists were examining the minds of consumers to determine their typical patterns of behavior in response to advertising copy.[70] The irony of rendering advertising simultaneously scientific and deceptive was not lost on contemporaries. In a 1915 short story, "Honestly—If Possible," Sinclair Lewis, whose novels constituted a sustained critique of American commercial culture, had his Madison Avenue protagonist "write advertisements that were deliberate, careful, scientific lies."[71] Playing off a common trope of the day, the crafting of advertising copy was a form of scientific deception.

This new approach, grounded on the management of emotions, did not spell the end of the use of testimonials, although a new generation of scientifically minded experts did look down upon the older practice. Well into the 1910s, advertisers continued to promote the deployment of testimonials under the rubrics of "good will" and "personality." Admitting that it was widely considered the "houn' dawg" of advertising, C. B. McCuaig argued that testimonials could still be profitably used if administered "geographically." Associations with a locally or regionally identifiable celebrity could still serve as a means of guaranteeing trust in one's product.[72] As the president of the Schulze Baking Company observed, commerce remained "conducted through the medium of human relationships," and consumers "will buy from concerns in which they have confidence, and will refuse to respond to the appeal of those whom they distrust."[73] In many ways the design of testimonials and the new psychological advertising were not so different in kind. As historian Roland Marchand has documented, the solidification of a modern and scientific industry in the 1920s and 1930s was accompanied by the "repersonalization" of advertising through fictional trade figures such as Betty Crocker, branding products in a manner not so different from the testifying celebrities of old.[74]

The use of testimonials in advertising emerged during a period when the act of witnessing and observing was a matter of concern in a number of public and professional arenas. The criticisms leveled against testimonial advertising did not originate solely within the professionalizing strategies of a new generation of marketers. They also emerged in response to broader cultural concerns about the reliability of direct, individual testimony. As exemplified by his performance during the Orchard trial, Münsterberg represented the kind of Progress Era intellectual that sought to replace human judgment, due to its untrustworthy subjectivity, with supposedly indifferent mechanical interventions. Still, just as the jury system was not supplanted by the psychologist's technical measurements of those involved in litigation, more informal forms of witnessing continued to survive and flourish within advertising. The testimonial was rebuffed, but it was ultimately rehabilitated during this period.

Testimonial advertising also illustrated a crucial way of generating trust in commerce that was distinct from the methods used in sciences and the law. First, with testimonial advertising, authority remained tied to the particular identity of an often notable and readily recognizable individual. Trust is not secured through the production of anonymous, interchangeable language of standardization but rather through the very personal experience and testimony of the particular individual. It is through the public constitution of an endorser's personal experience with the product that reliability and authority are generated. Second, whereas the legal and scientific witness must provide a guarantee that their testimony matches in some reliable way a truth to nature, the testifying subject in advertising only has to guarantee a product's value and worth, which is something quite different from professing a mimetic truth to nature. It is here that the highly recognizable celebrity rather than the technical expert can play an important role as a reliable witness. In the example of the Cardiff Giant, those who provided testimonials argued that an exhibit that risked being a hoax could still be worth the price of admission if it was desirable and pleasurable to view. Just because the object may not have been authentic did not mean that it lacked commercial and entertainment value. While the endorser of a product attempts to sway the audience's opinion, one must bear in mind that the critique of this style of gaining trust has coexisted with it from the start.

NOTES

1. P. T. Barnum, *Humbugs of the World: An Account of Humbugs, Delusions, Impositions, Quackeries, Deceits and Deceivers Generally, in All Ages* (New York: Carleton, 1866), 53–55.
2. See especially James W. Cook, *The Arts of Deception: Playing with Fraud in the Age of Barnum* (Cambridge, MA: Harvard University Press, 2001). Other key studies of Barnum include Neil Harris, *Humbug: The Art of P. T. Barnum* (Boston: Little Brown, 1973); A. H. Saxon, *P.T. Barnum: The Legend and the Man* (New York: Columbia University Press, 1989); Bluford Adams, *E Pluribus Barnum: The Great Showman and the Making of U.S. Popular Culture* (Minneapolis: University of Minnesota Press, 1997); Andrea Stulman Dennett, *Weird and Wonderful: The Dime Museum in America* (New York: New York University Press, 1997); Benjamin Reiss, *The Showman and the Slave: Race, Death, and Memory in Barnum's America* (Cambridge, MA: Harvard University Press, 2001); Steven Belletto, "Drink Versus Printer's Ink: Temperance and the Management of Financial Speculation in *The Life of P. T. Barnum*," *American Studies* 46, 1 (2005): 45–65.
3. All too often subjectivity in the legal and commercial realm gets sidestepped, see Susanna L. Blumenthal, "The Default Legal Person," *UCLA Law Review* 54, 5 (2006): 1135–1265; and Mary S. Morgan, "Economic Man as Model Man: Ideal Types, Idealization and Caricatures," *Journal of the History of Economic Thought* 28, 1 (2006): 1–27. On the nineteenth-century decoupling of psychology and economics as human sciences, rendering the latter as a form of social physics, see Margaret Schabas, "Victorian Economics and the Science of the Mind," in *Victorian Science in Context*, ed. Bernard Lightman (Chicago: University of Chicago Press, 1997), 72–93; and Harro Maas, *William Stanley Jevons and the Making of Modern Economics* (Cambridge: Cambridge University Press, 2005), 151–180.
4. Michael Leja, *Looking Askance: Skepticism and American Art from Eakins to Duchamp* (Berkeley: University of California Press, 2004).
5. Donald S. Napoli, *The Architects of Adjustment: The History of the Psychological Profession in the United States* (Part Washington, NY: Kennikat Press, 1980); John M. O'Donnell, *The Origins of Behaviorism: American Psychology, 1870–1920* (New York: New York University Press, 1985); Jill G. Morawski, ed., *The Rise of Experimentation in American Psychology* (New Haven: Yale University Press, 1988); Kurt Danziger, *Constructing the Subject: Historical Origins of Psychological Research* (Cambridge: Cambridge University Press, 1990); Elizabeth Lunbeck, *The Psychiatric Persuasion: Knowledge, Gender, and Power in Modern America* (Princeton: Princeton University Press, 1994); John Carson, *The Measure of Merit: Talents, Intelligence, and Inequality in the French and American Republics, 1750–1940* (Princeton: Princeton University Press, 2007).
6. Bruno Latour and Steve Woolgar, *Laboratory Life: The Construction of Scientific Facts* (1979; Princeton: Princeton University Press, 1986); Steven Shapin and Simon Schaffer, *Leviathan and the Air-Pump: Hobbes, Boyle, and the Experimental Life* (Princeton: Princeton University Press, 1985); Steven

Shapin, *A Social History of Truth: Civility and Science in Seventeenth-Century England* (Chicago: University of Chicago Press, 1994).

7. Shapin and Schaffer, *Leviathan and the Air-Pump*, 66. See also Peter Dear, "Totius in Verba: Rhetoric and Authority in the Early Royal Society," *Isis* 76 (1985): 145–161; and Charles Bazerman, *Shaping Written Knowledge: The Genre and Activity of the Experimental Article in Science* (Madison: University of Wisconsin Press, 1988), 59–79.
8. Donna J. Haraway, "Modest Witness: Feminist Diffractions in Science Studies," in *The Disunity of Science: Boundaries, Contexts, and Power*, ed. Peter Galison and David J. Stump (Stanford: Stanford University Press, 1996), 428–441, 429.
9. See Theodore Porter, *Trust in Numbers: The Pursuit of Objectivity in Science and Public Life* (Princeton: Princeton University Press, 1995), esp. 89–90.
10. Lorraine Daston and Peter Galison, *Objectivity* (New York: Zone Books, 2007). Although often implicated in concerns about fakery, photography as a process became the predominant model for scientific truth-making. On the epistemic status of nineteenth-century photography, see Allan Sekula, "The Body and the Archive," *October* 39 (1986): 3–64; John Tagg, *The Burden of Representation: Essays on Photographies and Histories* (Basingstoke: Macmillan, 1988); Shawn Michelle Smith, *American Archives: Gender, Race, and Class in Visual Culture* (Princeton: Princeton University Press, 1999); Jennifer Tucker, *Nature Exposed: Photography as Eyewitness in Victorian Science* (Baltimore: Johns Hopkins University Press, 2005).
11. See Martin Rudwick, *The Great Devonian Controversy: The Shaping of Scientific Knowledge among Gentlemanly Specialists* (Chicago: University of Chicago Press, 1985); and Stuart McCook, "'It may be Truth, but it is not Evidence': Paul du Chaillu and the Legitimation of Evidence in the Field Sciences," *Osiris* 11 (1996): 177–197, 190.
12. Because legal concepts of evidence and testimony were influential in the formulation of early modern scientific epistemology, and the role of forensic evidence has drawn increased cultural attention in recent years, science studies scholars have begun to explore the similarities and differences between these two realms. The English Common Law tradition with its historical and inductive approach to evidence, as opposed to Continental Roman law's emphasis on rationalistic deduction, was a core cultural resource that Boyle himself drew upon in developing his experimental epistemology in the seventeenth century. See Barbara J. Shapiro, *'Beyond Reasonable Doubt' and 'Probable Cause': Historical Perspectives on the Anglo American Law of Evidence* (Berkeley: University of California Press, 1991); Shapiro, "Testimony in Seventeenth-Century English Philosophy: Legal Origins and Early Development," *Studies in History and Philosophy of Science* 33, 2 (2002): 243–263; Rose-Mary Sargent, *The Diffident Naturalist: Robert Boyle and the Philosophy of Experiment* (Chicago: University of Chicago Press, 1995). Scholars have explored the more recent difficulties that scientific experts in the areas of fingerprinting, handwriting analysis, and genetics have faced in getting courts to admit their evidence as reliable. What the history of modern

forensics has illustrated is that despite some common roots in the early modern era, practitioners of science and law frequently have differing ideas about the kinds of evidence and testimony that may be deemed desirable and credible. See Sheila Jasanoff, *Science at the Bar: Law, Science, and Technology in America* (Cambridge, MA: Harvard University Press, 1995); Jennifer Mnookin, "Scripting Expertise: The History of Handwriting Identification Evidence and the Judicial Construction of Reliability," *Virginia Law Review* 87, 8 (2001): 1723–1845; Ian A. Burney, *Bodies of Evidence: Medicine and the Politics of the English Inquest, 1830–1926* (Baltimore: Johns Hopkins University Press, 2000); Burney, *Poison, Detection, and the Victorian Imagination* (Manchester: Manchester University Press, 2006); Simon Cole, *Suspect Identities: A History of Fingerprinting and Criminal Identifications* (Cambridge, MA: Harvard University Press, 2001); Tal Golan, *Laws of Men and Laws of Nature: The History of Scientific Expert Testimony in England and America* (Cambridge, MA: Harvard University Press, 2004). For recent attempts to apply sociology of knowledge approaches to the law, see Bruno Latour, *La fabrique du droit: Une ethnographie du conseil d'Etat* (Paris: Découverte, 2002); and Mariana Valverde, *The Law's Dream of a Common Knowledge* (Princeton: Princeton University Press, 2003).

13. Classic histories of the advertising industry include Daniel Pope, *The Making of Modern Advertising* (New York: Basic Books, 1983); Stephen Fox, *The Mirror Makers: A History of American Advertising and its Creators* (New York: Morrow, 1984); Roland Marchand, *Advertising the American Dream: Making Way for Modernity, 1920–1940* (Berkeley: University of California Press, 1985), 52–87; T. J. Jackson Lears, *Fables of Abundance: A Cultural History of Advertising in America* (New York: Basic Books, 1994); Elspeth H. Brown, *The Corporate Eye: Photography and the Rationalization of American Commercial Culture, 1884–1929* (Baltimore: Johns Hopkins University Press, 2005), 159–216.
14. On the rise of product testing, see Lawrence B. Glickman, "A Strike in the Temple of Consumption: Consumer Activism and Twentieth-Century American Political Culture," *Journal of American History* 88, 1 (2001): 99–128; and Timothy Messer-Kruse, "The Crusade for Honest Weight: The Origins of an Overlooked Progressive Movement," *Journal of the Gilded Age and Progressive Era* 5, 3 (2006): 241–286.
15. Warren Susman, "'Personality' and the Making of Twentieth-Century Culture," in *Culture as History: The Transformation of American Society in the Twentieth Century* (New York: Pantheon, 1984), 271–285. See also Karen Haltunnen, *Confidence Men and the Painted Women: A Study of Middle-Class Culture in America, 1830–1870* (New Haven: Yale University Press, 1982); T. J. Jackson Lears, "From Salvation to Self-Realization: Advertising and the Therapeutic Roots of Consumer Culture, 1880–1920," in *The Culture of Consumption: Critical Essays in American History, 1880–1980*, ed. Richard Wightman and Lears (New York: Pantheon, 1983), 1–38; John F. Kasson, *Rudeness and Civility: Manners in Nineteenth-Century Urban America* (New York: Hill and Wang, 1990); Judy Hilkey, *Character is Capital: Success*

Manuals and Manhood in Gilded Age America (Chapel Hill: University of North Carolina Press, 1997); Ian Nicholson, *Inventing Personality: Gordon Allport and the Science of Selfhood* (Washington: American Psychological Association Press, 2003). For a critical assessment of this literature, linking the notion personality to debates about immigration rather than consumption, see Andrew Heinze, "*Schizophrenia Americana:* Aliens, Alienists and the 'Personality Shift' of Twentieth-Century Culture," *American Quarterly* 55, 2 (2003): 227–256.

16. Walter A. Friedman, *Birth of a Salesman: The Transformation of Selling in America* (Cambridge, MA: Harvard University Press, 2004), 22–26.
17. The hoax is also analyzed in Barbara Franco, "The Cardiff Giant: A Hundred Year Old Hoax," *New York History* 50, 2 (1969): 421–440; and Elizabeth Pritchard Stewart, "Who Shall Decide when Doctors Disagree? Hoaxes and American Men of Science in the Nineteenth Century," (PhD dissertation, American University, 2003). On tourism of sacred and wondrous places, see John F. Sears, *Sacred Places: American Tourist Attractions in the Nineteenth Century* (New York: Oxford University Press, 1989); David E. Nye, *American Technological Sublime* (Cambridge, MA: MIT Press, 1995); Suzanne K. Kaufman, *Consuming Visions: Mass Culture and the Lourdes Shrine* (Ithaca: Cornell University Press, 2005).
18. *The American Goliah: A Wonderful Geological Discovery*, 2nd ed. (Syracuse: Redington and Howe, 1869); and *The Onondaga Giant, or the Great Archaeological Discovery* (Syracuse: Nottingham and Tucker, 1869).
19. *Onondaga Giant*, 10.
20. "Obituary—John A. Clarke," Syracuse *Journal* (September 21, 1872), Onondaga Historical Association vertical files of press clippings, hereafter referred to as OHA files.
21. Belletto, "Drink Versus Printer's Ink," 47.
22. *American Goliah*, 8–9.
23. *American Goliah*, 30–31.
24. See "Advertisement," Syracuse *Daily Standard*, October 26, 1869, OHA files.
25. "The Onondaga Giant," Syracuse *Journal*, October 27, 1869, OHA files.
26. "Equally as Great," Syracuse *Journal*, October 23, 1869, OHA files.
27. See, for example, "The Cardiff Giant," *Harper's Weekly* (December 4, 1869), 776; W. A. McKinney, "A History of the Cardiff Giant Hoax," *The New Englander* (1875): 759–769; G. A Stockwell, MD, "The Cardiff Giant, and Other Frauds," *Popular Science Monthly* (1878): 197–203; Andrew Dickson White, "The Cardiff Giant: The True Story of a Remarkable Deception," *Century Magazine* (1902): 948–955.
28. I discuss the various responses to the Cardiff Giant in greater detail in Michael Pettit, "'The Joy in Believing': The Cardiff Giant, Commercial Deceptions, and Styles of Observation in Gilded Age America," *Isis* 97, 4 (2006): 659–677.
29. See especially John Harley Warner, "The Rise and Fall of Professional Mystery: Epistemology, Authority, and the Emergence of Laboratory

Medicine in Nineteenth Century America," in *The Laboratory Revolution in Medicine*, ed. Andrew Cunningham and Perry Williams (New York: Cambridge University Press, 1992).

30. James Harvey Young, *The Toadstool Millionaires: A Social History of Patent Medicines in America before Federal Regulation* (Princeton: Princeton University Press, 1961); and Young, *The Medical Messiahs: A Social History of Health and Quackery in Twentieth-Century America* (Princeton: Princeton University Press, 1967).
31. See Sarah Stage, *Female Complaints: Lydia Pinkham and the Business of Women's Medicine* (New York: W.W. Norton and Co., 1979); and Elysa Engelman, "'The Face That Haunts Me Ever': Consumers, Retailers, Critics, and the Branded Personality of Lydia E. Pinkham" (PhD dissertation, Boston University, 2003).
32. Barnum, *Humbugs of the World*, 15–16. One must question how far these claims were simply rhetorical devices, as advertisements for sarsaparilla and other cures were included in some of his publicity material. See *Barnum's American Museum: Illustrated* (New York: William Van Norden and Frank Leslie, 1850).
33. Marlis Schweitzer, "'The Mad Search for Beauty': Actresses' Testimonials, the Cosmetics Industry, and the 'Democratization of Beauty,'" *Journal of the Gilded Age and Progressive Era* 4, 3 (2005): 255–292. Schweitzer's chapter in this volume is a revised and expanded version of this article.
34. See Nicola Beisel, *Imperiled Innocents: Anthony Comstock and Family Reproduction in Victorian America* (Princeton: Princeton University Press, 1997); Helen Lefkowitz Horowitz, "Victoria Woodhull, Anthony Comstock, and the Conflict over Sex in the United States in the 1870s," *Journal of American History* 87, 2 (2000): 403–434; Andrea Tone, "Black Market Birth Control: Contraceptive Entrepreneurship and Criminality in the Gilded Age," *Journal of American History* 87, 2 (2000): 435–459; Molly McGarry, "Spectral Sexualities: Nineteenth-Century Spiritualism, Moral Panics, and the Making of U.S. Obscenity Law," *Journal of Women's History* 12, 2 (2000): 8–29; Alyssa Picard, "'To Popularize the Nude in Art': Comstockery Reconsidered," *Journal of the Gilded Age and Progressive Era* 1, 3 (2002): 195–224.
35. Anthony Comstock, *Frauds Exposed; or, How the People are Deceived and Robbed, and Youth Corrupted* (New York: J. Howard Brown, 1882), 5.
36. On the confidence man, see Johannes Dietrich Bergman, "The Original Confidence Man," *American Quarterly* 21, 3 (1969): 560–577; Gary Lindberg, *The Confidence Man in American Literature* (New York: Oxford University Press, 1982); Haltunnen, *Confidence Men and the Painted Women*; Kasson, *Rudeness and Civility*; Stephen Mihm, *A Nation of Counterfeiters: Capitalists, Con Men, and the Making of the United States* (Cambridge, MA: Harvard University Press, 2007).
37. David H. Leeper, *The Eye Opener or Man's Protector* (Kirkville, MO: Journal Printing, Co., 1892), 15.
38. Ben H. Kerns, *The Grafter* (Topeka, KS: Crane and Company, 1912), 29.

39. On the rise of subjective vision, see Jonathan Crary, *Techniques of the Observer: On Vision and Modernity in the Nineteenth Century* (Cambridge, MA: MIT Press, 1990).
40. On the traffic between commercial and scientific uses of illusions, see Albert A. Hopkins, *Magic, Stage Illusions, and Scientific Diversions* (New York: Munn, 1897).
41. On the earlier historical moment that stressed illusions as products of individual physiological difference, see Crary, *Techniques of the Observer*, 67–96.
42. On the introduction of psychological expertise into advertising techniques, see Stuart Ewen, *Captains of Consciousness: Advertising and the Social Roots of the Consumer Culture* (New York: McGraw-Hill, 1976); Kerry W. Buckley, *Mechanical Man: John Broadus Watson and the Beginnings of Behaviorism* (New York: Guilford Press, 1989), 134–147; Lears, *Fables of Abundance*, 196–234; Stuart Ewen, *PR!: A Social History of Spin* (New York: Basic Books, 1996).
43. Walter Dill Scott, *Theory and Practice of Advertising* (1903; New York: Small, Maynard and Company, 1916), 168. On Scott's psychology of selling, see David P. Kuna, "The Concept of Suggestion in the Early History of Advertising Psychology," *Journal of the History of the Behavioral Sciences* 12, 4 (1976): 347–353; Ludy T. Benjamin, Jr., "Science for Sale: Psychology's Earliest Adventure in American Advertising," in *Diversity in Advertising: Broadening the Scope of Research Directions*, ed. Jerome D. Williams, Wei-Na Lee, and Curtis P. Haugtvedt (Mahwah, NJ: Lawrence Erlbaum, 2004), 21–39, 28–31; Friedman, *Birth of a Salesman*, 172–189.
44. Scott, *Theory and Practice of Advertising*, 175–177.
45. Ibid., 177–181.
46. Ibid., 191.
47. Hugo Münsterberg, *On the Witness Stand: Essays on Psychology and Crime* (1908; New York: Clark Boardman Co., 1925). On Münsterberg's career, see Matthew Hale, Jr., *Human Science and Social Order: Hugo Münsterberg and the Origins of Applied Psychology* (Philadelphia: Temple University Press, 1980); Frank J. Landy, "Hugo Münsterberg: Victim or Visionary?" *Journal of Applied Psychology* 77, 6 (1992): 787–802; Jutta and Lothar Spillman, "The Rise and Fall of Hugo Münsterberg," *Journal of the History of the Behavioral Sciences* 29, 4 (1993): 322–338. On his forensic psychology more specifically, see Golan, *Laws of Men and Laws of Nature*, 211–253; Ken Alder, *The Lie Detectors: The History of an American Obsession* (New York: The Free Press, 2007); Alison Winter, "A Forensics of the Mind," *Isis* 98, 2 (2007): 332–343, 333–335.
48. Münsterberg, *On Witness Stand*, 15.
49. Ibid., 41–43.
50. See Hugo Münsterberg, "Nothing but the Truth," *McClure's Magazine* 29 (September 1907): 532–536; Münsterberg, "The Third Degree," *McClure's Magazine* 29 (October 1907): 614–622; Münsterberg, "Hypnotism and Crime," *McClure's Magazine* 30 (January 1908): 317–322; Münsterberg, "The Prevention of Crime," *McClure's Magazine* 30 (April 1908): 750–756.

51. Lightner Witmer, "Mental Healing and the Emmanuel Movement," *The Psychological Clinic* 2, 8 (1909): 239–250, 241. Similar criticisms can be found in Joseph Jastrow, "Chips from a Psychologist's Workshop," *The Dial* (May 16, 1914): 426–427.
52. The laboratory-oriented psychology of Scott, Münsterberg, and Witmer was largely displaced in the American imaginary by psychoanalysis largely through the testimony of celebrity journalists and authors in the press. On the role of celebrity testimonials in the promotion of psychoanalysis, see Joel Pfister, "Glamorizing the Psychological: The Politics and the Performances of Modern Psychological Identities," in *Inventing the Psychological: Toward a Cultural History of Emotional Life in America*, ed. Pfister and Nancy Schnog (New Haven: Yale University Press, 1997), 167–213. On the resistance of academic psychologists to psychoanalysis during these same years, see Gail A. Hornstein, "The Return of the Repressed: Psychology's Problematic Relations with Psychoanalysis, 1909–1960," *American Psychologist* 47, 3 (1992): 254–263.
53. On the Haywood trial, see J. Anthony Lucas, *Big Trouble: A Murder in a Small Western Town Sets Off a Struggle for the Soul of America* (New York: Simon and Schuster, 1997).
54. Münsterberg, "Experiments with Harry Orchard," (1907), Hugo Münsterberg Papers, Boston Public Library, Mss Acc 2450, pg. 6. Hereafter cited as HMP. On the conflict between experimental psychology and physiognomy during this period, see Brown, *Corporate Eye*, 23–64.
55. Münsterberg, "Experiments with Harry Orchard," 7.
56. Hugo Münsterberg to Editor of *McClure's Magazine*, July 14, 1907, HMP, Mss Acc 2358; Münsterberg to Clarence Darrow, July 14, 1907, HMP, Mss Acc 2311.
57. John H. Wigmore, "Professor Münsterberg and the Psychology of Testimony," *Illinois Law Review* 3, 7 (1909): 399–445. See also Wigmore to Münsterberg, November 11, 1908, HMP, Mss Acc 2244.
58. John Henry Wigmore, *A Treatise on the Anglo-American System of Evidence* (1904; Boston: Little, Brown, 1940), vol. III, 58. Francis L. Wellman, *The Art of Cross-Examination* (New York: Macmillan Co., 1904), 135.
59. Münsterberg, *On Witness Stand*, 65.
60. See Merle Curti, "The Changing Concept of 'Human Nature' in the Literature of American Advertising," *Business History Review* 41, 4 (1967): 335–357; Marchand, *Advertising the American Dream*, 66–69; Brown, *The Corporate Eye*, 164–168.
61. *McLean v. Fleming*, 96 U.S. 245 (1878).
62. *Pillsbury v. Pillsbury*, 64 Fed. 841 (1894).
63. *McCann v. Anthony*, 21 Mo. App. 83 (1886).
64. *Britton v. White Manufacturing* 61 Fed 93 (1894).
65. On the challenge mounted by psychologists to the "unwary purchaser norm," see Michael Pettit, "The Unwary Purchaser: Consumer Psychology and the Regulation of Commerce in America," *Journal of the Behavioral Sciences* 43, 3 (2007): 379–399.

66. See Harry M. Marks, *The Progress of Experiment: Science and Therapeutic Reform in the United States, 1900–1990* (Cambridge, NY: Cambridge University Press, 1997).
67. Herbert W. Hess, "History and Present Status of the 'Truth-in-Advertising' Movement," *Annals of the American Academy* 101, 1 (1922): 211–220.
68. Newton A. Fuessle, "Copy that Appeals to the Emotions," *Printers' Ink* 97, 3 (October 12, 1916), 50–56.
69. See "First Conviction under Law against Untrue Advertising," *Printers' Ink* 75, 5 (May 4, 1911), 26–28; and Roy W. Johnson, "'Psychology' the Name, and Psychology the Practical Thing," *Printers' Ink* 75, 5 (May 4, 1911), 70–71.
70. On these issues, see T. J. Jackson Lears, *Fables of Abundance: A Cultural History Advertising in America* (New York: Basic Books, 1994).
71. Sinclair Lewis, "Honestly—If Possible," *Saturday Evening Post* (October 14, 1915), reprinted in Anthony Di Renzo, ed., *If I Were Boss: The Early Business Stories of Sinclair Lewis* (Carbondale: Southern Illinois University Press, 1997), 88.
72. C. B. McCuaig, "Making the Testimonial Earn Its Keep," *Printers' Ink* 98, 6 (February 8, 1917), 74–75.
73. Paul Schultze, "When Business Personality Becomes an Asset," *Printers' Ink* 95, 5 (May 4, 1916), 17–22, 17.
74. Marchand, *Advertising the American Dream*, 352–359. Among those somewhat erroneously credited with the wholesale reintroduction of testimonials was psychologist turned advertising executive, John B. Watson. For an analysis of this mythos, see Buckley, *Mechanical Man*, 140–141.

CHAPTER 3

"After a Season of War": Sharing Horticultural Success in the Reconstruction-Era Landscape

Marina Moskowitz

The 1866 edition of *Vick's Annual Catalogue and Floral Guide* contained the following letter, attributed to George Ford of Lawrence, Kansas. Writing on the fourth of January 1864, the author requested a catalogue from the company, explaining:

> The Flower Seeds we purchased from you last spring came up remarkably well…The Asters were very fine, some seventy plants being in full bloom at the time of the *Quantrell Raid*, and made, together with Snap Dragons, Dianthus, Heddewigs, Phloxes, Petunias and other fine varieties, a very gay and beautiful appearance, and were the means, Providentially, of saving our house from pillage and destruction. Quantrell, with a dozen of his gang, came to destroy the place, but Quantrell said to my wife it was too pretty to burn, and should be saved. Thus you see that the beauty of cultivated nature softened the heart of a notorious bushwacker and cold-blooded murderer. We shall cultivate flowers as long as we remember this horrible rebellion.[1]

Ford's remarkable story was only one of dozens of voices testifying to the value of seeds purchased from James Vick. While Ford's narrative of salvation was certainly the most dramatic, the testimonial letters together created an aura of success that both loyal and potential customers could share. This particular catalogue was one of the first I studied as part of a larger project on the nineteenth-century seed trade. This specific letter somewhat falsely led me to believe that such sources would provide reflection on the cataclysmic event of the Civil War as it happened and immediately thereafter. So at first I was disappointed to realize that Ford's letter (which was followed in later editions of the catalogue by an epic poem describing the event) was an anomaly among the hundreds of letters, in dozens of catalogues, I have now read.

In fact, the many testimonial or commendatory letters published each year by seed dealers such as the Vick, Buist, Bliss, and Briggs companies tended to be more prosaic (figure 3.1). Rather than Ford's tale of survival in a time of national turmoil, most letters included in the seed catalogues of the 1860s and 1870s shared smaller-scale rewards, such as neighborhood acclaim for an abundant garden; prizes for horticultural specimen deemed the best at county or state fairs; or financial gain from prolific crops with good market value. As I looked at more of these writings, the absence of significant comment on the Civil War and its aftermath began to speak as loudly as George Ford's letter had. In planting their fields and gardens each year, and perhaps writing of their experiences doing so, consumers of seeds went about the task of reconstruction in a literal and personal way. As one newspaper editor wrote in a letter reprinted by the Vick Company, "It is time for the ladies to be looking up their flower seeds, to start their plants for transplanting, to see to it that they shed joy in the New England homes, after a season of war, mourning, and captivity even."[2] The entrenched pattern of turning to seed catalogues each January to plan for spring plantings provided a routine for those looking to maintain or reestablish their local landscapes, and by extension, their customary patterns of life. This maintenance of the status quo in the practice of horticulture tempered, whether consciously or instinctively, the upheaval of the previous years at war as well as the calls for significant change in the American economy and society. At the same time, the potential conservatism of these acts of cultivating the home terrain was countered by the expanding market relations possible in the newly reunited nation.

George Ford found comfort in not only planting his garden, but also writing about it. He shared his experience with a seed seller who was, in all realms but the commercial, a stranger to him, but by doing so, joined a vast community of consumers. What practices and routines lay behind George Ford's letter? And why did these epistolary exchanges take root in the seed trade?[3] Testimonial letters were used to meld two potentially divergent messages, encapsulating on the one hand the geographic range of the trade in seeds and on the other the intimacy that was still possible in the realm of commerce.

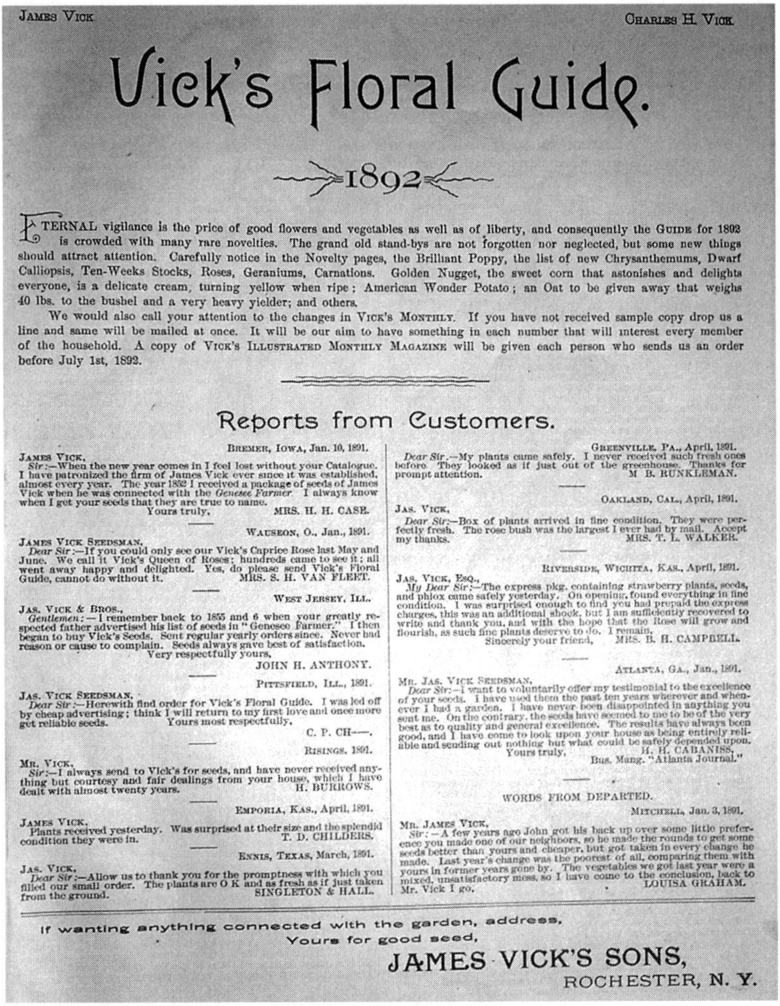

James Vick   Charles H. Vick

Vick's Floral Guide.

1892

ETERNAL vigilance is the price of good flowers and vegetables as well as of liberty, and consequently the Guide for 1892 is crowded with many rare novelties. The grand old stand-bys are not forgotten nor neglected, but some new things should attract attention. Carefully notice in the Novelty pages, the Brilliant Poppy, the list of new Chrysanthemums, Dwarf Calliopsis, Ten-Weeks Stocks, Roses, Geraniums, Carnations. Golden Nugget, the sweet corn that astonishes and delights everyone, is a delicate cream, turning yellow when ripe; American Wonder Potato; an Oat to be given away that weighs 40 lbs. to the bushel and a very heavy yielder; and others.

We would also call your attention to the changes in Vick's Monthly. If you have not received sample copy drop us a line and same will be mailed at once. It will be our aim to have something in each number that will interest every member of the household. A copy of Vick's Illustrated Monthly Magazine will be given each person who sends us an order before July 1st, 1892.

Reports from Customers.

Bremer, Iowa, Jan. 10, 1891.

James Vick,
Sir:—When the new year comes in I feel lost without your Catalogue. I have patronized the firm of James Vick ever since it was established, almost every year. The year 1852 I received a package of seeds of James Vick when he was connected with the *Genesee Farmer*. I always know when I get your seeds that they are true to name.
Yours truly, MRS. H. H. CASE.

Wauseon, O., Jan., 1891.

James Vick Seedsman,
Dear Sir:—If you could only see our Vick's Caprice Rose last May and June. We call it Vick's Queen of Roses; hundreds came to see it; all went away happy and delighted. Yes, do please send Vick's Floral Guide, cannot do without it. MRS. S. H. VAN FLEET.

West Jersey, Ill.

Jas. Vick & Bros.,
Gentlemen:—I remember back to 1855 and 6 when your greatly respected father advertised his list of seeds in "Genesee Farmer." I then began to buy Vick's Seeds. Sent regular yearly orders since. Never had reason or cause to complain. Seeds always gave best of satisfaction.
Very respectfully yours,
JOHN H. ANTHONY.

Pittsfield, Ill., 1891.

Jas. Vick Seedsman,
Dear Sir:—Herewith find order for Vick's Floral Guide. I was led off by cheap advertising; think I will return to my first love and once more get reliable seeds. Yours most respectfully,
C. P. CH——.

Risings, 1891.

Mr. Vick,
Sir:—I always send to Vick's for seeds, and have never received anything but courtesy and fair dealings from your house, which I have dealt with almost twenty years. H. BURROWS.

Emporia, Kas., April, 1891.

James Vick,
Plants received yesterday. Was surprised at their size and the splendid condition they were in. T. D. CHILDERS.

Ennis, Texas, March, 1891.

Jas. Vick,
Dear Sir:—Allow us to thank you for the promptness with which you filled our small order. The plants are O K and as fresh as if just taken from the ground. SINGLETON & HALL.

Greenville, Pa., April, 1891.

Dear Sir.—My plants came safely. I never received such fresh ones before. They looked as if just out of the greenhouse. Thanks for prompt attention. M B. RUNKLEMAN.

Oakland, Cal., April, 1891.

Jas. Vick,
Dear Sir:—Box of plants arrived in fine condition. They were perfectly fresh. The rose bush was the largest I ever had by mail. Accept my thanks. MRS. T. L. WALKER.

Riverside, Wichita, Kas., April, 1891.

Jas. Vick, Esq.,
My Dear Sir:—The express pkg. containing strawberry plants, seeds, and phlox came safely yesterday. On opening, found everything in fine condition. I was surprised enough to find you had prepaid the express charges, this was an additional shock, but I am sufficiently recovered to write and thank you, and with the hope that the Rose will grow and flourish, as such fine plants deserve to do. I remain,
Sincerely your friend, MRS. B. H. CAMPBELL.

Atlanta, Ga., Jan., 1891.

Mr. Jas. Vick Seedsman,
Dear Sir:—I want to voluntarily offer my testimonial to the excellence of your seeds. I have used them the past ten years wherever and whenever I had a garden. I have never been disappointed in anything you sent me. On the contrary, the seeds have seemed to me to be of the very best as to quality and general excellence. The results have always been good, and I have come to look upon your house as being entirely reliable and sending out nothing but what could be safely depended upon.
Yours truly, H. H. CABANISS,
Bus. Mang. "Atlanta Journal."

WORDS FROM DEPARTED.

Mitchell, Jan. 3, 1891.

Mr. James Vick,
Sir:—A few years ago John got his back up over some little preference you made one of our neighbors, so he made the rounds to get some seeds better than yours and cheaper, but got taken in every change he made. Last year's change was the poorest of all, comparing them with yours in former years gone by. The vegetables we got last year were a mixed, unsatisfactory mess, so I have come to the conclusion, back to Mr. Vick I go. LOUISA GRAHAM.

If wanting anything connected with the garden, address,
Yours for good seed,
JAMES VICK'S SONS,
ROCHESTER, N. Y.

Figure 3.1 Testimonial letters submitted to *Vick's Floral Guide*, 1892.
Source: Author's collection.

Seeds as Commodities

After a war that made stark the divisions between agrarian and industrial economies, purveyors of seeds had a unique position as a trade that bridged that divide. This particular trade intrigues me precisely because it sits at the intersection of agrarian and industrial economies and cultures that is so characteristic of the nineteenth century. I believe there is an important "borderland" (to adapt a term from the landscape historian John Stilgoe), with both geographic and temporal aspects, between the Jeffersonian vision of an agrarian society and the modern industrial realm.[4] The seed trade was an early and widespread business in the United States, and yet one that defies what are now stereotypical notions of factories and industrial work. Still, members of the trade did not identify solely with the agrarian sector either. In verbal and visual representations of their work and work sites, the seed trade blurred the distinctions between agricultural and industrial settings, rural and urban sites, and even, manual and mechanized labor. By expanding traditional agricultural production while introducing distribution methods of the industrial era, firms moved seeds from the realm of informal trade and gift exchange into a commercial marketplace.

While drawing on both economic systems for aspects of production and distribution, the seed trade was also among the first to develop successful national markets. In presenting itself as resident in the borderland between agriculture and industry, the seed trade recognized that its market was a hybrid as well. The consumer market for seeds was vast, in both geographic and socioeconomic terms. While the start of a demographic shift from rural to urban areas certainly did begin in the nineteenth century, that shift did not imply a decline in planting, but rather a greater variety of market sectors. For example, the rise in urban populations led to a rise in market gardens, cottage kitchen gardens, leisure-time flower gardens, and garden suburbs with vast lawns. Most seed companies catered indiscriminately to those who planted for sustenance, economic pursuit, or leisure.

Many seed companies employed print culture as the means of reaching this broadening audience. While it could be argued that all businesses benefited from developments in print technology over the course of the nineteenth century, there does seem to have been a special relationship between, or even overlap of, seed sellers and the printing trade.[5] From Bernard M'Mahon to James Vick, several important nineteenth-century American seed sellers were also trained as printers and published their own catalogues, while the larger seed companies that flourished in the late nineteenth century often included on-site printing works to produce their marketing materials. Seeds were broadcast not only in the soil but also through the postal networks of the expanding United States.

Still, farmers and gardeners had to be convinced that it was worthwhile to buy seeds, when they could perfectly well harvest them from their own fields and plots. In addition to this initial hurdle, purveyors of seeds sought to encourage repeat business, in an attempt to inculcate what we would now call brand loyalty. In order to shift the public's view of seeds from products of the domestic economy to commodities, the trade developed a variety of marketing techniques, including the use of testimonial letters.

Seed companies recognized the important bond between seller and buyer in a trade where the commodity sold was difficult to judge or value before its use. As the Burpee Company wrote in their 1872 catalogue:

> The relations of the Planter to his trusted Seedsman are more intimate than those of the buyer and seller in any other line of business; with other goods the buyer can largely judge of the quality and value by the sample, while with seeds the purchase is altogether a matter of confidence. To merit and maintain this confidence is the constant aim of the conscientious Seedsman. He cannot go into the open market to buy his supplies, but must prepare a year and two years ahead to have suitable acreage planted with selected stocks especially for seed, which he can recommend of his own knowledge...[6]

This idea of a personal recommendation from the seed seller was echoed effectively through testimonial letters because in this instance purveyors and consumers were involved in the same horticultural pursuits. Many nineteenth-century industries developed mechanized production processes that, while replicating and replacing earlier craft-based work, could not themselves be replicated on a domestic scale or without significant capital investment. Seed growers, however, shared their work processes with the farmers and gardeners who would eventually buy their goods. Thus, the words of consumers helped amplify the sense of trust fostered by the trade.

The George Ford letter is intriguing for not only its content but also its context. Though I have seen testimonial letters in seed trade catalogues as early as the 1850s, they flourished in the 1860s and 1870s. It is instructive to look at these early uses, which predate a boom in advice literature on advertising, from the introduction of *Printers' Ink* in 1888 as an advertising industry trade journal to the publication of numerous marketing manuals at the turn of the twentieth century. Such later writings codified practices with which firms such as Vick, Buist, and Briggs experimented a generation earlier. While I am certainly not claiming that the seed industry was the sole originator of the use of testimonials, there is no question that the early reliance on printed catalogues supporting mail-order distribution provided a venue for such letters to be published. While display advertisements in periodicals might have had space for a handful of quotations, the mid-nineteenth century catalogues sometimes contain as many as eight pages of letters, printed tightly in a small typeface. The firms tended to group letters under headings such as "Reports from My Customers," "Commendatory," or indeed, "Testimonials."[7] The B. L. Bragg firm of Springfield, Massachusetts, wrote of the need to limit the letters they printed lest they overtake the rest of the catalogue: "That our seeds have given excellent satisfaction is confirmed by the many testimonials that we have received, some of which we print in full in this volume of our farm manual. We have many others which if printed would make a volume in themselves."[8] Through these pages, printed year after year by several of the major companies, patterns of testimony do emerge. The letters tend to mention very specific plants, they laud the company as being better than others they have tried, they tend to include some personal measure of achievement, and they often offer corroboration of their success through the admiration of others.

Seed companies did invoke the opinions of experts in the field, such as the editors of agricultural and horticultural periodicals; these names might be attached to actual letters or might simply take the form of quotations from the press, as when Briggs and Brother divided their general heading, "What They Say of Us," into two sections, "From the Press" and "From the People," to which they referred together as "the great engine of society."[9] If companies distributed wholesale as well as retail, they might also employ the testimony of merchants, whose own livelihood would depend on the quality of the seeds they bought and sold. The Buist Company of Philadelphia explained these different markets, "The glowing testimonials that we are constantly receiving from all parts of the country endorsing our seeds, a few of which we annually publish in this Almanac, show the esteem in which they are held by both the planter, merchant and gardener; the one pronounces them the best he has ever planted, and the other the most reliable and satisfactory he has ever sold to his patrons."[10]

The companies occasionally employed publicly recognizable names, such as the Rev. Henry Ward Beecher, whose endorsement graced several competitors' pages in the 1860s, or the author Anna Warner, whose 1866 letter to the Vick Company was accompanied by a short story, originally published in *Harper's Weekly*, which featured the company.[11] More often, however, the companies presented the experiences of ordinary customers, who shared the occasionally extraordinary moments of their lives. Testimonial letters were so effective in this broad and varied market because no particular status was needed to voice success; all parties could claim equal authority. The words of a well-established market gardener who relied on a given company's seeds for income were no more authoritative than the story of a self-described amateur gardener whose flowers were the envy of her neighborhood. Having some sort of professional credential or expertise might lend credence to a testimonial, but *not* having this experience could equally well convince buyers that such results were attainable by anyone. As a letter from Rev. R. H. Waggoner of Hillsdale, Michigan, noted, "The seeds I obtained from you gave great satisfaction. The marvel with all is that with the care, or more properly the neglect, they receive in a common garden they should come equal to your recommendation."[12] Here, as in many of the letters, it is the status of the common gardener writing in appreciation that, in fact, becomes a valuable marketing tool.

Because most of the authors writing letters to the seed trade held this status as "everyday" consumers rather than offering specialist expertise, and because the catalogues provided space for such a large number of the letters to be printed, testimonials could be used to mirror the variety of products on offer. Seed houses offered more individual items for sale than perhaps any other nineteenth-century trade, packaging the variety of nature enhanced by the science of hybridization. For every letter praising a newly bred, brightly colored, double-blossomed zinnia that drew attention to the writer's front garden, there was another lauding the market success of a large and prolific breed of cabbage.[13] At the same time, these letters, and the different commodities they vouched for, exhibited the breadth of the consumer market for seeds: in the years following the Civil War, this was a truly national market, transcending differences in region, livelihood, socioeconomic status, gender, and, potentially, race. Though, of course, not all of those who bought seeds from the myriad outlets where they could be purchased had the time, inclination, or, indeed, literacy skills to write letters about their experiences, the variety among testimonial authors was suggestive of the wide reach of this particular trade.[14]

In the present day, one of the questions asked of testimonials is whether they are "real," in the sense of actually being written by contented consumers; television advertising adds an extra layer to this question, as even words that originate with a consumer might be presented by an actor. Are these endorsements in fact written by company marketers as part of larger advertising campaigns? Such present-day questions niggle at the historian—were these letters written by nineteenth-century customers and sent in, as is often suggested by the text, with an order for the next year's seeds, or were they written by members of the firm, who wrote all the rest of the catalogue text, including instructions for planting and descriptions of plants? Although it is difficult to give an absolutely confident response to the thousands of letters printed in mid- to late- nineteenth-century seed trade catalogues, there is strong evidence that—in this trade, at this time—the letters genuinely were written by consumers. A close look at the context in which these letters are placed reveals an incredible similarity between the different companies' catalogues in some of the key features—planting instructions, varietal descriptions, and certainly in the printed illustrations, which tended to be widely shared between companies. But the testimonial letters actually show much greater variety than that. Their very specificity—with attributions of full names and hometowns that often supported only small populations—would have aroused suspicion if the authors were not recognizable figures in a community, especially if the letter claimed, as so many of them did, that a particular garden was the talk of the neighborhood.[15]

Even in this early history of the use of marketing testimonials, the companies themselves were aware of the skepticism with which these types of letters might be met, and they went out of their way to assert their authenticity and their spontaneous, "unsolicited" praise. Seed purveyors explained their inclusion of consumer opinion; for example, Henry Dreer wrote in his 1866 catalogue, "Self-praise is no recommendation, nor are newspaper puffs reliable. We hold that the unsolicited testimonials of our customers are far more satisfactory, and, therefore, take the liberty of offering a few extracts from letters received from our friends, in various sections of the country, as an evidence of the reliability of our seeds...."[16] The Buist company went so far as offer evidence of the letters:

> For the past few years we have taken the liberty of publishing extracts from a few of the many complimentary letters we are continually receiving, in order to satisfy those who are strangers to our house, that BUIST'S GARDEN SEEDS will always afford them the utmost satisfaction. The disinterested opinion of our customers will certainly be more convincing than any remarks we could possibly make. All letters of this character will always be separately filed, and kept open for the inspection of any customer.[17]

Interestingly, some firms that did not print testimonial letters still addressed the topic; they acknowledged the many customers who wrote to them, but cited space restrictions, such as J. J. Bell of Binghamton, New York, who wrote, "What People Think of our seeds and prices could be illustrated by printing hundreds of letters which daily we receive from customers saying our seeds are not only the cheapest but the Best they have ever planted. We omit these for lack of space but will try to convince every new customers of our ability to fill our orders with greater dispatch than heretofore."[18] The Bliss Company did publish letters until about 1880 but after that date offered instead their "extensive and constantly increasing business as evidence that our endeavor... is duly appreciated."[19] Thus, while testimonial letters were initially reproduced by firms at least in part to document the reach of their market, here the Bliss Company argues that the market reach is testimony in itself. Still, even when these statements seem defensive, they are centered more on issues of accurate quotation, and unprompted praise, than they are about the actual existence of the correspondents. Through these varied approaches, however, a focus on correspondence with customers emerges and is explained by the nature of the trade. The question that the issue of veracity raises—why would people write these letters?—is balanced in explaining the inclusion of testimonial letters in promotional materials by the question of why people would read the letters. (Or, why would seed companies presume customers would read them?)

Certainly, patterns of testimony do emerge, and at times I have noted worryingly close language between two specific letters. For example, the Vick Company printed in its 1868 *Illustrated Catalogue and Floral Guide* a letter from Mrs. H. P. Morrison of Cambridge, Ohio, which said "I feel as though it would be ungrateful in me not to say something to you about my flowers, the seed of which I purchased of you last Spring . . . We were surrounded with beauties inexpressible, all summer, at very little expense."[20] The following year, the same company printed another letter, this from Annabel Lewis, of Ryerson Station in Greene County, Pennsylvania: "I feel as though it would be ungrateful in me not to say something to you about my flowers—the seed of which I purchased of you last spring. My seed almost all germinated, producing flowers far beyond my expectation . . . All the neighbors that saw them say they never saw the like before."[21] Still, it is just as likely that these similarities arise because individual authors recognize a form to follow in the letters they have read in previous catalogues, as opposed to one author, or a team, churning out drafts. Templates may have existed, but these appear to be borrowed from the conventions of nineteenth-century letter writing, rather than codified marketing practices.

These conventions were an element of both social and business practices, and numerous guides to these practices offered both general advice on letter writing and model letters for specific situations. While advising originality of thought, these manuals nonetheless recommended following the templates provided; the testimonial segments of trade catalogues might have supplied appropriate guides. Such manuals advised that, with varying degrees of formality depending on the relationship and situation between writer and recipient, correspondence should serve in the place of face-to-face communication. For example, the *New Parlor Letter Writer* of 1850 advised, "The art of Letter-Writing consists in a proper expression of those ideas on paper, which we should convey by conversation to a person were he present."[22] The *Pocket Letter Writer* of 1852 concurred: "the best instruction, perhaps, for this kind of writing, is to consider well what you are about to say, and write it exactly as you would tell it, if the person was present."[23] While such advice might seem commonplace, its application to commerce was increasingly relevant.

Commerce and Epistolary Culture

The seed trade was a pioneer in mail-order business. The face-to-face exchange of the traditional marketplace increasingly was replaced by written communication. Although over the course of the nineteenth century, some firms introduced blank order sheets tipped into their catalogues, much of the exchange between distributor and consumer was carried out by correspondence, to the extent that many of the catalogues offered advice on what information to be sure to include in these letters. Letter-writing manuals echoed these instructions, explaining exactly how to place orders by mail, and to separate the actual order from any other questions, suggestions, or commentary.[24] Indeed the Rochester *Democrat*, in the city that became known as Floral City because of the concentration of seed and nursery firms there, published a column, reprinted in the Briggs catalogue of 1872, entitled "The Art of Letter Writing," suggesting the correct form for such letters and gently chiding those who blamed the companies for missing or incorrect orders, when in fact their own lack of precision in writing had caused the problem.[25] Many larger catalogues included engravings depicting not only the plants being sold, but also the physical plants in which seeds were sorted, stored, packaged, and prepared for shipping. These images showed the various firms' mail rooms as busy hives of activity at the heart of the trade. Whether intentional or not, this emphasis on letter writing provided a context in which the testimonial letter seemed naturally to fit; in requesting a subsequent order or simply a new catalogue, authors might well mention the success they had had in previous seasons.

The catalogues themselves can be seen as an epistolary form. As the nineteenth century progressed, horticultural advice was incorporated directly into the business ephemera of the seed trade. With the rise of the mail-order trade, seed lists, such as the one circulated by Bernard M'Mahon at the turn of the nineteenth century, grew into the distinct genre of the seed catalogue. Certainly the annual catalogues constituted an important form of education in gardening, and their authors were self-conscious in this role of consumer education. James Vick wrote in his 1866 edition:

> [M]y Catalogue is not a list of hard names, dry and unmeaning to all but the experienced florist or botanist, but a valuable DIRECTORY, and a safe GUIDE FOR THE FLOWER GARDEN, one that may be consulted with profit by all, either in the purchase of seeds or their after treatment. The habits of each variety are clearly stated; the situation for which it is best adapted, both for the perfection of the plant and the beauty of the garden; the season of flowering; the distance apart at which the plants should be given in full with each variety, so that the most inexperienced need not fail.[26]

The Philadelphia seed seller Robert Buist called his annual seed catalogue the *Garden Manual and Almanac*; while he referred to it as a "very plain little work," he also wrote that "it contains plain facts, and useful directions and hints on the cultivation of Vegetables, just what the cottager and the inexperienced require; and an effort to encourage the taste for the cultivation of the garden from which a great saving is accomplished in the support of rural families."[27] Botanical knowledge and folk wisdom blended in the pages of catalogues, which offered instruction on plant origins, sowing and culture of specific plants, and tenets of garden design.

Most of the catalogues started with some form of "letter" from the seedsman to his "friends," with headings such as "Gossip with Customers," "friendly greeting," or "a New Year's gift."[28] These narratives couched commerce in the language of friendship, advice, and gift giving. They also used the friendly counsel on the planning, sowing, tending, and harvesting of fields, gardens, lawns, and other planted landscapes to maintain a personal touch in what was an increasingly far-flung business. James Vick and W. Atlee Burpee were the masters of this genre, which served to personalize a trade relationship conducted without face-to-face contact. By the etiquette of the day, as well as the business practice of mail order, such "letters" invited a response from the consumer. As a *Pocket Letter Writer* published in Cincinnati in 1853 advised, "All letters . . . require an answer. And in answering letters, always reply to any question that may have been asked, or suggestions made, before proceeding with your own thoughts and information."[29] If the seed seller's "gossip" and advice about plants constituted the "suggestions made," it made sense that at least some consumers responded with their experiences of following that advice. To that extent, the testimonial letters of the nineteenth-century seed trade might be considered to be "solicited," but because of this model of ongoing personal correspondence, as opposed to a commercial inducement to answer a particular slate of leading questions, there did not appear to be any discomfort with the use of these letters as a marketing tool.

On the rare occasions when customers of mail-order firms did come in contact with members of the company, the relationships established by previous correspondence were cemented. Robert Buist, a Philadelphia-based seed seller, wrote of his firm's experience at the Centennial Exhibition in 1876 in their hometown:

> In addition to the many enjoyments of the great Centennial, the occasion has given us the opportunity of meeting, for the first time, many of our customers and friends from various parts of the United States, whose trade has been conducted with us for many years exclusively by correspondence. The pleasure of becoming personally acquainted with those with whom we have been so familiar, by name only, has afforded us with great satisfaction, and trust will have a tendency to increase their confidence that we have so long enjoyed.[30]

Seed firms used their catalogues as a medium to display their correspondence, fostering a sense of intimacy in two ways. On the one hand, they replicated in print the experience of face-to-face exchange possible in a commercial site such as a seed store, while on the other, they encouraged commercial relations to follow the model of personal correspondence.

Seed sellers carefully tread this fault line between commercial and personal, professional and friendly. James Vick expressed his attitude toward his customers:

> Nothing connected with business gives me so much pleasure as to know that my customers are satisfied with the efforts I make to please them, and that they feel well repaid for their expenditure of money and labor in growing choice flowers. I feel far more than a commercial interest in the success of those to whom I furnish seeds, sympathising with all both in success and failure, and making every possible effort to insure success. It is gratifying to know, therefore, that unbounded success—success that delights and astonishes the growers is the rule, failure the exception.[31]

The companies encouraged consumers to share their horticultural success with them and, through the medium of the trade catalogue, with other consumers like themselves. In this way, not only did the firms retain a personal relationship with consumers, but they also tried to foster a sense of community among consumers who did not share geographic locale. The testimonial sections of catalogues were used to exemplify and publicize word-of-mouth recommendations. The examples printed in catalogues were simply codified forms of a broader consumer network recognized by the companies. As the Bliss Company wrote in 1881, "We owe a word to those of our friends who in so many instances have recommended us to others. Individual acknowledgment is impossible, but our gratitude for the attention is none the less."[32] Still, the idea of the testimonial letter being a recommendation to others stemmed in part from its subsequent use by the recipients; the extent to which consumers intended their words to reach a broader audience is unclear, but certainly many of those writing to companies would have been familiar with the printing of similar letters in catalogues and advertisements.

In this way, the letters were a hybrid between business and personal correspondence, in not only the eyes of the recipient but the eyes of the writers as well. Of course, in the way that testimonial letters often accompanied orders for goods, they can be considered business letters. But even beyond that, one model for such letters was the "testimonial" or recommendation letter offered in the context of employment. Though in this case consumers were recommending purchase from a seller or firm rather than hiring of an employee, the issues of honesty, efficiency, fitness to task, and trust were similar; many letters did comment favorably on the business practices of a particular firm. The eighty-two-year-old Abijah Reed of Hulberton, New York, wrote to the B. K. Bliss Company, "Allow me to say that in all my dealings with you I have found everything honorably and fairly done, and I am glad to believe that your enterprise has placed you among the first in your profession, and so long as I am able to give attention to the cultivation of flowers (and you continue the business,) I will be your customer."[33] Even when, as was often the case, letters commented on commodities, rather than the people who sold them, recommendation of these goods stood as a testament to trade with the seller, as a purveyor of reliable and high-quality goods. As Thomas Hill wrote in his 1878 *Manual of Social and Business Forms*, "Knowledge of persons recommended, of their fitness and capacity for the work they engage in, is always essential, before they can be conscientiously recommended to others...An individual giving a recommendation is, in a certain sense, responsible for the character and ability of the person recommended; hence, certificates of character should be given with caution and care." Hill's *Manual* and numerous other guides to letter writing offered guidance for such testimonials.[34] Such letters, and their printing in catalogues, drew consumers together by making them responsible to one another for not only the endorsement of a particular firm but also advice on specific plants to grow.

Still, the epistolary form of many of the testimonial letters is the more personal model of a thank you note. Many companies included free packets of seeds with orders, and it was also common practice to reward customers with chromolithographs depicting abundant displays of flowers, fruits, and vegetables. Many testimonial letters began with a note of thanks for these premiums, as when Mrs. C. S. Raymond of Bridgewater, Connecticut, wrote to the Vick Company in 1865, "Accept my thanks for the Pansy seed, also for the other seed you have sent us gratuitously. I would like very much to send you a bouquet of the verbenas I have raised from your seed this Summer."[35]

Still, many letters considered even the purchased seeds as gifts, describing a value in the garden that seemed to exceed what was actually paid. For example, the Vick company presented a letter from Rev. J. W. Zimmerman of Vanceburg, Kentucky: "I have intended writing to you for some time to thank you for your truly valuable Catalogue, and also for your excellent seed. You know I got most of my garden seed from you last year, and I must say they all gave satisfaction; yea more—delight."[36] Similarly, Mrs. D. R. Foster wrote, "The Aster Seed you sent me...have produced flowers so beautiful and perfect in color, size, and every development, that I hasten to thank you for the great pleasure they afford us hourly...."[37] James Vick clearly saw the letters in light of this common form of etiquette, stating above a raft of testimonials: "My Customers are all well pleased with the way in which I serve them. They think they not only receive the full worth of their money but a good deal more, and so every year send me thousands of letters expressing their thanks, though I have never in one case asked anything of the kind."[38] Robert Buist explained the cyclical nature of such correspondence, "Such encouraging reports stimulate us to still greater efforts to please our customers and friends, to whom we return our warmest thanks and kindest remembrances."[39] Although they worked to commodify their product, the seed trade continued to draw on the tradition of gift exchange, through which seeds had been transferred from person to person, and place to place, for generations, or indeed centuries.

Reading vast numbers of these letters on end, I was puzzled by what begins to sound like outright bragging—I was reminded of the frequent advice of writing manuals, "Never write anything you would blush to see in print."[40] But the model of a letter of gratitude to a company, whether for a specific gift or the general worth of the product purchased, provided a means of subsuming personal pride within the broader context of corporate praise. The bestowing of small gifts and the trope of the thank you note employed as testimony for the company show the attempts to gain and maintain their customers' trust in an increasingly far-flung business. For the seed trade, the period of Reconstruction was a time to forge a national market, by not only courting a broad base of consumers but also reflecting it in their promotional materials. The inclusion of testimonial letters in seed catalogues both asserted and encouraged the existence of a broad community of consumers, and fused their local landscapes into a national one.

Notes

1. *Vick's Illustrated Catalogue and Floral Guide* (Rochester, NY: James Vick, 1866), i.
2. *Vick's Illustrated Catalogue and Floral Guide* (Rochester, NY: James Vick, 1868), inside front cover.
3. Although I am not arguing that the seed trade originated the use of testimonial advertising, there is no question that in the American marketplace, purveyors of seeds made strong use of this marketing practice by the middle of the nineteenth century. The trade in proprietary medicine shows many parallels to the seed trade, from its basis in botanical specimen to the market practices based on consumer testimony; this field is being explored in current research by Elysa Engelman on the Lydia Pinkham Company and Susan Strasser on medicinal herbs.
4. John R. Stilgoe, *Borderland: Origins of the American Suburb, 1820–1939* (New Haven: Yale University Press, 1988).
5. Sandra Markham has explored this relationship in the Rochester, New York area in her excellent article, "Living Preachers, Through Voiceless Lips: Printing for the Nursery Industry, 1840–1920," *Ephemera Journal* 9 (2001): 13–30. For more general discussion of the use of business ephemera in the

nineteenth century, see Kenneth Ames, "Trade Catalogues and the Study of History," in *Accumulation and Display: Mass Marketing Household Goods in America, 1880–1920* (Winterthur: Henry Francis DuPont Winterthur Museum, 1986), 7–14; and Robert Jay, *The Trade Card in Nineteenth-Century America* (Columbia: University of Missouri Press, 1987).

6. *Burpee's Farm Annual* (Philadelphia: W. Atlee Burpee and Co., 1892), 17.
7. *Vick's Illustrated Catalogue*, 1866, i; *Dreer's Garden Calendar for 1866* (Philadelphia: Henry A. Dreer, 1866), inside back cover; *Buist's Almanac and Garden Manual* (Philadelphia: Robert Buist, Jr., 1882), 138.
8. B. L. Bragg and Co., *Hampden Agricultural Warehouse and Seed Store* (Springfield, MA: B. L. Bragg, 1888), i.
9. "Advance Retail Price List," (Rochester, NY: Briggs and Brother, 1873), 11.
10. *Buist's Almanac and Garden Manual* (Philadelphia: Robert Buist, Jr., 1877), 3.
11. *Spring Catalogue and Amateur's Guide* (New York: B. K. Bliss and Son, 1868), inside front cover; *Vick's Illustrated Catalogue and Floral Guide*, 1868, i; *Vick's Illustrated Catalogue and Floral Guide* (Rochester, NY: James Vick, 1867), iii, and back cover. In the world of advertising, Beecher is perhaps best known for the testimonial statement he gave to Pears' Soap in the 1880s, in which he famously drew a connection between cleanliness, Pears', and godliness. Tim Shakleton, "Introduction," *Bubbles: Early Advertising Art from A. F. Pears Ltd.*, ed. Mike Dempsey (London: Fontana, 1978), 3.
12. *Vick's Illustrated Catalogue*, 1866, iv.
13. *Vick's Illustrated Catalogue*, 1866, p. ii; James J. H. Gregory, *Annual Circular and Retail Catalogue* (Marblehead, MA: Pease, Triall, and Fielden, 1874), 5.
14. Although the remainder of this essay focuses on the mail-order trade in seeds, most of the firms that sold through catalogues had other outlets as well, distributing seed packets, often packaged in "branded" display boxes, to a variety of retailers. By the latter half of the nineteenth century, developments in print technology meant that many seed packages were identifiable by image, as well as text. Thus, the assumption of literacy at the heart of mail-order distribution, and the practice of testimonial letter writing, was not a requisite of the seed trade itself.
15. Even in the seven years since Marlis Schweitzer and I began this project, the research resources available to historians hoping to corroborate at least the existence of testimonial letter writers (if not some proof for their actual authorship) have increased greatly with the proliferation of Internet-based genealogy sites. Using sites such as www.ancestry.com, www.cornerstonegenealogy.com, or www.familysearch.org, to name but a few examples, it is possible to trace the existence of specific figures whose historical records in local history sources might otherwise be less accessible. I have been able to document the existence of a broad geographic sample of testimonial writers, including several quoted in this essay, providing reassurance about the veracity of the sources used in this trade in this time period.
16. *Dreer's Garden Calendar for 1866*, inside back cover.
17. *Buist's Almanac and Garden Manual*, 1882, 137.

18. J. J. Bell, *Book on Summer Gardening* (Binghamton, NY: J. J. Bell, 1895) n.p.; see also *Hovey's Illustrated Catalogue and Guide* (Boston: Hovey and Co., 1869), 11; *Washburn's Amateur Cultivator's Guide to the Flower and Kitchen Garden* (Boston: Washburn and Co., 1869), 11.
19. B. K. Bliss and Sons, *Handbook for the Farm and Garden and Catalogue* (New York: B. K. Bliss and Sons, 1881), 2.
20. *Vick's Illustrated Catalogue and Floral Guide*, 1868, iv.
21. *Vick's Illustrated Catalogue and Floral Guide* (Rochester, NY: James Vick, 1869), inside front cover. Just as an example of the type of corroboration possible, genealogical records on the Internet do reveal an "Annabell Lewis" living in Greene County, Pennsylvania within a few years of the date of the letter; the daughter of Daniel Lewis, Annabell married Brice Riggs in August of 1872. http://www.cornerstonegenealogy.com/brides.htm, accessed March 25, 2007.
22. *The New Parlor Letter Writer* (Auburn, MA: James Alden, 1850), iii.
23. *The Pocket Letter Writer* (Worcester: S. A. Howland, 1852), iv.
24. See, for example, Thomas Hill, *Manual of Social and Business Forms* (Chicago: Moses Warren Co, 1878), 87; and James D. McCabe, *The National Encyclopedia of Business and Social Forms* (Philadelphia: National Publishing Co., 1879), 174.
25. Briggs and Brother, *Illustrated Catalogue* (Rochester, NY: Briggs and Brother, 1872), 3.
26. *Vick's Illustrated Catalogue and Floral Guide*, 1866, 2.
27. Robert Buist Company, *Buist's Almanac and Garden Manual* (Philadelphia: Robert Buist, Jr., 1887), 2.
28. *Vick's Illustrated Catalogue and Floral Guide*, 1868, 2; Bragg, p. i; *Vick's Illustrated Catalogue and Floral Guide* (Rochester: James Vick, 1872), 1.
29. *The Pocket Letter Writer* (Cincinnati: U. P. James, 1853), 10.
30. *Buist's Almanac and Garden Manual*, 1877, 3.
31. *Vick's Illustrated Catalogue*, 1866, i.
32. B. K. Bliss and Sons, 1881, 2.
33. B. K. Bliss, *Spring Catalogue and Amateur's Guide* (Springfield, MA: Benjamin Bliss, 1866), inside front cover.
34. Thomas Hill, *Manual of Social and Business Forms* (Chicago: Moses Warren Co, 1878), 94. See also, *A New Letter-Writer for the Use of Gentlemen* (Philadelphia: Porter and Coates, 1877), 28.
35. *Vick's Illustrated Catalogue*, 1866, back cover.
36. *Spring Catalogue and Amateur's Guide*, inside front cover.
37. *Vick's Illustrated Catalogue*, 1866, i.
38. *Vick's Illustrated Catalogue*, 1868, i.
39. Robert Buist Company, 1877, 3.
40. See, for example, J. A Dacus, *A Guide to Success, with Forms for Business and Society* (St Louis: Scammell and Co., 1879), 113.

CHAPTER 4

"The Ten Year Club": Artificial Limbs and Testimonials at the Turn of the Twentieth Century

Edward Slavishak

The turn of the twentieth century witnessed a massive increase in the scope of the American artificial limbs industry. Although a brisk market in prostheses emerged in the United States after the Civil War, it was only in the late nineteenth century that amputations from mechanical accidents occurred with enough frequency to make the dismembered worker, and not the injured soldier, the industry's vision of the common man. Regional and national manufacturers competed for urban and rural clientele with promises of comfort, ability, and rejuvenation. By 1910, artificial limbs were so common in the popular marketplace that Sears, Roebuck and Company catalogues advertised manufacturers' sales pamphlets. Such was the nature of prosthetic advertising in the late nineteenth and early twentieth centuries; one item of marketing literature frequently referred to others. Prospective customers were expected to follow a paper trail in order to learn all that they could before making an educated purchase. At the heart of this paper trail lay the customer testimonial.[1]

In the 1870s, writer William Rideing noted what he considered to be a new trend in the marketing of artificial limbs to Civil War amputees. Manufacturers began including testimonial sections in limb catalogues as another way to impress upon prospective customers the quality of their products. Rideing defined these testimonials as the "experiences of crippled men whose infirmities have been relieved . . . by the dexterity of artisans in human-repair shops." His description touched upon three of the main claims that limb makers hoped to make for their products—the promise of physical relief, the positioning of patentees as skilled craftsmen, and the argument that prosthetic reconstruction could make one human again. In the decades after Rideing's discovery, manufacturers' marketing strategies ran the gamut from elaborate displays at industrial exhibitions to 500-page treatises on the science and artistry of prostheses. Yet a consistent pattern also emerged in their advertising ephemera, one that placed the reactions and encouragements of satisfied customers center stage. In order to guarantee themselves repeat business and to recruit new customers, limb makers sought to establish a community of consumers around the use of artificial arms and legs. Rather than simply telling prospective customers that thousands of people in their situation existed in the nation, limb makers used the rhetorical strategy of testimonial to reify the supposed bonds forged between people who had experienced amputation.[2]

Most advertising catalogues from artificial limb companies ended with a collection of customer commendations that conformed to a standard model (figure 4.1). First, testimonial writers provided a brief account of the dismembering accident or disease. Second, writers gave a favorable review of the prosthesis' performance, offering specific details of daily function and ease of movement. Next, writers affirmed the manufacturer's supremacy, typically claiming that they would not trade the model in question for any sum of money. Many letters then ended by welcoming the correspondence of prospective customers.

Limb companies solicited such testimonials directly from their clientele. Writers frequently began their letters by referring to companies' requests for feedback and expressing their pleasure in honoring them. Some manufacturers even offered direct guidance as to what correspondents should cover. The J. F. Rowley company of Chicago asked customers four specific questions to get them started: whether they experienced any chafing in the socket of their artificial legs, whether their leg stumps slipped when they sweated, whether the wax in the prosthetic sockets melted in hot weather, and whether they experienced any problems with their mechanical ankle joints. When the A. A. Marks company of New York included hundreds of testimonials in its 1907 catalogue, it explained that it had been "necessary to cut out all irrelevant matter in order to give each writer his share of the space allotted to the chapter." Even with such editing, the allotted space—156 pages—allowed Marks to present an overwhelming number of opinions from people who had experienced artificial arms, legs, hands, and feet. In the logic of this strategy, manufacturers did not necessarily expect prospective customers to

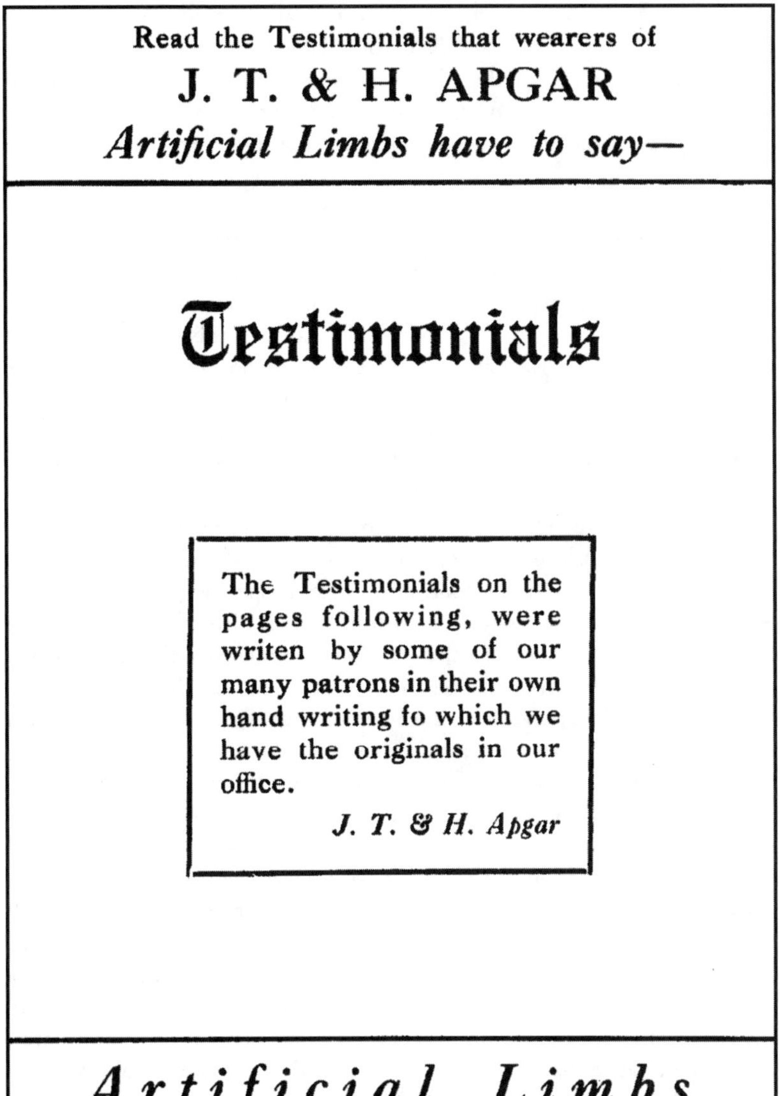

Read the Testimonials that wearers of

J. T. & H. APGAR

Artificial Limbs have to say—

Testimonials

The Testimonials on the pages following, were writen by some of our many patrons in their own hand writing fo which we have the originals in our office.

J. T. & H. Apgar

Artificial Limbs

that "act" humane

Figure 4.1 Candor and proof. From J. T. and H. Apgar, *Catalogue of Artificial Limbs*, 1910.

wade through nearly 800 individual testimonials. Instead, the onslaught of brief biographical sketches and laudatory claims was meant to impress the reader with the scope of the Marks manufacturing and distribution network. Here was a company that offered not only prosthetic products but also decades of experience that had forged a seeming community of grateful consumers.[3]

Testimonials buttressed limb makers' key claims about their products—especially concerning the successful illusion of covered artificial limbs, the exceptional range of motion made possible by their use, and the physical comfort experienced when wearing them. For every testimonial writer who claimed that "not one-quarter of the inhabitants of this city" knew about the presence of the prosthesis, there were dozens who simply chronicled the miles they had walked and tasks they had performed with the mechanical aid. That some letters were more outlandish than others only served to highlight customers' enthusiasm for particular models of prostheses. A man writing to J. F. Rowley from Kentucky in 1911 illustrated the type of hyperbole that exalted limb makers: "Rowley, your limbs are so near perfect it is a pity you could not add one thing more—flesh and blood." Beyond the essential function of promoting the use of specific products and the patronage of specific manufacturers, testimonials also offered glimpses of the purported miracle of prosthetic reconstruction—men (and much less frequently, women) who had won an unexpected second chance in life. The Connecticut tightrope-walker who rejoiced that his career had been only temporarily halted, not destroyed, by the loss of his right leg joined thousands of other Americans in affirming that economic success and personal well-being went hand-in-hand after the purchase of an artificial limb.[4]

Yet the real work done by testimonials—the true advantage of the advertising technique for companies that used it—was the trio of psychological cues that such correspondence offered. Manufacturers relied on testimonials from satisfied consumers to convey three messages to prospective buyers. First, letters written by actual customers were meant to suggest a level of candor that was perhaps not expected from the companies themselves. In the name of transparency, limb makers stressed that they willingly threw open their archives of letters in order to show that they had complete confidence in the quality of their wares. Of course, the fact that such letters were solicited, selected, and even edited limited the risks involved in publishing their contents. Second, testimonials made tangible the atomized population of amputees in the United States and beyond. Emphasizing the devastating sense of isolation that amputees were told they should feel, manufacturers presented themselves as leaders of an intimate consumer movement that bridged social and geographic chasms. Finally, and perhaps most significantly, testimonials signaled membership in a network that promised to be long-lived. When the Rowley company founded its "Ten Year Club" in the early twentieth century, it did so in order to reward loyal customers who had used a single Rowley leg for a decade or more. Yet the notion of a Ten Year Club also epitomized the advertising promises of artificial limbs. Here was a techno-medical product meant to reverse the deteriorating physical, economic, and social effects of dismemberment by granting amputees the one aspect of life that they were coached to miss most—longevity.

This chapter analyzes testimonials printed in the catalogues of five artificial limb manufacturers from the turn of the twentieth century. A. A. Marks of New York City, the oldest company, was established in 1853. By 1905, the company owned an office and factory on Broadway and a lumber mill in Connecticut. The J. F. Rowley Company began manufacturing artificial legs in Chicago in the 1870s. William Feick established Feick Brothers in Pittsburgh in 1881. The George Fuller company succeeded Douglas Bly's well-regarded Rochester prosthetics firm in 1877. Finally, John T. Apgar formed his company in New York City in 1900. Of the five firms, only Feick Brothers sold all manner of surgical instruments and corrective apparatuses. Accordingly, artificial limbs comprised a small but significant part of Feick Brothers promotional catalogues. The other four firms focused all research and investment on devices for amputees—artificial limbs, stump sockets, suspenders, hosiery, crutches, and hand-propelled carts. The array of devices offered in any given catalogue could overwhelm the reader with technical detail and reminders of trauma. The testimonial became the leading advertising form for turn-of-the-century manufacturers because of its ability to create a favorable image of both the products available and the people using them.[5]

"All one could expect": Commercial Candor

Testimonials were first used in prosthesis marketing in the mid-nineteenth century by Frank Palmer's American Artificial Limb Company. In addition to dozens of reports from American military surgeons, European doctors, and the faculty of American medical schools, Palmer's 1865 catalogue contained twenty-five letters from customers who confirmed the quality and comfort of the limbs. The company noted:

> The testimony of wearers of the limbs will be, to the mass of the public, the best possible evidence of their merit. The Appendix contains letters from persons in every walk of life, who join in the warm expression of their approval of these substitutes, arising from personal experience of their use.[6]

Palmer's formula, in which testimonials were believable because of their aura of "personal experience," became the standard justification for their use in limb catalogues. Testimonials were common in the 1870s and 1880s because, as the *St. Louis Globe-Democrat* noted, "the Civil War left an immense number of stumps." The volume of printed testimonials increased dramatically as the size of prosthesis advertising materials grew. By 1887 the George R. Fuller company compiled over 500 testimonials and endorsements for its 230-page commercial review.[7]

When limb makers turned their attention to the industrial worker as a typical customer, the use of testimonials and correspondence networks became even more prominent. The market was growing. Economist Mark Aldrich has shown that while death rates from railroad accidents declined in the United States after the 1880s, injury rates from train mishaps more than doubled from 1890 to the 1910s. Similarly, injury rates for railroad employees rose steadily to a peak in the 1910s. The inverse relationship between injury and death rates was caused in part by surgical advances systematized after the Civil War that enabled physicians to save lives by removing limbs and limiting infection. A recent study of all forms of turn-of-the-century industrial accidents in the United States concluded that the period was marked by "exceptionally acute" injury rates, which only declined after the implementation of workers' compensation programs in the 1910s.[8]

The most lucrative markets for prostheses by 1910 were urban areas with large manufacturing workforces and high railroad traffic. Massive industrial cities like Pittsburgh, according to one contemporary study, produced upwards of 500 industrial amputees in a year in the first decade of the century. Leg amputations occurred most often when pedestrians, workers, or passengers fell beneath moving trains, when miners had legs crushed in partial tunnel collapses, or when industrial workers were caught between heavy materials and vehicles. Arm amputations tended to occur more often in factory employment that required movement of the hands in and around swiftly moving machinery. Industrial clientele and city dwellers in general thus became the focus of manufacturers as the Civil War market declined in the late nineteenth century. Although manufacturers acknowledged that most customers were of limited financial means, they devoted the most space in their catalogues to their most innovative products. These were also the most expensive, suggesting some incongruity between what manufacturers claimed as their public service role and their recognition of what maximized profits. The largest catalogues, those published by the A. A. Marks company, featured testimonials written by a cross-section of the American workforce: 36 percent manual workers, 22 percent professionals and business owners, 15 percent clerical workers, and 14 percent farmers. Regardless of who was most typical within the prosthetic clientele, it was increasingly clear by the 1890s that the business was changing. The New York City limb maker who grumbled in 1896 that business was poor because "veterans are dying off" would have to shift his marketing focus in the next decade to remain competitive.[9]

Part of the objective of letter-writing was to make consumers believe that they had access to every scrap of information available on artificial limbs. When state distribution programs offered limbs to Civil War veterans, contracts between states and manufacturers allowed little shopping around on the part of amputees. North Carolina and Mississippi led the way in purchasing prostheses for Confederate veterans, allocating over $80,000 and $30,000 respectively, while the federal government allocated funds for Union veterans. It was only when accident victims were expected to pay for their own limbs, especially in the context of turn-of-the-century industrial cities, that judging between competing products became paramount. Companies warned prospective customers that charlatans lurked behind every advertisement for the "best" limbs. A railroad worker from Rhode Island counseled fellow amputees in 1904 that there was "as much difference in artificial limbs as there [was] in folks, and sometimes more." With variety came a series of bewildering choices for amputees.[10]

Feick Brothers of Pittsburgh noted that there had been "entirely too much mystery thrown about the making of artificial limbs" by manufacturers eager to confuse the public. The company used this claim to argue that other manufacturers had inflated prices by alluding to "secret methods" that made their limbs superior. Limb makers presented testimonials simultaneously to discredit rivals' claims of specialization and to establish their own technological proficiency. Equipped with lengthy lists of actual amputees who wore artificial limbs, companies stressed, the prospective customer could have all questions answered. In 1905, customer G. A. Corbett of Wisconsin wrote to the A. A. Marks company of the fundamental role that men like himself played: "I consider it my duty, and everyone else that wears an artificial limb, to tell the public, especially those that have to wear them, their candid opinions of the legs they are wearing."[11]

The first step in conveying a sense of utter candor through testimonials was to emphasize the impossibility of fully replacing natural arms and legs. Although all limb makers claimed to have perfected the mechanics of human motion, they also argued through correspondence that no manufacturer should claim too much about prosthetic function. Elmer Brewer, an Iowa farmer, wrote that his artificial arm was "all one could expect" from a prosthesis company. E. H. Hammond of Sheridan, Wyoming, admitted to J. F. Rowley that "the best is bad enough, and the best is what we must have." Realistic expectations, companies suggested, would prepare the customer for the difficulties of learning to use the limb and make him pleasantly surprised by the eventual result. John Byrne of Connecticut reasoned that "we all know" that prostheses could not "be expected to do the same amount of work as the natural one," yet amputees must struggle to make the most of them. Comparisons between natural and artificial limbs effectively served to blur the lines between the two. By using the trope of prostheses that delivered the "nearest approach to nature," companies claimed humility at the prospect of approximating natural design even as they boasted about their mastery of the process. Isaac Collins concluded his 1904 testimonial by declaring, "This artificial leg with rubber foot can't be excelled unless you get the blood circulating in it."[12]

A recurring element in testimonials stressed the ability of a particular limb to eradicate problems associated with other brands. In a similar fashion to the "natural versus artificial" debate, the focus on problems common to limbs served as a way of staking out the manufacturer in question as the exception to the rule. It was a false type of candor, then, but one meant to resonate with amputees who either had not purchased a limb before or had done so and had been dissatisfied with the results. Testimonial writers often explained the attributes of their limbs in the negative, noting the types of inconveniences that their particular limb did *not* cause. A soldier from Venezuela praised the A. A. Marks company's artificial leg for what it was not: "It is not heavy, neither does it tire me, nor pain my stump." By reminding readers of the potential for excessive weight, fatigue, and pain in daily use, Marks posited the existence of a community of sufferers who might never find relief if they did not learn about the Marks enterprise.[13]

Technical or sensitive subjects that might otherwise not appear in advertising material found their way into customers' letters. William Jessop wrote of his initial concern that his Apgar artificial leg would emit the same "disagreeable odor" that he had experienced with other limbs. Adam Ehrlin of Ohio rejoiced that his Marks limb had finally freed him from a creaking ankle joint that had plagued him while using a competitor's model. A doctor from Iowa referred to non-Marks models of artificial limbs as "rattle-traps," suggesting that only Marks had solved the problem of noisy prostheses. Indeed, the "unpleasant squeaking and rattling of joints" appeared often in testimonials as an embarrassing fact of life for people wearing inferior products. Writers' emphasis on odor, noise, and the details of their stumps' condition brought the minutiae of prosthetic living to the foreground. This was novel for advertising materials that otherwise encouraged the omission of any detail that might detract from the successful illusion of able-bodied movement. Gone were mid-Victorian concerns with artifice and insincerity when dealing with others; limb catalogues instead spread the gospel of social manipulation that characterized early twentieth-century business culture as a world of appearances. Testimonials dredged up the hidden aspects of prosthetic living in order to convince the prospective customer that he was now in the know.[14]

The grim pragmatism offered in such testimonials echoed contemporary medical texts that turned attention from the accident and toward the assumed recovery. Limb makers and their clients adopted the surgical community's focus on the usefulness of stumps as the key component of dismemberment. By the turn of the century, surgeons stressed that it was no longer necessary to save as much of an arm or leg as possible to offer an accident victim the best chance of optimal use. Instead, surgeons began amputating limbs in a fashion that best adapted them to use with prosthetics, even if it meant removing part of the limb that could otherwise be saved. This prosthesis-centric approach to amputation complemented limb makers' insistence on revealing customers' efforts to maintain their stumps. Indeed, advertising catalogues ranked care of stumps as one of the most pressing issues for prospective customers.[15]

Manufacturers noted that there was much to be lost in terms of function and comfort if amputees attempted to wear artificial limbs without first confirming that their limbs were in proper order. The J. T. and H. Apgar company of New York, for instance, advertised its course of treatment for stumps that, if followed religiously by the customer, would make the use of an artificial limb as pleasant as possible. All manufacturers specified stump care programs and frequently used testimonials to remind readers that positive reviews and tales of amazing physical ability were contingent upon such hard work. The rewards, they promised, were impressive. Many writers noted that it took considerable adjustments to become accustomed to artificial limbs as a facet of one's daily life. C. S. Powers of Valley Falls, New York, explained that when he first used his new limb, he "experienced considerable difficulty and embarrassment in manipulating same." Powers stated, however, that after a brief period of time, he could "perfectly control" his motion. Writers used the condition of their stumps, then, to explain the comfort experienced with a particular brand of limb and to commend the manufacturer further for his quality and care. Correspondents' assertions of sturdiness ("My stumps are hard as nails") indicated the physical state that made prosthetic reconstruction comfortable and implied that it was a particular limb maker that had delivered them to that state.[16]

In order to impart a sense of candor in the midst of hard-sell advertising copy, limb makers turned to the correspondence of happy customers who could give an insider's view of the trials and triumphs of learning to live prosthetically. The intended impression for the reader was that people outside the company were suddenly giving away the company's secrets (even if they all turned out to be flattering). Writers themselves recognized the power of the presumed independent observer, one declaring that "a satisfied customer is the best advertisement." Others shrewdly denigrated their own writing skills, distancing their rhetorical powers from the power of the prosthesis to convince the amputee through its sheer mechanical achievement. An Indiana man noted in 1901, "I am not much on commendatory letters, but will give you the best I have got and let the readers decide for themselves." A Rowley customer signed off in 1910, "No use occupying any more space—the goods speak for themselves." In the entrepreneurial spirit of plain talking and straight dealing, testimonials from customers attempted to remind potential purchasers that reading pages and pages of customers' reactions was ultimately unnecessary.[17]

"My life was a misery before I got one": An End to Isolation

If correspondents stressed that testimonials could only do so much to aid in the selling of a product, there was a more ambitious goal in mind that would eventually serve the company just the same. Testimonial sections were designed to forge letter-writing networks for the exchange of information about the shared experiences of the injured. Amputees were promised a useful connection with others across the country who understood the pains of dismemberment. Thus, when writers solicited correspondence from those who were searching for the best arm or leg, they (through the company) encouraged other amputees to bypass the company temporarily. The steamboat worker from Kentucky who declared himself "ready and willing to give any information . . . to anyone in need" was one of thousands of people scattered throughout and beyond the nation who sought each other based on their use of artificial limbs. Another man from New Jersey encouraged "everybody that has need of a leg" to visit him and observe him in action. A. A. Marks encouraged prospective buyers to read through its testimonials and provide the company with a list of men with whom they wished to correspond. Marks would subsequently send the list of addresses. With such a system in place, testimonial sections essentially allowed the reader to shop for pen pals as well as prosthetic goods.[18]

The viability of "consuming brotherhoods" at the turn of the century depended on the availability of both discretionary income and specific types of consumption that conformed to prevailing gender roles. Sociologist Mark Swiencicki has argued that not only was the late nineteenth and early twentieth century a period of "enormous" male consumption of goods and services, but that even working-class men participated voraciously. Sports, social and labor clubs, saloons, variety theaters, and gambling halls all encouraged what Swiencicki labeled "organizational consumption"—homosocial groupings that revolved around the use of goods and services and for which "membership" could be purchased directly or indirectly. Much of this male consumption took place in environments of fun and camaraderie, such as that enjoyed by the four million American men who claimed membership in fraternal organizations in 1900. Yet fraternal organizations had traditionally provided practical functions of reciprocity as well. The group identity fostered by limb makers was meant to be equally collegial and expedient.

In this way, the loose network of prosthesis customers was a combination of new forms of consumption-based fraternity and the traditional form of trauma-based fraternity seen prominently after the Civil War. Veterans groups promoted commemoration and *commiseration*, sanctioning members' emotional displays over wounds, lost comrades, and battle experiences. Studio photographs of veterans groups in the late nineteenth century often featured physical contact and elaborate poses that would be considered highly intimate by mid-twentieth-century standards.[19]

This intimacy was acceptable because it accompanied a narrative of physical and patriotic sacrifice. Similarly, limb manufacturers made intimacy between customers acceptable by couching it in terms of science, shared trauma, and capitalism. The pooling of resources that was central to fraternal groups in the United States and Europe before 1900 surfaced in customer correspondence as the sharing of tips and anecdotes. As scholars in disability studies have demonstrated, the historical construction of physical disability as an individual problem resulted in the widespread perception of specific forms of physical impairment as *sui generis*. In this framework, dismemberment became not only an end to the productive life of wage-earning but also to the mundane assumption that others shared one's experiences. Limb catalogues from the early twentieth century are vivid examples of the practice by which those who had experienced accidental trauma were instructed to believe in the overwhelming isolation brought on by their physical state. The solution, notes disability scholar Simi Linton, was to think of oneself as a "patient, client, and consumer."[20]

Limb makers expected amputees to huddle together by writing about what worked best in the prosthetics market. Though we cannot gauge the volume of correspondence that actually occurred according to the model set out by the companies, the model itself tells us much about the decision to highlight testimonials as a means to an end. Their vision of a collective masculinity contrasts sharply with the traditional notion of rugged independence as a prerequisite for active, male citizenship in the United States. For example, labor historian John Williams-Searle has shown that late nineteenth-century Midwestern railroad workers changed the way in which they viewed bodies damaged on the job. Trainmen initially treated work injuries as evidence of valiant, manly effort, but constricting labor markets and rising accident rates eventually made them fear both accidents and the bodily reminders of risky working lives. If self-determination in a capitalist society depended on the economic productivity brought by able-bodiedness, then workers without the full use of their limbs complicated a narrative in which experience on the job resulted in economic security and a strong character. Williams-Searle argues that unions adopted images of injured workers as useful mobilization tools but failed to implement programs to aid injured members who appeared irrevocably pathetic. The artificial limb catalogue and its testimonials posited a different dynamic, in which the pathos generated by representation was to be swept away by a commercial fix.[21]

The image of amputees presented by limb makers was one of isolated individuals who suffered their condition silently until brought together by sympathetic entrepreneurs. The Apgar company explicitly referred to its customers as "sufferers," using therapeutic language as it explained the process of ordering and fitting artificial limbs. It was through the process of purchasing that sufferers became non-sufferers. Customers themselves used bleak terms for their group—"sufferers," "the afflicted," "unfortunates," "unfortunate sufferers," "poor persons," "poor sufferers," "fellow sufferers," and "unfortunate humanity" among them. When Rosemarie Garland-Thomson writes that "disability is a culturally fabricated narrative of the body, similar to what we understand as the fictions of race and gender," she underscores the political process through which such texts as limb catalogues have created an either/or system of the fit and the unfit. The disability system, notes Garland-Thomson, has equated female, disabled, and dark bodies as dependent and incomplete, in need of intervention. Testimonials offered a way out (or, a way back). The promised intervention would come through both the technical assistance of the manufacturer and the practical camaraderie of fellow consumers.[22]

The depressing nature of the generic groups was the "before" that complemented the post-purchase "after" of ability, movement, and optimism. Feick Brothers of Pittsburgh declared in 1896:

> In the nature of things the only persons who are at all interested or put any thought upon the subject are those who wear the limbs, those who make them and the surgeons who prepare the stumps. And thus it usually happens, that when the necessity first arises for an artificial limb the patient has no friend or acquaintance who has any *practical* knowledge of the subject, and if by chance he has a friend who wears such an appliance, this friend may know only the work of a single manufacturer... This is not as it should be.[23]

In much the same way that disabled organizations in Great Britain and France encouraged members to forget their losses by immersing themselves in the company of other amputees, limb makers suggested that the most debilitating aspects of dismemberment were the various forms of isolation that accompanied it. An English customer noted to A. A. Marks in 1908: "sometimes I almost forget my loss, and that is saying a great deal." The best prosthetic illusion was that which came close to tricking the wearer himself. Forgetting loss was a matter of refusing to dwell on the past, and thus eliding the moment at which masculine independence became feminized vulnerability and destitution.[24]

Testimonials printed in catalogues rarely included much detail about the accidents that took customers' arms and legs. Even the exceptional letters that provided accident narratives used them as brief stepping stones along the path toward recovery:

> On August 29, 1906, I left my home, 338 Katon Avenue, Jersey City, to take a train on the Central Railroad of New Jersey, at Eighth St. Station, Bayonne, New Jersey, and while getting on the car, which I thought had stopped, it suddenly moved, I lost my footing, and the train passed over my two legs. I was taken to Bayonne Hospital and an operation was performed and both legs amputated. After being in the hospital about three months I made up my mind to have made artificial legs and gave you the order. After they were made by you I walked three blocks on them the same day I left the hospital, without feeling the loss of my natural ones. Since that time I am able to walk upstairs and do light work without the use of crutches. I am very thankful that I am able to work and am perfectly satisfied that you have the best patented limbs in the world, and would recommend them to all sufferers.
>
> Yours truly,
> Antonio Ielardia
> 277 E. 152nd St., New York[25]

Testimonials accomplished an act of replacement, training amputees' attention away from their lost limbs and toward the buoyant people among whom they suddenly found themselves. J. F. Rowley attributed its customers' successful walking both to the personalized treatment they received from the company and to the "moral encouragement" gained from seeing and reading about other amputees using artificial limbs.

This feeling of belonging was crucial to people who were told to be particularly sensitive to the situations and crowds in which they stood out. Marks detailed the humiliation that amputees confronted in their daily lives, as passersby pointed and gossiped about them:

> To be frequently asked: "How did it happen?" "Did you lose your arm in the war?" "Were you in a railroad collision?" or to have such utterances as: "Poor, unfortunate man!" "How he must have suffered!" "What a terrible loss!" whispered within your hearing, may, for a while, be accepted in good part, but their repetition becomes annoying and odious.[26]

Testimonial writers contributed to this argument by establishing the disguise of artificial limbs as an antidote to the unwanted attention of strangers. A cattleman from Australia commended Marks' limbs for making one "look as if he had nothing the matter with him." A Michigan attorney wrote of the "mental comfort" that wearing a quality limb gave him, as opposed to the constant self-doubt that came with wearing a problematic (noisy, smelly, ungainly) limb. A teacher from Indiana admitted that the greatest mental advantage of an artificial limb was its ability to relieve the wearer of "much embarrassment" in the course of public life. Once properly disguised, amputees could forget that which set them apart from others and instead concentrate on the connections that they could make with supposedly like-minded individuals.[27]

In the acutely pragmatic discourse of turn-of-the-century catalogues, the goal of artificial limbs was to return amputees to active lives. This generally implied wage-earning, but numerous examples of athletic and leisurely pursuits expanded the definition of "active" beyond the workday. The Apgar firm declared that a man who wore one of their limbs could not be "classed as a cripple," because movement and function were so thoroughly restored. The implication was clear—men worked, while cripples sat idle. The restoration of activity was meant to eliminate the intense social isolation presumably caused by the amputee's lack of a productive economic role. Rowley lamented that without artificial limbs at their disposal, amputees' "prospects for the future present a decidedly gloomy appearance." Apgar explained that in order "to keep his place in the race of human existence," a man in the United States required full use of his arms and legs; otherwise, "the unfortunate cripple" had to give way to "those less unfortunate in this respect." Studies of amputation and prosthetic rehabilitation in Europe have shown that physiologists and surgeons measured success in prosthetic rehabilitation by the ability of the amputee to perform the same occupational tasks that he had performed previously. Rather than mere survival or absence of pain, then, the ability of an amputee to earn a wage, ice skate, walk three miles, or ride a horse loomed as the desired endpoints of the prosthetic process in Europe and the United States.[28]

These promises defined masculinity across class lines as a standard, assumed repertoire of action. Disability studies scholars have stressed that gender consists of everyday bodily movements and comportments assembled into binary, prescriptive categories. Men whose bodies could not perform such activities or adopt such poses could alleviate the pressures of a bodily centric, capitalist culture through a consumer transaction. Testimonial writers echoed the refrain of successful function with the use of an artificial limb. More than any other feature, it was the chronicle of resumed work that characterized writers' tales. Charles Chrisley of Virginia divulged, "I never thought that I would be restored to my usefulness as I am," indicating that he could still meet the demands of farm work since his accident. Herman Hastings of Massachusetts wrote to A. A. Marks in 1904, "From the fact of having the artificial limb I obtained several prominent [clerical] positions, which otherwise would have never been opened to me." Railroad workers, grocers, chauffeurs, bakers, longshoremen, and silk weavers all declared that their working lives and wages were reclaimed. A ticket collector on the Weehawken Ferry in New Jersey wrote to the Apgar company in the spring of 1909, noting his ability to work as usual with an artificial limb. In his position as a public figure, the collector dealt with large crowds each day. Not only did he not stand out as an object of unwelcome attention, but he could serve the public as well as any able-bodied employee.[29]

A Canadian magician who professed to be skilled at the art of illusion told this tale to A. A. Marks:

> When I appear on stage my steps are elastic and never betray the fact that I wear an artificial leg. After having worn your leg about six weeks, I invited the surgeon who amputated my limb to witness my performance; he invited in turn his medical class. When I was called upon to show my artificial limb, you should have seen the expression on those students' faces—they could hardly believe it.[30]

Extreme examples served the dual purpose of accentuating the illusion of able-bodiedness brought by prostheses and highlighting the uplifting trope of a man on the job, doing what he had previously done. The fact that this man was a magician added a colorful element to the story, but it also highlighted the notion that artificial limbs allowed *skilled* workers to perform to the utmost of their abilities.

An end to isolation also meant incorporation into a happier, healthier existence. Stock phrases interwoven throughout testimonials—"It seems as though I were living in a new world," "It has done more for me than I ever dared hope for"—emphasized rebirth, all the more remarkable because it was shared with people in neighboring towns and distant countries. A writer from Maine declared: "I only wish all who are thus afflicted might be able to call on A. A. Marks, who will add much happiness to their lives." A doctor from Brooklyn agreed: "I am fully conscious that it is a great misfortune for any person to lose a limb and I realize how much that affliction is mitigated by you in making limbs to such a high degree of perfection as you have attained in that line." The "affliction" of dismemberment, wrote a farmer from Oklahoma, was so mitigated by the replacement that "the terror [was] removed" physically and psychologically. A farmer from Alabama summed up these sentiments for fellow Marks customers, "My life was a misery before I got one."[31]

And so it came back to the reading of testimonials and the sharing of information with other amputees. A. A. Marks explained in 1907:

> It was customary in former times to give with each testimonial the full post-office address of the writer; but the frequency of complaints by the writers

> as well as the readers, has induced us to locate by counties and states only and furnish complete addresses when asked for. Artificial limb wearers move about the same as other persons. Among eight hundred, a large proportion change their locations every year and cannot be reached by the old addresses. For this reason it is better to give up-to-date addresses as they are needed and called for. Any person desirous of communicating or conferring with testimonial writers can make a list from this chapter and send it to us. Immediately upon its receipt we will send addresses that have been corrected to date.[32]

The announcement offered numerous cues to suggest the vitality of the prosthetic project: a manufacturer that frequently updated its contact list; customers so eager to reach each other that they complained when their letters went astray; and the image of a dynamic population constantly on the move and hard to constrain.

In the decidedly male world of artificial limb catalogues, Bertha Deily of Zion Hill, Pennsylvania, invited any interested parties to visit her home to see her artificial leg. Deily represented the less than 10 percent of correspondents appearing in catalogues who were women, and the even smaller percentage of female customers who solicited correspondence. As such, Deily was welcomed into the fraternity of the prosthetically reconstructed as one more instance of the Apgar company's geographic reach (in this case, turning her eastern Pennsylvania residence into a virtual showroom). Edward Stewart of Bridgeport, Connecticut, told Apgar: "You can use this publicly for the benefit of those who are in doubt whose limb to get. You can also refer any prospective customer to me privately, and I will answer all letters." Manufacturers' amateur sales forces grew via the enlistment of individuals like Deily and Stewart. William Sparks invited all prospective customers to his New York City home, where he would "try to entertain them" by performing tasks both mundane and extraordinary. Although few letters promised such entertainment directly, the exchange of information was meant to offer emotional rewards as well as functional ones. The epitome of the community ideal stressed in testimonials came in a letter from W. L. Corgan of St. Louis to the A. A. Marks company: "Brothers, don't be discouraged if you get a leg or two cut off, for if you are the right kind of stuff, there is lots of fun here for you yet."[33]

"As long as I live": The Benefits of Membership

Prosthetic manufacturers pushed amputees to affiliate with each other, to create and maintain a series of direct and indirect communications in order to counter the lonely experience of dismemberment. An offshoot of this effort was an attempt to position the company as the facilitator or mediator of all exchanges. Thus, the final message conveyed in artificial limb testimonials was that loyalty to a particular firm was rewarded through symbolic membership in an enduring organization. Customers who persevered with their prosthetic products could enjoy the company's success by proxy. J. F. Rowley led in this respect, establishing a "Ten Year Club" for individuals who had worn a Rowley leg for a decade or more and wished to correspond with both veterans and newcomers to the world of artificial limbs. In its 1911 catalogue, the company supplied one hundred letters from customers designated as Ten Year Club members, including their addresses. Frank Palmer attempted a similar scheme in 1865, when he announced the establishment of a "Roll of Honor" to exchange biographical information on the "thousands of soldiers and sailors" who lost limbs during the Civil War. Although Palmer's American Artificial Limbs Company sought a "mass of narrations" to exhibit the "heroic fortitude" of those who fought, a related goal was to glorify the company that served these men.[34]

The advertising appeal of the Ten Year Club or the Roll of Honor lay in their vision of a venerated company history combined with promises of an auspicious future. Writers' tales of being abandoned by their former limb makers revolved around both practical implications (the inability to find replacement parts or take advantage of warranties) and emotional wounds (losing jobs or giving up all hope of living "normally" again). Brooklyn resident William Broach noted in 1909: "Six years ago I had the misfortune to lose my leg; some months after I had an artificial limb made by another firm which was absolutely worthless, as it was simply impossible for me to wear it, and after he got his money he ignored me entirely." The aura of loyalty produced by such gimmicks as the Ten Year Club was designed to counteract amputees' inclination to think myopically about their prospects.[35]

Testimonials selected for publication often emphasized a lengthy track record with a manufacturer's wares. In 1904 a train dispatcher from New York wrote to A. A. Marks that "eight years of constant wear without a cent for repairs must appeal with force to wearers of artificial feet." It was not simply longevity that made particular limbs appealing, but the economics of longevity—the promise that devices that worked well cost less over the course of time than cheaper models that required greater upkeep. A railroad clerk from Illinois had even more experience with Marks' limbs, noting that four artificial legs in forty years had allowed him to keep up with men half his age. The implications of such statements were that both prosthesis and individual survived, even thrived, thanks to the genius of the inventor and his company.[36]

In addition to identifying with other amputees, customers were shown that they could also relate closely to their artificial limb. In 1903 Harry Dunn of New York wrote, "If I go without it only a few hours I feel out of place and miss it nearly as much as I did the original." An Oregon laborer declared that his artificial leg had become his "best friend; without it my life would be miserable." A teacher from Newfoundland wrote of his joy over the replacement limb for "my old friend No. 1" that he had been wearing for six years. Companies that reprinted these letters counseled readers to identify their own worth with their bodies' performance. There was no suggestion that personhood could be defined by any criteria other than physical function. Such was the professed ease and comfort of artificial limbs that some testimonials featured astounding degrees of hyperbole. Edward Marshall, a journalist who lost a leg while covering the Spanish-American War, praised his prosthesis in dramatic terms: "I almost wish that it may be necessary to amputate the right leg, as I can certainly handle the left one much better than I can the one which is still flesh and blood." By presenting prostheses as enjoyable, faithful companions, writers turned the life of an amputee into a symbiotic relationship with a company and its merchandise.[37]

In the same way that manufacturers expected amputees to incorporate artificial limbs into their bodies, they also hoped that customers would view themselves as being incorporated into the longevity of the company. When Apgar customer William Jessop wrote from Brooklyn in 1910, "You delivered the leg to me in December 1905, and it has been part of me ever since," he captured well the concept of complete prosthetic assimilation. The limb became part of the amputee, the amputee became part of the company, and the company became part of American technological innovation. A loose insert that A. A. Marks included in its 1910 catalogue declared that because "A NAME IS EVERYTHING," the firm had "set a standard of efficiency that no other firm in the world has ever equaled." James Butler wrote to Marks that his limb had been "a great help in [his] daily labor" as a fisherman. His thoughts on the future were simple: "I hope and believe it will be so as long as I live."[38]

Constructing testimonial networks was just one of a variety of strategies that limb makers used to make their firms accessible to customers. By encouraging prospective customers to see themselves in the company and its clientele—an effort taken to an extreme by the Artificial Limb Manufacturing Company of Pittsburgh, which had a staff composed entirely of amputees—limb makers packaged and repackaged the community ideal. The *Chicago Tribune* ran a seemingly fictional story in 1900 about a local man who had lost both legs when he was hit by a train. When he arrived at an unnamed prosthesis dealer in town, he was shocked to see staff members climbing, jumping, and working machinery at a rapid pace on the sales floor. The amputee tried out his new limbs, only to claim that he would never be able to function as a "sound limbed man" again. The owner then had each staff member parade by to lift the pant legs and lower the socks that covered artificial limbs, thereby proving the company's empathetic relationship with customers. Rowley claimed in 1911 that most of its stockholders were amputees who had such confidence in the company's ability to solve the problem of movement after amputation that they invested in the venture. An Apgar customer stressed in 1909 that patentee John Apgar, "on account of wearing one himself," exhibited a "fellow feeling" for those who required prostheses.[39]

The intimacy implied by advertising copy survived in the letters of correspondents, yet it began in the factory or sales office. Feick Brothers boasted that its employees had "successfully fitted many hundreds of artificial limbs" while maintaining its pledge to "first-class work and honest treatment for all." Such a pledge placed some responsibility on the customer to travel to the sales office. Feick Brothers preferred customers to come to their establishment on Sixth Street in Pittsburgh when making a purchase. Their catalogue noted that if their employees could "examine the stump personally," they could then give the best assessment on what type of product would work. The company did allow transactions by mail, however, asking customers who chose this method to provide a "careful description of the amputation and the condition of the stump," to aid in selection and sizing. More information was needed as well; customers had to send measurements for the shoulder strap that would secure artificial legs, the exact specifications of the end of their stump for fitting the socket, and the circumference of their thighs at five-inch increments. For all transactions completed by mail, Feick provided "printed formulas" for taking measurements and written directions for supplying the manufacturer with any details that he might need to know.[40]

A. A. Marks, too, stressed the importance of a precise fitting that could be done via the mail but would ideally happen in person. Marks noted that there were many limb makers in the world but very few "fitters," trained experts who took time with individual customers to assure comfort. Marks promised those customers who dealt directly with the firm "the genuine, the best, and the most approved." The company emphasized the spectacle of visiting its Broadway offices and showroom, repeatedly using images of a seven-floor building with amputees on the front sidewalk. The company also printed testimonials that reinforced this notion, like a Wisconsin customer's claim that "no one can help but feel at home" in their showroom. Customers who ordered Marks limbs through third-party dealers, on the other hand, were warned to be vigilant by specifically asking for the Marks limb and then checking their delivered model for authentic Marks patent stamps. Despite the company's call for customers to visit an office, Marks noted in 1914 that most of the people who supplied testimonials had been "supplied without leaving their homes." Payment could also be made through the mail. Marks required a deposit of at least one half of the total cost before making limbs to order. The firm even printed money conversion tables for foreign customers who found it more convenient to send "any money that may be most available."[41]

The Apgar company devised a course of stump treatment that would presumably guarantee comfort for those who used an Apgar leg. Customers placed under John Apgar's "personal supervision" were expected to visit the sales office for consultation. The company boasted that it kept no inventory but instead made each limb to order after its employees had measured all aspects of a customer's stump. Alternately, Apgar accepted measurement sheets sent through the mail (preferably completed by a physician). For amputations below the knee, Apgar offered to send a "skilled representative" to customers who lived in the New York area in order to measure and make a cast of the stump. Apgar's emphasis on expertise and patent-holding was not unique, but it went as far as noting that the measurement sheet used to produce artificial legs was itself patented.[42]

Rowley offered not just the prosthesis but a system of rehabilitation that it called an "education in the use of the Rowley Leg." Customers were to mail in measurements taken by a physician or other expert. In the meantime, customers had to purchase and wear the company's patented stump protector until the prosthetic leg had been manufactured and customized. When the test fitting arrived, amputees were expected to make their way to one of the company's establishments in Chicago, Pittsburgh, St. Louis, Kansas City, Omaha, Indianapolis, Cincinnati, or Detroit. Rowley promised to send an employee to meet customers at the nearest train station and transport them to the office. The personal fitting session, according to the company's catalogue, was the time when the customer realized that the "only sure way to comfort" was through working one-on-one with experts. Finally, the Rowley firm offered "lessons in walking" with a trained "corps of instructors" who were themselves amputees. During this fitting and instructional period, Rowley encouraged customers to have their mail sent to the office and enjoy nearby restaurants and theaters. The intimate treatment contrasted with what Rowley termed the "businesslike conditions" that governed the purchase of a limb from competitors. Marks illustrated this idea well in a diagram of the interior of its factory (figure 4.2). The building's second story held both a large work floor with nine employees tending to their tasks and two private offices in which customers could be seen in consultation with the company's fitters. Just beyond the closed door of one of the offices, a Marks employee stood with his arms folded, watching the progress of a man walking toward him with the help of an artificial leg.[43]

The close links that customers apparently felt between themselves and the companies meant that their correspondence often approached the level of private letters. A satisfied Apgar customer echoed many writers in the

Figure 4.2 The promise of intimate customer service. Detail from A. A. Marks, *Manual of Artificial Limbs*, 1907.

use of phrases like "as you know," a device that rendered the customer and company so intimate as to make the staff aware of any individual's specific experiences. Firms' efforts to individualize their operations in the personage of a single inventor found resonance with customers who appreciated special treatment. William Walsh of Brooklyn noted: "I cannot find words with which to express my thanks to Mr. Apgar for the leg he made for me, and I heartily recommend his leg to my fellow men." A New Jersey writer told John Apgar, "I pray God to spare you your health and strength to help all those unfortunates whom you come in contact with." D. W. Tucker of Trumbill, Ohio, sent his regards to "all the boys in the shop" at Rowley's Pittsburgh sales office. A soldier addressed A. A. Marks in 1904 as "my good friend and benefactor of suffering humanity." Testimonials counseled prospective customers that they could not only be linked to fellow amputees but could also make new friends at the local prosthesis house.[44]

J. F. Rowley used a mechanical metaphor to introduce the concept of its Ten Year Club in 1911:

> As in all other machines an artificial leg consists of parts and the intrinsic value of these parts determine the value of the whole leg, which of course represents the parts assembled or combined.[45]

Here was a metaphor for both the Ten Year Club and the prosthetic community as a whole—a loose collection of people who came together symbolically and perhaps literally in order to commiserate, challenge each other, and inspire further purchases from the sponsoring manufacturer. Induction into the Ten Year Club brought no material rewards, tangible symbols of membership, or discounted merchandise from the company. The club was designed to confer a specific type of status upon people who had displayed a level of consumer loyalty that could be put to work, transformed into an ideal vision of customers working with each other and the manufacturer for the happiness of all.

Conclusion

The hyperbole of testimonials raised comment even within the industry. In their 1896 catalogue, the owners of the Feick Brothers firm, who positioned themselves as both expert craftsmen and industry watchdogs, noted, "As to the matter of testimonials, while some are of value, it is a well known fact that many are to be had for the asking, and these of the most extravagant and laudatory kind." Feick Brothers' challenge to the utility of testimonials for customers represented a small manufacturer's defensive swipe at the success of its larger competitors. It certainly did not signal a moratorium on the use of customer comments in pamphlets and catalogues. Limb makers did not expect testimonials to stand alone, instead, they were to work in tandem with all that preceded them in advertisements—mechanical diagrams, scientific explanations of human motion, price lists, and so on. Rowley appealed to prospective customers' ability to investigate claims and decide for themselves: "All we ask is that the reader weigh carefully our array of incontrovertible facts herein shown and draw his own conclusions." Readers were to approach testimonials as one of many types of proof. Rowley repeatedly defended the veracity of its catalogue images, using photographic authority as a means of establishing its superiority. "This cut," the company's catalogue noted, "is a half-tone from a photograph of a Rowley Leg and is a fairly good picture, and is not a drawing made by some artists, but is actual and real."[46]

Feick Brothers suggested that testimonials could not be granted a similar status of "actual and real." Yet the veracity of turn-of-the-century testimonials was always beside the point. Limb catalogues contained several elements that undercut the authority of testimonials—their sheer number (producing a monotonous reading experience), the writers who begged readers to ignore their words as amateurish and poorly expressed, and the exaggeration and melodrama pervading many missives. It was the appeal of hearing from others, of sharing experiences that could otherwise appear to be isolating and peculiar, that made testimonials prominent features in limb catalogues. As a sales technique, moreover, the testimonial possessed the cunning ability to speak for the manufacturer without *directly* speaking for the manufacturer. By selecting and editing letters, limb makers assembled arguments that they had already created in other sections of their catalogues. Testimonials offered a kind of genuine evidence buttressed by their genial and seemingly simple quality. Manufacturers insisted that these were commendations written by people who were experienced in the life of an amputee and entirely uninterested in the tactics of advertising. Testimonial writers were ideal spokesmen for artificial limb companies because they represented the content and optimistic successes that manufacturers believed customers wanted to be. Published correspondence served the company by prompting amputees to see themselves as among allies.

NOTES

1. On the advertising and business history of the artificial limbs industry in the United States, see Lisa Herschbach, "Fragmentation and Reunion: Medicine, Memory and Body in the American Civil War" (Ph.D. diss. Harvard University, 1997); Stephen Mihm, " 'A Limb Which Shall Be Presentable in Polite Society': Prosthetic Technologies in the Nineteenth Century," in *Artificial Parts, Practical Lives: Modern Histories of Prosthetics*, ed. Katherine Ott, David Serlin, and Stephen Mihm (New York: New York University Press, 2002), 282–299; and Edward Slavishak, " 'Artificial Limbs and Industrial Workers' Bodies in Turn-of-the-century Pittsburgh," *Journal of Social History* 36 (Winter 2003): 365–388.
2. William Rideing, "Patched Up Humanity," *Appletons' Journal* 13 (June 19, 1875): 784.
3. J. F. Rowley Co., *An Illustrated Treatise on Artificial Legs* (Chicago, 1911), 126; A. A. Marks, *Manual of Artificial Limbs* (New York, 1907), 257.
4. J. T. and H. Apgar, *Catalogue of Artificial Limbs* (New York, 1910), 45; Rowley, *An Illustrated Treatise on Artificial Legs*, 129; Marks, *Manual of Artificial Limbs* (1907), 326.
5. Amputees could receive free limb catalogues through doctors or by mailing applications that appeared in newspapers and promotional pamphlets. The Fuller company distributed a twenty-five-page pamphlet in 1887 that excerpted its 230-page catalogue. Marks' 1893 circular for the World's Fair in Chicago advertised the company's free 430-page catalogue. Displays at

industrial exhibitions also touted limb makers' wares. A. A. Marks, for one, displayed models of its limbs at exhibitions in Atlanta, Philadelphia, New Orleans, and Augusta, Georgia in the 1880s and 1890s.

6. American Artificial Limb Company, *The Palmer Arm and Leg* (Philadelphia, 1865), 5.
7. *St. Louis Globe-Democrat*, February 24, 1900; George R. Fuller, *Anatomical Artificial Limbs* (Rochester, 1887).
8. Mark Aldrich, *Death Rode the Rails: American Railroad Accidents and Safety, 1828–1965* (Baltimore: Johns Hopkins University Press, 2006), 323, 327; John Fabian Witt, *The Accidental Republic: Crippled Workingmen, Destitute Widows, and the Remaking of American Law* (Cambridge, MA: Harvard University Press, 2004), 26, 187.
9. Crystal Eastman, *Work-Accidents and the Law* (New York: Charities Publication Committee, 1910), 11–13; *Brooklyn Daily Eagle*, September 6, 1896. For more on the nature of industrial accidents between 1890 and 1915, see Slavishak, "Artificial Limbs and Industrial Workers' Bodies in Turn-of-the-century Pittsburgh." The correspondents' distribution is based on the 1914 A. A. Marks catalogue. Of the 638 testimonials printed, 502 offered occupational information: 182 were from manual workers, including skilled craftsmen and common laborers; 112 were from professionals, mostly merchants, manufacturers, and teachers; 74 were written by clerical workers, mostly in stores, telegraph offices, railroad offices, and banks; 70 were written by farmers; only seven testimonials came from military personnel.
10. Ansley Herring Wegner, *Phantom Pain: North Carolina's Artificial-Limbs Program for Confederate Veterans* (Raleigh: North Carolina Department of Cultural Resources, 2004), 32–35; Marks, *Manual of Artificial Limbs (1907)*, 283. On the emergence of state pension programs after the Civil War, see also Laurann Figg and Jane Farrell-Beck, "Amputation in the Civil War: Physical and Social Dimensions," *Journal of the History of Medicine and Allied Sciences* 48 (October 1993): 454–475; and Jennifer Davis McDaid, "With Lame Legs and Money: Virginia's Disabled Confederate Veterans," *Virginia Cavalcade* 47 (Winter 1998): 14–25.
11. Feick Brothers, *Illustrated Catalogue and Price List of Surgical Instruments*, 3rd ed. (Pittsburgh, 1896), 552; Marks, *Manual of Artificial Limbs* (1907), 284.
12. Marks, *Manual of Artificial Limbs* (1907), 269, 273, 283; Rowley, *An Illustrated Treatise on Artificial Legs,*173.
13. Marks, *Manual of Artificial Limbs* (1907), 280.
14. Apgar, *Catalogue of Artificial Limbs*, 39; Marks, *Manual of Artificial Limbs* (1907), 298, 324, 330; Karen Halttunen, *Confidence Men and Painted Women: A Study of Middle-Class Culture in America, 1830–1870* (New Haven: Yale University Press, 1982), 208–209. On illusion and bodily management, see also John F. Kasson, *Rudeness and Civility: Manners in Nineteenth Century Urban America* (New York: Hill and Wang, 1990), 112–146.
15. Warren Stone Bickham, "Amputations," in *Surgery: Its Principles and Practice*, ed. William Williams Keen (Philadelphia: W. B. Saunders Co.,

1909), 806. See also Philip Wilson, "Principles of Design and Construction of Artificial Legs," *Publications of the Red Cross Institution for Crippled and Disabled Men* 2 (July 10, 1918): 8.

16. Apgar, *Catalogue of Artificial Limbs*, 10–11, 40; Marks, *Manual of Artificial Limbs* (1907), 397.
17. Apgar, *Catalogue of Artificial Limbs*, 48; Rowley, *An Illustrated Treatise on Artificial Legs*, 130, 170. The Apgar catalogue noted: "The testimonials on the pages following were written by some of our many patrons in their own hand writing fo [*sic.*] which we have the originals in our office."
18. A. A. Marks, *Manual of Artificial Limbs* (New York, 1914), 257. In 1889, a writer for the *Journal of the Franklin Institute* estimated that Marks had 9,000 limbs in use. See "On Marks' Artificial Limbs," *Journal of the Franklin Institute* 127 (May 1889): 336.
19. Mark Swiencicki, "Consuming Brotherhood: Men's Culture, Style and Recreation as Consumer Culture, 1880–1930," *Journal of Social History* 31 (Summer 1998): 781, 791; Mary Ann Clawson, *Constructing Brotherhood: Class Gender, and Fraternalism* (Princeton: Princeton University Press, 1989), 7; John Ibson, *Picturing Men: A Century of Male Relationships in Everyday American Photography* (Washington, DC: Smithsonian Institution Press, 2002), 45. See also David Deitcher, *Dear Friends: American Photographs of Men Together, 1840–1918* (New York: Harry N. Abrams, 2001), 118.
20. Clawson, *Constructing Brotherhood*, 41. Presentation style factored greatly in the process of making discussions about products acceptable to men. Brent Shannon, "ReFashioning Men: Fashion, Masculinity, and the Cultivation of the Male Consumer in Britain, 1860–1914," *Victorian Studies* 46 (Summer 2004): 624, notes that turn-of-the-century advertisements for male corsets emphasized athletic and "surgical" features rather than focusing on the ability of the device to improve one's figure. All manufacturers surveyed here adopted this gendered marketing strategy for artificial limbs. For disability studies approaches to forms of disability as "isolable phenomena," see Simi Linton, *Claiming Disability: Knowledge and Identity* (New York: New York University Press, 1998), 134–135.
21. John Williams-Searle, "Cold Charity: Manhood, Brotherhood, and the Transformation of Disability, 1870–1900," in *The New Disability History: American Perspectives*, ed. Paul K. Longmore and Lauri Umansky (New York: New York University Press, 2001), 158–159, 179–180.
22. Apgar, *Catalogue of Artificial Limbs*, 34, 38, 40, 42; Marks, *Manual of Artificial Limbs* (1907), 288; Rosemarie Garland-Thomson, "Integrating Disability, Transforming Feminist Theory," in *Gendering Disability*, ed. Bonnie G. Smith and Beth Hutchison (New Brunswick: Rutgers University Press, 2004), 77, 79.
23. Feick Brothers, *Illustrated Catalogue and Price List of Surgical Instruments*, 552.
24. Seth Koven, "Remembering and Dismemberment: Crippled Children, Wounded Soldiers, and the Great War in Great Britain," *American Historical Review* 99 (October 1994): 1195–1196; Marks, *Manual of Artificial Limbs* (1914), 262. In the 1910s, the British Disabled Society adopted testimonial

techniques used by American limb makers for decades, asking for photographs and autobiographical blurbs from men who used prosthetics.

25. Apgar, *Catalogue of Artificial Limbs*, 50.
26. A. A. Marks (1914), 183. On the emphasis that popular writers placed on the conspicuity of amputees in public, see David D. Yuan, "Disfigurement and Reconstruction in Oliver Wendell Holmes's 'The Human Wheel, Its Spokes and Felloes,'" in *The Body and Physical Difference: Discourses of Disability*, ed. David T. Mitchell and Sharon L. Snyder (Ann Arbor: University of Michigan Press, 1997), 71–88.
27. Marks, *Manual of Artificial Limbs* (1907), 333, 353, 366.
28. Apgar, *Catalogue of Artificial Limbs*, 5, 9; *Rowley, An Illustrated Treatise on Artificial Legs*, 5. On the work of labor scientist Jules Amar in France, see Roxanne Panchasi, "Reconstructions: Prosthetics and Rehabilitation of the Male Body in World War I France," *Differences* 7 (Fall 1995): 109–164. Whereas labor reformers and industrial critics documented the existence of thousands of working-class amputees, the variety of stories relayed through testimonials was meant to convince the reader that anyone could find happiness with the right artificial limb. An Apgar customer implied that class distinctions meant little for the company's clientele: "In my estimation your patent legs are the best that have been put on the market within the reach of both rich and poor." Symbols of class distinction, however, were built into the very limbs said to erase hierarchies. Manufacturers could not claim that peg-legs and hook-arms were on par with expensive models featuring articulated joints and the fusion of rubber, wood, metal, and rawhide, except in the vague sense that all products enabled users to resume their established social roles.
29. Russell P. Shuttleworth, "Disabled Masculinity: Expanding the Masculine Repertoire," in *Gendering Disability*, ed. Bonnie G. Smith and Beth Hutchison (New Brunswick: Rutgers University Press, 2004), 167; Marks, *Manual of Artificial Limbs* (1907), 280, 315; Apgar, *Catalogue of Artificial Limbs*, 38.
30. Marks, *Manual of Artificial Limbs* (1907), 265.
31. Ibid., 259, 312, 394, 404.
32. Ibid., 257.
33. Apgar, *Catalogue of Artificial Limbs*, 38, 39, 48; Marks, *Manual of Artificial Limbs* (1907), 286. Marks catalogues from 1905, 1907, and 1914 reprinted similar sets of letters in each edition. Of 758 testimonials printed in the 1905 catalogue, 62 were from women (8.2 percent). Two of these 62 were written by mothers on behalf of their sons.
34. Rowley, *An Illustrated Treatise on Artificial Legs*, 123–124; American Artificial Limb Company, 44. By 1911, Rowley claimed to have over 2000 members in its Ten Year Club, with many more excluded on the technicality that they had purchased a new Rowley leg after only eight or nine years of use.
35. Apgar, *Catalogue of Artificial Limbs*, 41.
36. Marks, *Manual of Artificial Limbs*, 260, 261.
37. Ibid., 267, 296, 351, 396. Susan Wendell writes of her experience with myalgic encephalomyelitis: "I am learning not to identify myself with my body, and this helps me to live a good life with a debilitating chronic illness."

See Susan Wendell, "The Suffering and Limited Body," in *Gendered Bodies: Feminist Perspectives*, ed. Judith Lorber and Lisa Jean Moore (Los Angeles: Roxbury Publishing Co., 2007), 187.

38. Apgar, *Catalogue of Artificial Limbs*, 39; Marks, *Manual of Artificial Limbs* (1907), 274. On prosthetic assimilation and incorporation at the turn of the century, see Tim Armstrong, "Prosthetic Modernism," in *Modernism, Technology, and the Body: A Cultural Study* (New York: Cambridge University Press, 1998), 77–105; and Mark Seltzer, *Bodies and Machines* (New York: Routledge, 1992). On the advertising argument of innovation in prosthetics manufacturing, see Erin O'Connor, "'Fractions of Men': Engendering Amputation in Victorian Culture," *Comparative Studies in Society and History* 39 (October 1997): 767. O'Connor writes: "Fixed up nearly as good as new by the same system that crippled him, the prosthetic man became a symbol of all that was possible in the modern world of manufacture, a walking advertisement for the personal and social benefits to be had from a full-scale embrace of machine culture."
39. *Cities of Pittsburgh and Allegheny: Leading Merchants and Manufacturers* (New York: Historical Publishing Company, 1886), 193; *Chicago Tribune*, March 2, 1900; Rowley, *An Illustrated Treatise on Artificial Legs*, 10; Apgar, *Catalogue of Artificial Limbs*, 41.
40. *Illustrated Catalogue and Price List of Surgical Instruments, Illustrated Catalogue and Price List of Surgical Instruments* 552, 554–556, 558.
41. Marks, *Manual of Artificial Limbs* (1907), 284; A. A. Marks, "Highest Award for Artificial Limbs at the World's Columbian Exposition, Chicago, 1893," *Manual of Artificial Limbs* (1893), 2; Marks, *Manual of Artificial Limbs* (1907) (1914), 139, 256–257. Marks, like most artificial limb manufacturers, allowed for payment on an installment plan for "those in indigent circumstances." The firm required promissory notes signed by the customer and endorsed by a "reliable business person" with a sound credit rating. Payments could then be made weekly or monthly. On the economics of limb-purchase for industrial workers, see Slavishak, "Artificial Limbs and Industrial Workers' Bodies in Turn-of-the-century Pittsburgh," 382.
42. Apgar, *Catalogue of Artificial Limbs*, 11, 17.
43. Rowley, *An Illustrated Treatise on Artificial Legs*, 10, 44, 74, 77, 84–87. In contrast to the prevailing emphasis on direct contact between customer and manufacturer, the George Fuller company stressed mail-order transactions as the heart of the enterprise, with the slogan, "Limbs made without the presence of patient at the factory, and a good fit guaranteed." For companies like Fuller with small sales offices in multiple cities (Boston, Philadelphia, and Buffalo by the turn of the century), mail-order business was a relatively inexpensive means of reaching amputees beyond the local area.
44. Apgar, *Catalogue of Artificial Limbs*, 38, 45, 46; Rowley, *An Illustrated Treatise on Artificial Legs*, 126; Marks, *Manual of Artificial Limbs*, 358.
45. Rowley, *An Illustrated Treatise on Artificial Legs*, 123.
46. Feick Brothers, *Illustrated Catalogue and Price List of Surgical Instruments* 552; Rowley, *An Illustrated Treatise on Artificial Legs*, 6, 48.

CHAPTER 5

"The Mad Search for Beauty": Actresses, Cosmetics, and the Middle-Class Market[1]

Marlis Schweitzer

"Actresses as a rule know no more about making themselves beautiful than does the average woman; neither are they naturally more beautiful," wrote actress Margaret Illington Banes in a 1912 article entitled "The Mad Search for Beauty." "The truth of the matter is," she continued, "that no actress—or any woman—can impart the secrets of beauty to another, any more than the rich man can impart the secrets of business success to some other man."[2] Disturbed by recent trends in the theatrical profession that required actresses to present themselves as "beauty specialists," Banes argued that stage stars captivated audiences because they had numerous opportunities to appear onstage dressed in the height of style; "under the same circumstances," she concluded, most women "would look quite as well."[3]

But Banes' sober argument against the "mad search for beauty" seems to have done little to deter women from trying to reproduce themselves in the image of their favorite stars. By the 1910s, actresses were both highly respected and eagerly sought after for advice on fashion, cosmetics, and other beauty issues. Female theatregoers across the United States avidly followed stage stars' offstage lives, exchanged the latest stage gossip as a form of cultural capital, and employed a variety of techniques to recreate stage fashions, copying actresses' hairdos, dress styles, and other accessories. Thanks to growing coverage of actresses' onstage and offstage exploits in newspapers and magazines, many women felt extremely close to actresses they had never met but who represented an appealing vision of modern womanhood. For working- and middle-class women, in particular, the actress's ability to achieve social advancement and transform herself into a stylish, respectable lady on- and offstage implied that with the right clothes and a few lessons in deportment, they could do the same.[4]

Watching this trend, manufacturers of cosmetics, corsets, and other fashion products realized that an association with stage actresses was the surest way to expand into new markets while distinguishing themselves from the competition.[5] Echoing Banes' contention that the actress was no more beautiful than the average woman, they emphasized the artificial processes that transformed leading ladies from attractive women into exceptional beauties and implied that their products could do the same for every woman. Indeed, whereas Banes highlighted the artificiality of the actress's onstage appearances to dissuade women from emulating stage stars, advertisers used the revelation that the actress was *not* "naturally more beautiful" to promote the notion that every woman had the right, the capacity, and the obligation to make herself as beautiful as possible. Through the figure of the actress, these manufacturers promised that every woman would realize her full potential if she simply adjusted her daily beauty regime to incorporate a range of new products and practices.

This essay explores the various interrelated developments that drew the cosmetics industry to use testimonials from Broadway actresses as part of a larger strategy to expand its consumer base. Although some companies had featured actresses in their advertisements decades prior to the 1910s, lingering associations between female performers and prostitutes, two groups of women who "painted" their faces for a living, had limited the actress's appeal to middle-class consumers. It was only in the early twentieth century, when stage actresses finally gained a higher degree of social respectability, that advertisers could fully exploit their names and images to promote new products and encourage new patterns of consumer behavior.

Early Celebrity Testimonials: Scandal and Redemption

Celebrity testimonials first attracted widespread attention in the late nineteenth century when the craze for collecting celebrity photographs, or "cartomania," was at its height.[6] Advertisers capitalized on this consumer phenomenon by inviting (and sometimes paying) noted medical professionals, military officers, preachers, and performing artists to testify to the quality and worthiness of their products, inviting consumers to join, through consumption, a community of familiar faces.[7] Perhaps the most successful and long-standing testimonial campaign of this period was that launched by A. and F. Pears Ltd in 1882 featuring British actress Lily Langtry, "the world's most beautiful woman." In exchange for £132 (a somewhat strange fee that reportedly reflected her weight at the time), the former mistress of Edward VII agreed to let the company publish advertisements with her image and the following statement: "Since using Pears' Soap for the hands and complexion *I have discarded all others*" [emphasis in original].[8] Riding the wave of her enduring international fame, Pears' displayed Langtry's statement in its newspaper, magazine, and trade card advertisements for two decades.[9]

Following Pears' lead, American beauty culturist Harriet Hubbard Ayer approached Langtry to endorse her line of Mme. Recamier Preparations, offering the actress a furnished apartment in exchange for her statement. Ayer also enlisted the services of popular American actresses Lillian Russell, Cora Brown Potter, and Fanny Davenport, and the internationally renowned French actress Sarah Bernhardt, who each received payment in cash or kind.[10] Yet while Ayer ran advertisements throughout most of the 1880s in reputable publications such as *The New York Times*—a testament to her ability to attract a respectable clientele—most cosmetics companies struggled to win over middle-class consumers in this period. Although undoubtedly intrigued by the Pears' and Mme. Recamier advertisements, most middle-class women seem to have shied away from buying beauty products endorsed by stage stars, anxious about public perception of cosmetics use in general, not to mention the questionable morality of the actresses who endorsed them.[11]

For their part, actresses happily complied with advertisers' requests to promote their products, lending their names and images to an ever-widening range of products that included everything from chocolates, corsets, and cigars to dentifrice, pianos, and patent medicine (figure 5.1).[12] Australian opera diva Adelina Patti, one of the first stars to follow Lily Langtry in endorsing Pears' Soap, was so eager to lend her name for advertising purposes that she earned the nickname "Testimonial Patti."[13] The program for her 1904 "farewell performance" in Salt Lake City, for example, includes testimonials for Crème Simon, a cold cream; the Apollo Piano Player; Steinway and Sons; and Hill's Pure California Olive Oil.[14] But performers' indiscriminate endorsement of anything and everything ultimately undermined the value of the testimonial as a marketing tool by raising questions about the truthfulness of their statements and suspicions about the products they promoted. By the late 1890s, a series of scandals involving the use of fake or "tainted" testimonials by patent medicine companies, that is, some companies featured made-up testimonials while others included statements from individuals who claimed that the advertised product could do things it could not, further tarnished the testimonial's reputation, and many companies decided to avoid the form altogether.[15]

Figure 5.1 Images of actress Lily Langtry, the "world's most beautiful woman," appeared in countless advertisements for goods ranging from beauty products to health tonics. Trade card advertising "Brown's Iron Bitters."

Source: Author's collection.

The testimonial scandal cast a pall over the advertising industry, which found itself the subject of theatrical satires and parodies.[16] In an effort to restore dignity to the profession and refute lingering charges of charlatanism, advertising agents and the agencies they represented reinvented themselves as professional businessmen, promoting a scientific, rational approach to advertising that suited the needs of major clients such as National Biscuit (Nabisco), Domino, Pond's Extract Company, Unilever, and Libby.[17] Yet despite turning their backs on testimonials, advertising agents recognized the need to maintain a sense of intimacy and personal connection with consumers and explored a range of strategies to achieve such an effect, the most notable of which was the introduction of cute, cartoonlike trade characters. In 1913 advertising agent Charles W. Hurd argued that such recognizable trade characters as "The Campbell Kids, the two grape juice children, Phoebe Snow, the Gold Dust Twins, the Dutch Boy Painter and the host of them all testify to the value of the product." Like the testimonial, these characters "do not merely identify the product but they *identify satisfaction with it*, which must be regarded as a highly important thing."[18] As Hurd's comments suggest, advertising agents acknowledged the value of testimonial advertising but were wary of relinquishing control to potentially unreliable sources. Trade characters promised to do everything the testimonial could, without raising troubling questions about the truthfulness of their claims or their fidelity to a particular product; such characters *belonged* to the company they represented and (unlike performers like Adelina Patti who appears to have seized every advertising opportunity that came her way) did not diminish the value of the product by promoting a range of other goods, including those of the competition.[19] For manufacturers eager to control the kinds of messages associated with their products, trade characters represented the ideal solution to the problematic testimonial.

But advertising agents soon recognized that despite their appealing malleability, trade characters, along with other "pretty picture" illustrations, were failing to have the desired effect on consumers because they lacked "real human interest and sincerity."[20] Drawing on new research in consumer psychology, agents instead proposed using photographs of "living models" to promote brand-name products, trusting that consumers would more readily identify with images of real men and women than with cartoonlike trade characters. "It is my opinion that the *real* has a much greater appeal to a large majority of the public than the work of an artist, which cannot carry the same personal element, could ever have," explained Edward A. Olds of the Packer's Tar Soap Company in 1910. "The effect of the use of actual people, whether in photographs or some other medium that preserves the human characteristics of the model, is sure to carry a certain amount of personality to the reader." Alan C. Reilly of the Remington Typewriter Company agreed that advertisements with photographs of real people "stand out distinguished from the herd of illustrations by their own individuality."[21]

Celebrity testimonials, often accompanied by photographs, gave advertisers another way to infuse their products with "human interest," and the testimonial's return after a decade of relative obscurity can be read as a logical response to the perceived need for advertisers to connect with consumers on a more personal, emotional level. As Richard Fox and Elspeth Brown have shown, advertisers increasingly shifted focus from a rational "reason-why" approach to advertising copy to a "soft sell" approach that played more directly to the emotions.[22] In 1911, advertising trade journal *Printers' Ink* ran a five-part series on the testimonial, in which it presented case studies of successful campaigns and outlined important rules for advertisers interested in starting one of their own. While acknowledging that several prominent advertising agents continued to condemn testimonials "lock, stock, and barrel," the journal concluded that testimonials could encourage consumer loyalty if advertisers chose respected, knowledgeable sources, and took steps to ensure that their products lived up to the claims being made.[23] Ironically, the very strategy the advertising industry had rejected for over a decade as unable to confer distinction on advertised goods and win consumer trust was now being hailed as a way to achieve these goals. Despite the public's continuing skepticism, what made the testimonial such an effective advertising strategy was its ability to make a direct appeal to consumers through its association with people they could (supposedly) trust. Within such a shifting environment, advertisers once again turned to the actress for support.

Testifying Actresses

By the 1910s, actresses had graduated from social pariahs to fashionable trendsetters, thanks to a series of related factors that included growing efforts to professionalize the actor's craft; increased social, including romantic, interactions between Broadway stars and elite society; the promotional efforts of press agents and "star-making" producers; and perhaps most importantly, the emergence of a modern culture oriented toward display and show.[24] As historian Kathy Peiss observes, "In a society in which appearances were fluid and social rank unstable, the question of how to represent oneself was a pressing one. Strategies of appearance . . . became even more important."[25] Middle-class women, once wary of an association with the stage, now looked upon actresses as role models who could help them acquire the necessary skills to survive in modern society. Broadway actresses (or their press agents) responded to and encouraged this emulative behavior by sharing advice on matters of fashion and beauty in public lectures and articles published in major urban dailies and leading magazines ranging from *Harper's Bazar* [*sic*] and *Cosmopolitan* to *The Ladies' Home Journal* and *The Saturday Evening Post*.[26]

Observing the degree to which "women read and absorb with emulative eagerness all information relative to the mysteries of their [the actresses'] toilets," advertisers returned to the testimonial as a viable marketing strategy, with some notable changes.[27] Indeed, what most distinguished the celebrity testimonials of the 1910s from similar advertisements in the late nineteenth century was the type and quality of the advertised products. Whereas advertisers in the 1890s focused primarily on the selling power of the name and image regardless of the actual commodity being promoted (i.e., railways, cigarettes, patent medicine, corsets, etc.), advertisers in the 1910s acknowledged the need to present consumers with a strong argument for using the advertised product, and therefore relied on the actress's status as an expert in matters of fashion and beauty. Although some companies continued to question the value of using an actress's testimonial over that of a more "respectable" woman—for example, a society lady or a business professional—others preferred to trade upon the actress's expertise and celebrity to fulfill the female consumer's perceived desire to learn from women who embodied modern success, adventure, and beauty.[28]

Yet while middle-class anxieties about immoral actresses had considerably eased by the 1910s, beauty product manufacturers took great pains to select *appropriate* performers to endorse their products, carefully negotiating issues of race, class, and morality. Not surprisingly, the most desirable testimonials came from respectable, white performers with obvious aspirations for class mobility: opera singers, ballerinas, and leading ladies of the "legitimate" stage, many of whom had elite social connections. By contrast, chorus girls, burlesque dancers, vaudeville comics, coon singers, and other performers associated with "lowbrow" entertainment rarely appeared in advertisements for fashion goods, cosmetics, or other beauty products; instead, many of these performers posed suggestively for cigarette cards, the pocket-sized photographs that many tobacco companies offered as premiums, and other advertisements targeted at men.[29] Black, Asian, and Latina performers were likewise absent from most mainstream advertising pages in this period, although advertisements featuring black artists, most notably dancer and musical comedy star Aida Overton Walker, did appear in African-American publications.[30]

Concerns over race and class help to explain why manufacturers tended to privilege stage actresses over film actresses throughout this period. Indeed, while cinema had become one of the most popular forms of entertainment in the United States by 1910, film actresses rarely appeared in advertisements before 1916, the year Mary Pickford began endorsing Pompeian Beauty products.[31] Growing concerns among middle-class critics about the cinema's potentially disastrous effect on American youth and the medium's lingering association with working-class audiences offer two reasons for this apparent absence.[32] Another factor in advertisers' perceived preference for stage stars was the development of the motion picture star system itself. Although film actors became known to the public by name as early as 1909, these "picture personalities"—as film historian Richard de Cordova describes them—were not yet full-fledged "stars." "Knowledge about the picture personality was restricted to the player's professional existence—," de Cordova explains, "either to his/her representation in films or to his/her previous work in film and theater." It was only in 1914, the year when magazines and newspapers began to include information on film stars' private lives, that film actors became stars in their own right and therefore desirable testimonial subjects for manufacturers looking to appeal to a large national market.[33]

In addition to observing great care when selecting women to endorse their products, beauty product manufacturers emphasized the actresses' status as experts in the related fields of art and beauty, occasionally going so far as to name their products after popular performers. Such an association could be extremely risky, however, unless advertisers selected a star with broad appeal. In 1914, *Printers' Ink* surveyed leading advertisers on the relative merits of using a star's name for advertising purposes. Although several respondents worried that "the value to sales of the name of an actress or prominent person is only of a temporary nature," others expressed their preference for the practice. For "Parisian perfumer" V. Rigaud, the decision to name its new perfume after popular American opera singer Mary Garden proved to be a highly effective strategy for breaking into the American market. Playing into the public's perception of Garden as a stylish and respectable yet undeniably modern woman, Rigaud launched a multimedia campaign that included advertisements in *Vogue*, *Vanity Fair*, and *The Criterion of Fashion*, and window displays with a full-length photograph of Garden as Salome, along with booklets, folders, envelope inserts, counter-cards, and window-cards "to aid dealers in selling."[34] "As it is," explained *Printers' Ink*, "Mary Garden isn't so classical that she appeals only to the 'high-brows,' and still she isn't of the musical comedy sort whose followers may desert her in a season." The Rigaud example illustrates the extreme care with which advertisers selected performers to represent their brands. As an attractive, stylish, and, perhaps most importantly, *American* opera star, Garden represented a classy yet accessible image. Her dual status as a star and an artist distinguished her from other, lesser players and musical comedy performers, thereby reaffirming her social position and opera's superiority over commercial Broadway theatre.[35]

American beauty manufacturer Swift & Co. enjoyed similar success with the launch of Maxine Elliott Toilet Soap in 1912, emphasizing Elliott's

"The Star of Soapdom"
Maxine Elliott
Toilet Soap
Every woman realizes that one of the chief requisites of beauty is a clear complexion.
Maxine Elliott
Toilet Soap
with its purity and fragrance is a toilet necessity—an aid to beauty.
It is a complexion soap of the most delicate texture. It lathers freely, cleanses thoroughly and leaves the skin cool, smooth, refreshed. Made in this assortment:
Buttermilk and Violet
Buttermilk and Roses
Buttermilk and Glycerin
Buttermilk
10 cents the cake
50 cents the box of 6
At Your Druggists

Figure 5.2 This advertisement for Maxine Elliott Toilet Soap includes Elliott's image, although some dealers apparently preferred versions of the ads without her image.

Source: *The Theatre Magazine* (December 1912): xxxi.

distinctive beauty, acting abilities, and business acumen as the owner and manager of the Maxine Elliott Theatre in print ads and displays (figure 5.2). One of the company's most memorable window displays was a miniature reproduction of the front of the Maxine Elliott Theatre, complete with electric lights, depicting several scenes from the actress's most recent play.[36] The company further highlighted its close relationship with Elliott by distributing product samples in the theatres where she appeared on tour. Swift & Co. was nevertheless careful to "[avoid] a too strong featuring of the actress to the detriment of the Swift product." While the company sent dealers photographs of Elliott for display purposes, the newspaper cuts simply showed boxes of the soap *without* a picture of the actress. *Printers' Ink* reported that many dealers preferred these cuts, believing that her picture would distract consumers from the actual product. In thus privileging the product over the actress, Swift & Co. demonstrated how a company could successfully use a celebrity's name and image while maintaining some distance from the actual celebrity.[37] Although Swift & Co. obviously retained their association with Maxine Elliot the person, they clearly hoped that Maxine Elliott Toilet Soap would soon be able to exist as a brand unto itself.

For stage actresses, an association with brand-name goods was a simple, profitable, and effective promotional strategy, especially when advertisements featuring their testimonials appeared in the pages of such leading magazines as *Vogue* or *Harper's Bazar.* Moreover, for those whose careers were often circumscribed by male producers, managers, and directors, testimonial advertising represented one area where they assume a greater degree of creative control over their professional lives. Acting independently or through an agent, these women made arrangements with advertisers that allowed them to profit from their own success, enhance their public profile, and promote themselves as fashion and beauty experts.

Yet while actresses may have been free to make business arrangements with advertisers as they saw fit, not all advertisers or store managers were willing to pay to use a performer's name or image.[38] While touring the United States in 1907, Australian opera diva Nellie Melba learned that store managers were profiting from the "Melba madness" sweeping the country by naming countless goods after her without requesting permission to do so. When she confronted one shop owner about this practice, he unapologetically asserted his right to use her name, explaining, "Melba's name is not her own. I am as much entitled to use it as she is."[39] The shop owner's proprietary stance is consistent with contemporary attitudes toward public figures. Theatre historian Benjamin McArthur notes that by 1907, the courts had made a clear distinction between the rights of public and private individuals. "A private individual had the right to prohibit reproduction of his picture," he explains, "[b]ut public characters... surrendered the right to keep their pictures out of the press. They belonged to the public."[40] Viewed as public property—and therefore readily accessible commodities, objects to be purchased and consumed as one would an item from a department store or mail-order catalogue—celebrity performers found it increasingly difficult to control and shape their public personae. Melba, however, was unwilling to let others benefit unfairly from her success and promptly patented her name.[41]

Melba's assertive action offers one of the more extreme examples of the efforts undertaken by actresses to control the circulation of their names and images. Other actresses took similar steps to ensure that they had the right to approve all photographs used for advertising purposes. "[W]hen [an actress] goes to have her photograph taken," Margaret Illington Banes explained to the readers of *The Green Book Album*, "[she] takes a whole day for the ordeal, and the operator, instead of snapping at most a dozen negatives, take hundreds of these, all are discarded except those few which show the sitter at her best."[42] Maxine Elliott was notorious for her exacting approach with photographers. Before every portrait session, she would insist on looking through the camera to ensure that the background was to her liking. Despite photographers' requests, she rarely smiled or altered her rather somber facial expression, insisting that she knew what worked best.[43]

"American Beauty" Lillian Russell also took matters into her own hands when she launched a line of beauty products in 1914. Both the company name, "Lillian Russell's Own Toilet Preparations," and the advertising copy strongly emphasized Russell's personal involvement with the company's day-to-day business operations. "My Own Toilet Preparations made by my own chemist, in my own laboratory, are the only toilet preparations which are authorized to use my name or likeness, and have my endorsement," Russell announced to the readers of *Vanity Fair* in a January 1914 advertisement.[44] In April 1915 she responded to charges from competitors that her products were "not of my own manufacture and that I only permitted the use of my name and portrait to fool the public," by reiterating her dedication to the company. "I am in my laboratory every day," she explained in an ad published in *Vogue, Vanity Fair*, and *Harper's Bazar*, "and personally inspect all materials and preparations and supervise all details of production and distribution." To further refute her critics, she offered to donate $10,000 to charity if anyone could prove "that Lillian Russell's Own Toilet Preparations are not solely and exclusively my own," and invited women to "call at my laboratory any day between three and five o'clock."[45] Despite her best efforts, however, sales for Lillian Russell's Own Toilet Preparations were disappointing, and plans to distribute the products in beauty salons proved to be more of a liability than a profit-making endeavor. With business failing, Russell's partners refused to pay her monthly royalty payments, and she was forced to sue them for the $5,000 they owed her. The company folded in 1917, leaving Russell with only $10,000 out of the $25,000 in stock that had originally been allocated to her.[46]

Ironically, perhaps, while actresses struggled to control the messages associated with their names and images, advertisers struggled to ensure that the actresses who provided testimonials for their products remained loyal to them. Without a binding contract, they could do little to prevent actresses from giving testimonials to other products or abandoning their business obligations altogether. Although it is unclear whether most advertisers in this period paid actresses for their statements or simply solicited statements from them in exchange for free products, what is clear is that the process of acquiring and using testimonials from actresses (and other public figures) presented a number of unique challenges. Unlike the satisfied average consumer, that is, an amputee happy about his prosthetic leg or a farmer ecstatic about his latest crop, actresses seem to have treated the practice of giving testimonials as more of a business interaction than an act of generosity.[47] As noted in the Introduction, the issue of payment is often what distinguishes a "testimonial" from an "endorsement." However, in the early twentieth century, the line between a testimonial and an endorsement seems to have been much less distinct, particularly as so few legal regulations were in place; and this blurriness often worked in the actresses' favor.

In 1914 *Printers' Ink* addressed the issue of attracting and retaining celebrities for testimonial purposes and concluded that "[w]hen it comes right down to the point, it is all up to the manufacturer." For those dealing with temperamental actresses, the journal advocated an approach strikingly similar to that of a suitor, characterizing the relationship between the actress and advertiser as that of a haughty woman and her desperate lover. Actresses "must have flowers in her dressing-room every now and then," the article advised, in addition to free samples of the product for themselves and their friends. Playing up to the actress's whims was a necessary strategy to prevent her from "desert[ing] the manufacturer whose distribution she often controls to a greater or less degree."[48] Although this admittedly sexist approach may have worked for some, other manufacturers adopted a much less conciliatory approach to securing celebrity commitments. According to *Printers' Ink*, one trademark lawyer was advising his clients to get celebrities to sign a contract permitting the use of their names for a lengthy period of time and then copyright the names before the contract expired.[49] The manufacturer would then "own" the celebrities, or rather their names, which would effectively prevent them from endorsing any other products.

Still, despite advertisers' efforts to buy endorsers' names, the absence of any formal contractual law meant that they were ill-equipped to prevent actresses from making other business arrangements. In fact, some celebrities seem to have enlisted the assistance of agents for the express purpose of securing multiple endorsement deals, as the 1917 court case of British fashion designer, Lucile, Lady Duff Gordon reveals. In April 1915, while living and working in New York, Lucile signed a contract with American agent Otis F. Wood stipulating that for one year he had "the exclusive right, subject always to her approval, to place her indorsements [*sic*] on the designs of others." The contract also guaranteed Wood "the exclusive right to place her own designs on sale, or to license others to market them," for which he would take out any patents, copyrights, or trademarks deemed necessary to protect his client's name and designs. Lucile, in return, was to receive "half of 'all profits and revenues' derived from any contracts he might make."[50] Perhaps impatient for money, Lucile disregarded her contract with Wood and endorsed a variety of fashion products and accessories including an exclusive arrangement with Sears, Roebuck and Company to design gowns for their catalogue.[51]

In 1917 Wood sued Lucile for damages. The designer defended her actions by pointing out that Wood was not bound to do anything; he did not promise to make "reasonable efforts to place [her] indorsements [*sic*] and market her designs," and in her view, the contract was invalid. Following a series of appeals and counter-appeals by both defendant and plaintiff, Judge Cardozo of the New York Court of Appeals delivered a verdict in favor of the plaintiff, explaining:

> The law has outgrown its primitive stage of formalism when the precise word was the sovereign talisman, and every slip was fatal. It takes a broader view to-day. A promise may be lacking, and yet the whole writing may be "instinct with an obligation," imperfectly expressed. If that is so, there is a contract.[52]

Wood vs. Lucy, Lady Duff-Gordon [*sic*] codified the relationship between celebrities and the advertising agents working on their behalf and remains a landmark case in contract law. It did little, however, to stop celebrities from blatantly endorsing multiple products simultaneously. These abuses would continue largely unheeded until 1927 when *Printers' Ink*, the Better Business Bureau, the Association of National Advertisers, and other consumer advocacy groups began to agitate for change. That year film actress Constance Talmadge appeared in advertisements for eight different products, ranging from alarm clocks to inner tubes, in a single issue of *Liberty* magazine. Her multiple appearances provoked reactions ranging from laughter to outrage, posing serious questions about the use and misuse of celebrity endorsements and prompting calls for tighter regulations on the practice of soliciting and paying for testimonial statements.[53]

The relative freedom that actresses enjoyed with testimonial advertising thus presented a major challenge for companies wishing to convey a specific message to consumers. Still, for certain companies, especially those in the cosmetics industry, the benefits associated with the celebrity testimonial and/or endorsement more than outweighed the risks.

THE DEMOCRATIZATION OF BEAUTY

The cosmetics industry was one of the most active and innovative exponents of testimonial advertising in the 1910s, as a survey of the leading women's magazines suggests. Broadway actresses appeared in the pages of elite fashion and society magazines as well as more mainstream, middle-class publications promoting everything from soap and perfume to rouge and depilatories.[54] The operative question is "why?" Why were cosmetics manufacturers, more than other manufacturers, so eager to use actresses' testimonials? One possible explanation lies in the products themselves. As "invisible" aids to beauty, cosmetics could not be advertised onstage as readily as a hat, gown, or other items in an actress's stage wardrobe. Testimonial advertisements, however, allowed cosmetics manufacturers to highlight the extent to which their products enhanced the actress's appearance onstage and offstage, thereby attracting female fans looking to emulate their favorite stage stars. Indeed, as the following analysis suggests, actresses' testimonials played an integral role in the industry's attempt to break into new markets by reworking perceptions of "natural" and "artificial" beauty.

By the 1910s, hostile attitudes toward cosmetics, predominant throughout most of the nineteenth century, were subsiding. Most women, from working girls to society ladies, used some form of facial cream or powder, and more adventurous women were also beginning to apply color to their cheeks and lips. Despite this growing acceptance, however, a number of men and women (most of whom were middle class) continued to have reservations about the morality of "making up." It was one thing to apply cold cream to protect the skin; quite another to transform the face by applying color to the eyes, lips, and cheeks.[55] Most leading women's magazines reflected this generally cautious attitude toward makeup. While offering information on beauty culture in general, they avoided advocating cosmetics as a beautifying practice. Typical editorials instead urged women to cultivate their inner beauty through a healthy diet, regular exercise, and a positive attitude; others encouraged women to make their own beauty products at home. Not surprisingly, given this editorial position, few cosmetics companies advertised their products in magazines, relying instead on more traditional practices such as trade cards, posters, and word of mouth.[56]

But from approximately 1911 onward, beauty product manufacturers began to adopt a much more aggressive promotional strategy. Where once ads for cosmetics and other beauty products had been relegated to the back pages of questionable periodicals, they increasingly appeared in the nation's most authoritative fashion magazines, occupying half- and full-pages in the front sections.[57] Advertisers also took steps to challenge the traditional equation between goodness, morality, and physical appearance by insisting that beauty was something that could be acquired, not through good works, but through good purchases. Advocating the "democratization of beauty," they preached that it was not only possible for all women to be beautiful, but that it was also every woman's *responsibility* to be beautiful.[58] In this new equation, physical appearance was no longer a direct reflection of a woman's interior life, but rather was something that a woman could alter to express her individuality.[59]

Although potentially liberating for some women, this democratic rhetoric had disastrous consequences for others, most notably nonwhite women already excluded from other forms of social and economic democracy. As numerous historians have shown, advertisements for skin whiteners and other skin bleaching products exploited black women's desires for social acceptance by promising to transform or "erase" their "problematic" black skin, leaving them with a light complexion that would facilitate, at least theoretically, their assimilation into mainstream white society. Rather than allowing for a more expansive definition of beauty, such advertisements insisted that being beautiful meant being white.[60] Ads featuring successful, attractive, and undeniably white stage actresses did little to disrupt this racist ideology despite the emphasis on "democracy," making whiteness a necessary condition of social advancement and personal success.

Ironically, however, advertisers looking to promote their new consumerist doctrine of beauty first had to contend with actresses' own anxieties about admitting to using cosmetics. Although well-skilled in the art of stage makeup, many female performers hesitated to speak openly about their beauty practices prior to the 1910s, fearful of conveying the wrong impression or associating themselves with lowbrow performers. In a series of beauty articles published in *The Delineator* between February and October 1911, prominent Broadway actresses, including none other than Lillian Russell, Maxine Elliott, and Mary Garden, denied using commercial beauty products and instead emphasized the importance of cultivating inner beauty. "Keep your mind cheerful and your body clean, inside and out," advised vaudeville star Elsie Janis, "and then, being an American, with the American girl's natural endowment of attractiveness, you can't be very homely."[61] Other actresses likewise advocated a healthy diet, regular exercise, adequate sleep, and a positive attitude, instead of cosmetics. Although some performers admitted to using cold cream, most disavowed using cosmetics offstage.[62]

Younger actresses, representatives of a new generation more interested in experimenting with physical appearance, were more willing to discuss their beautifying practices in public, although they too took care to distinguish between the techniques they used onstage and offstage. In 1913, *The New York World* ran a series of articles describing the steps taken by emerging Broadway actresses as they "made up" for the stage.[63] Ostensibly lessons in stage makeup, these articles by reporter Eleanor Schorer offered highly specific information on the application of such products as cold cream, face powder, eyeliner, and rouge, and made a point of acknowledging any unusual or innovative application techniques, for example, Jane Cowl's use of an "Alice Blue" eye pencil or Laurette Taylor's use of rouge on her cheeks, lips, and eyebrows.[64] Accompanied by a series of sketches illustrating the different stages in the makeup process, the *World* articles seem to have served as practical guides for female readers looking to experiment with makeup.[65] It is worth noting, however, that none of the actresses interviewed by Schorer admitted to using cosmetics offstage, nor did Schorer ask them to discuss their private beautifying practices. This careful omission suggests that the context of the articles—that is, interviews with professional artists about the skills they have developed through years of careful study and practice—may have been a factor in the actresses' willingness to discuss their makeup techniques.

As beauty product manufacturers continued to redefine notions of natural beauty and adopt an aggressive advertising strategy, more and more actresses emerged as advocates of cosmetics, so much so that by 1915 many of the stars who had initially expressed reservations about such products in *The Delineator* were suddenly promoting them.[66] Others went so far as to echo industry rhetoric around the "democratization of beauty" in interviews and promotional articles. For example, in 1916, musical comedy star Anna Held, the former wife of producer Florenz Ziegfeld, argued that it was a woman's duty "to yourself and to the world to appear as attractive as arts and artifices will permit," and further suggested that those who refused to help themselves by "eschew[ing] make-up" were "vulgar."[67] A year later, theatre columnist Anne Archbald concurred, stressing that women who failed to care for their physical appearance were irresponsible not only to themselves, but to those around them. For the betterment of society, she argued, women were obliged to make themselves as beautiful as possible.[68] The means to achieving this perfection was, of course, through consumption. This emphasis on beautification as a social responsibility and the subsequent condemnation of those who "eschewed" cosmetics as "vulgar" indicates the degree to which issues of class were interwoven with the democratization of beauty. By encouraging middle-class women to incorporate a range of creams and other products into their daily beauty regime, actresses not only redefined "natural beauty" but also legitimated their own beautifying practices, thereby bolstering their emergent middle-class status. As the following section shows, beauty product manufacturers joined actresses in inverting the age-old prejudice that only disreputable women used cosmetics by insisting that the actresses who used cosmetics onstage and off did so out of a personal and professional obligation to maintain a natural, healthy appearance at all times.

Artificially Natural, Naturally Artificial

In October 1911, Brooklyn-based beauty specialist Forrest D. Pullen launched a major campaign to introduce *Créme Nerol* [*sic*], a new cold cream. The first full-page ad, which appeared in the October 15 issue of *Vogue*, displayed testimonials, photographs, and signatures from Broadway's most admired and respectable stars: actresses Margaret Anglin, Julia Marlowe, Billie Burke, Maxine Elliott, Mrs. Fiske, Frances Starr, and Julie Opp; and opera divas Luisa Tetrazzini, Geraldine Farrar, and Mabel Taliaferro (figure 5.3). The performers' statements characterize Créme Nerol as "an unsurpassed preparation," "a most agreeable cleanser and food for the skin," and "exceptional both as to quality and results." As the ad copy suggests, Pullen knew that consumers were more likely to believe statements from respected, fashionable

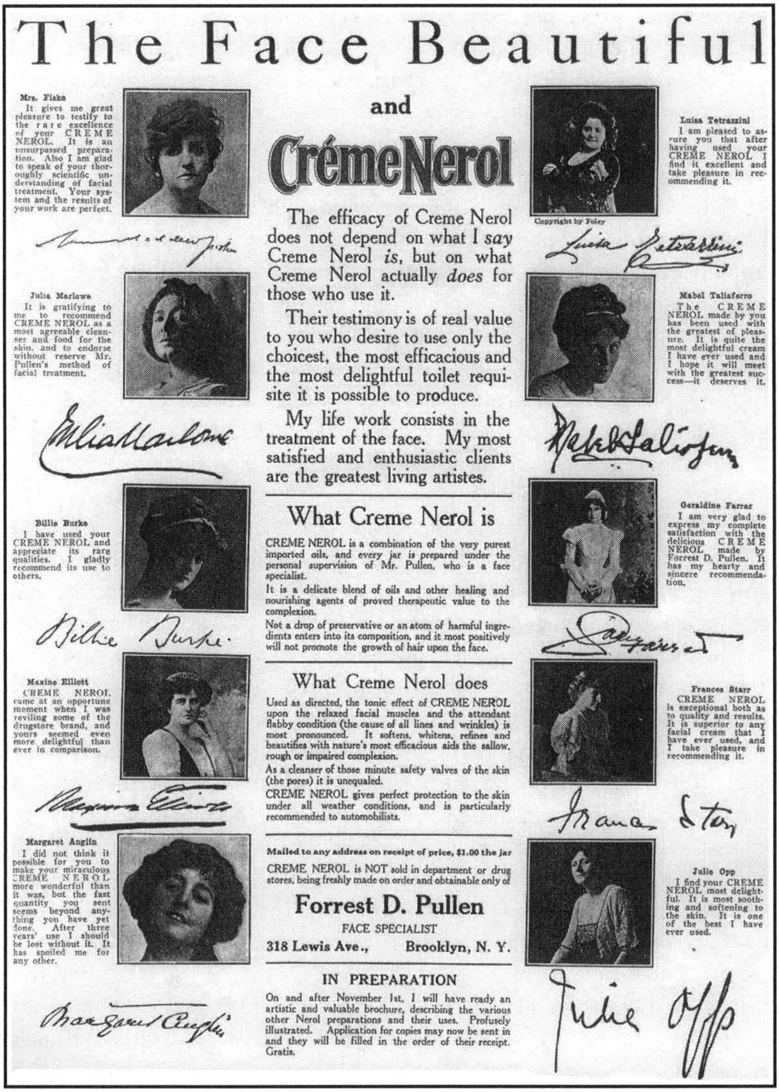

Figure 5.3 Forrest D. Pullen's *Créme Nerol* with testimonials from esteemed stars including Maxine Elliott, Julie Opp, Billie Burke, and Julia Marlowe.

Source: *Vogue* (October 15, 1911): 69.

actresses than the words of an unknown, faceless *male* beauty specialist (or from morally questionable chorus girls). "The efficacy of Créme Nerol does not depend on what I *say* Créme Nerol *is*," he explains, "but on what Créme Nerol actually *does* for those who use it." His comments further imply that

Créme Nerol is responsible for restoring and maintaining the natural beauty of stage favorites such as Billie Burke and Julia Marlowe. Significantly, while Pullen promotes the "efficacious" properties of Créme Nerol, his emphasis is on restoration, not *transformation*. His cold cream "softens, whitens, refines and beautifies . . . the sallow, rough or impaired complexion," returning it to its former (presumably more natural) state.[69]

Pullen's use of a constellation of well-known actresses and performing artists to promote his new cold cream represents a significant departure from Rigaud's decision to build its new perfume around the identity of opera singer Mary Garden. Rather than relying exclusively on the pulling power of one star's name and image, Pullen seems to have opted to impress potential consumers with the sheer number of stars using his product, a strategy that gave him greater control over the messages suggested by the individual performers' statements and photographs. If one actress chose to endorse a competitor's product, his cold cream would nevertheless maintain its integrity and reputation.

Perhaps sparked by Pullen's success, other beauty businesses also began soliciting actresses' testimonials.[70] These advertisements, especially those for rouge and other forms of "makeup" are notable for the way they combine testimonials with democratic rhetoric.[71] "If women who are not born beauties would give as much care to their appearance as those who are, this would be a world of beautiful women," declares the 1912 advertisement for Le Secret Gaby Deslys, a line of products named after the fashionable French musical comedy actress. Playing up to the idea that every woman could and *should* be beautiful, the Importers Company, manufacturers of Le Secret, advertise their products as "the means of *acquiring* beauty as well as the best method of *preserving* and *accentuating* it [emphasis added]." Although the ad promotes the notion that women who are not naturally beautiful can become beautiful by using Le Secret (consistent with the rhetoric of the "makeover"), the emphasis here is on *preservation* and *accentuation*, over transformation. Women who use Le Secret are not "making up" as much as they are highlighting their natural physical assets, just like Gaby Deslys. The ad alludes to Deslys' artful performance of beauty by pointing out that "even on close view and under glaring lights," the beauty products "absolutely defy detection." Furthermore, as the name Le Secret implies, women who purchase the beauty products (which include "a whitener for the neck and arms, a tint for the face, a silk sponge for its proper application, and a rouge [*sic*] for the lips, cheeks, and nails") will share a trade secret with the French star. Like Gaby, they will be able to enhance their "natural" beauty without being caught in the act.[72]

This emphasis on the actress's skillful employment of artificial means to achieve natural beauty is perhaps most noticeable in the advertisements created for Pond's Vanishing Cream in the mid-to-late 1910s. In 1914, the

Pond's Extract Company became one of the first major cosmetics companies to launch a national campaign directed at a predominantly middle-class market. Under the guidance of the J. Walter Thompson Company, its longtime advertising agency, Pond's stopped advertising its signature product, Pond's Extract, and focused instead on promoting Pond's Vanishing Cream and Pond's Cold Cream. Between 1914 and 1916, Pond's advertised these products separately until Thompson copywriter Helen Landsdowne Resor developed an innovative strategy to encourage women to incorporate both creams into their daily beauty regimen. Ads bearing the slogan, "Every normal skin needs these two creams," appeared in major newspapers and magazines throughout the country, including both *Vogue* and *The Ladies' Home Journal*. The campaign was an undisputed success; by 1920, sales for both creams had tripled, firmly establishing Pond's as one of the leading beauty businesses in the United States.[73]

Most accounts of the "two creams" campaign focus on Resor's brilliant marketing tactics and her persuasive copy, and overlook the extent to which actresses' testimonials played an integral role in Pond's strategy to win over middle-class consumers.[74] In 1914, the J. Walter Thompson Company incorporated celebrity testimonials into the ads for Pond's Vanishing Cream, enlisting the aid of popular performers such as vaudeville singer and impressionist Elsie Janis, legitimate stage star Frances Starr, and ballerina Anna Pavlova. Photographs of these and other prominent stage stars (most ads featured two or three performers) appeared in half- and full-page magazine advertisements, often embedded in the copy beneath a larger illustration.[75] The decision to feature performers from different artistic fields, including vaudeville, musical comedy, drama, and ballet, suggests that (like Pullen) the J. Walter Thompson Company wished to appeal to a variety of diverse tastes rather than rely on a single performer's ability to attract consumers. Women could chose to identify with one or all of the performers featured in the ads, depending upon their personal and artistic preferences. At the same time, the actresses' collective testimony leant an air of distinction to the advertised product and served as an authoritative proof of its quality.

While it is impossible to state conclusively that actresses' testimonials were responsible for the success of Pond's Vanishing Cream, the J. Walter Thompson Company's continued use of actresses in the campaign offers strong evidence that it believed this to be the case. By 1916, sales for Pond's Vanishing Cream had increased by as much as 60 percent, more than double the 27 percent growth experienced by Pond's Cold Cream. It is therefore likely that the J. Walter Thompson Company's decision to link the two creams was motivated by a desire to boost sales for the Cold Cream.[76]

As other historians have noted, the success of the "two creams" campaign depended on Pond's ability to convince middle-class women, including those who had never used cosmetics, to try new products and adopt new beautifying *practices*.[77] What these historians fail to observe, however, is the J. Walter Thompson's strategic deployment of actresses' testimonials to demonstrate how Pond's Vanishing Cream enhanced rather than transformed the women who used it. Actresses' testimonials and the copy surrounding their images suggested that women could improve their complexions and achieve a "natural" glow without compromising themselves or dramatically altering their appearance. The underlying message was that women wishing to disassociate themselves from more questionable beauty products like rouge had nothing to fear from vanishing cream.

The continued use of testimonials suggests that actresses played a crucial role in promoting the Vanishing Cream as an unthreatening, essential beauty product. Numerous ads emphasized the actress's professional responsibility to maintain a healthy, glowing complexion, and characterized her as a knowledgeable and skillful consumer. "Actresses and dancers, whose skin must always be at its loveliest...get from Pond's Vanishing Cream just the effect they have always wanted," explained one ad from 1915.[78] Another praised Pond's Vanishing Cream for helping actresses to maintain a "fresh, clear and brilliant" complexion despite the "demanding" and "exhaustive" nature of their work.[79] Women were invited to discover for themselves "why it is used by more women on the stage than any other cream," with the promise that they too would "obtain just the effect so marvelously attained on the stage."[80] *Every* woman, the ad promises, can have beautiful, "natural" skin if they use Pond's Vanishing Cream. Without explicitly stating that the women who use Pond's Vanishing Cream will look like the actresses endorsing the product, the use of the word "effect" nevertheless implies that their *skin* (if nothing else) will look similar. The word "effect" also alludes to the *invisibility* of the product and its attendant magical qualities. Women who use Pond's Vanishing Cream do not look like they are wearing cosmetics (the product "immediately sinks in—vanishes"), yet the "effect" of the cream, its ability to enhance and restore the skin to achieve a natural appearance, is apparent.

Conclusion

Upon returning to New York from Paris in 1916, actress Anna Held observed that attitudes toward the use of artificial beauty products had changed dramatically: "No woman of to-day sees a fresh-blown complexion but what she asks her self, 'I wonder where she buys it,' or says, 'How well she puts it on!'" Cosmetics were now considered a necessary part of a woman's daily life, and beauty was something found in a bottle rather than within.[81] Ironically, Margaret Illington Banes' revelation that actresses were "made up" rather than natural beauties played right into the hands of beauty product manufacturers. These companies promoted the democratization of beauty through the authentication of the artificially beautiful actress. Actresses' testimonials implied that any woman could, should, and *would* achieve a similarly elegant appearance if she purchased the right products. Perhaps more importantly, actresses' testimonials helped to underscore the relationship between wearing cosmetics and maintaining a natural look, a key point for cosmetics companies hoping to win over reluctant middle-class consumers. Actresses' photographs and testimonials implied that women who did not use cosmetics were somehow less attractive and less "natural" than those who did. A "natural" beauty was no longer the woman who eschewed cosmetics, but rather the woman who embraced them.

NOTES

1. A much earlier version of this essay received the K. Austin Kerr Prize from the Business History Conference in 2003 and later appeared in the online conference proceedings. See "Uplifting Makeup: Actresses' Testimonials and the Cosmetics Industry, 1910–1918," *Business and Economic History On-line* 1, 1 (2003). URL: http://www.thebhc.org/publications/BEHonline/beh.html. A later, greatly expanded, version of this essay appeared as " 'The Mad Search for Beauty': Actresses' Testimonials and the 'Democratization of Beauty,' " *Journal of the Gilded Age and Progressive Era* 4, 3 (July 2005): 255–292. Reworked sections of the *JGAPE* essay also appear in Marlis Schweitzer, *When Broadway Was the Runway: Theater, Fashion, and American Culture* (Philadelphia: University of Pennsylvania Press, 2009). Many thanks to *JGAPE* for permission to reprint this material here.
2. Margaret Illington Banes, "The Mad Search for Beauty: And the Slight Chance that the Average Actress Can Guide the Average Woman," *The Green Book Magazine* (May 1912), 953.
3. Illington Banes, "The Mad Search for Beauty," 956.
4. On female fans and their relationships with stage stars, see Susan Torrey Barstow, "Ellen Terry and the Revolt of the Daughters," *Nineteenth-Century Theatre* 25, 1 (Summer 1997), 20–21. See also Kim Marra, *Strange Duets: Impresarios and Actresses in the American Theatre, 1865–1914* (Iowa City: University of Iowa Press, 2006), 99–103; Veronica Kelly, "An Australian Idol of Modernist Consumerism: Minnie Tittell Brune and the Gallery Girls," *Theatre Research International* 31, 1 (2006): 17–36.
5. Philip Francis Nowlan, "Warding Off Saturation Point by Changing Advertising Appeal," *Printers' Ink* (September 2, 1917), 27–28. The leading source on American beauty culture in the nineteenth and twentieth centuries is Kathy Peiss, *Hope in a Jar: The Making of America's Beauty Culture* (New York: Metropolitan Books, 1998).
6. On "cartomania" and theatre photography in the late nineteenth century, see Alan Thomas, *The Expanding Eye: Photography and the Nineteenth Century*

Mind (London: Croom Helm, 1978); Ben L. Bassham, *The Theatrical Photographs of Napoleon Sarony* (Ohio: The Kent State University Press, 1982); William C. Darrah, *Cartes de Visite in Nineteenth Century Photography* (Gettysburg: W. C. Darrah, Publisher, nd); Barbara McCandless, "The Portrait Studio and the Celebrity," in *Photography in Nineteenth Century America*, ed. Martha Sandweiss (New York: Abrams, 1991).

7. Tim Shakleton, "Introduction," *Bubbles: Early Advertising Art from A. F. Pears Ltd.*, ed. Mike Dempsey (London, 1978), 3.
8. Lois Rather, *Two Lilies in America: Lillian Russell and Lily Langtry* (Oakland, CA: Rather Press, 1973), 50. Shakleton, "Introduction," *Bubbles*, 3.
9. Langtry's endorsement of Pears' was the subject of a parody in *Punch* magazine that became almost as famous as the original. See Dempsey, *Bubbles*, 48. Pears' also solicited a testimonial from religious leader Henry Ward Beecher, who famously drew a connection between cleanliness, Pears' Soap, and godliness. See Shakleton, "Introduction," *Bubbles*, 3. See also Sherry J. Caldwell, "Clean and Sober: Women Celebrity Endorsers and the 1883 Pears' Soap Campaign," *Theatre Symposium: Representations of Gender on the Nineteenth-Century American Stage* vol. 10 (Tuscaloosa, AL: University of Alabama Press, 2002): 100–113.
10. Rather, *Two Lilies in America*, 50.
11. On middle-class anxieties toward cosmetics and other beauty products in the nineteenth century, see Peiss, *Hope in a Jar*, esp. 48–60.
12. *Printers' Ink: A Journal for Advertisers—Fifty Years, 1888–1938* [special 50th anniversary edition] July 28, 1938, 111. See Folder 6, Box 2, Dentistry; Folder 8, Box 1, Chewing Gum; Folder labeled Advertising Cards, Box 15, Theater, Warshaw Collection of Business Americana, National Museum of American History, Behring Center, Smithsonian Institution [hereafter NMAH].
13. Irwin Leslie Gordon, ed. *Who Was Who: 5000 B.C. to Date: Biographical Dictionary of the Famous and Those Who Wanted to Be*, as included by Jone Johnson Lewis on "Women's History—Humorous Biographies," URL: www.historynet.com. Accessed May 27, 2002.
14. Patti, Adelina, Box 12, Theater, Warshaw Collection of Business Americana, NMAH.
15. I have not come across any primary documentation to explain what sparked these scandals or any identification of the specific companies involved. I expect that the scandals were provoked, at least in part, by the efforts of anti-patent medicine muckrakers, but again have been unable to prove this. There seems to be a tacit assumption among historians that these scandals occurred; the *Printers' Ink* 50-year retrospective collection references them several times, and advertising historian Stephen Fox alludes to the testimonial's "lingering unsavory association with patent medicines." However, there is still considerable research needed to uncover the scope of the anti-testimonial campaign. See *Printer's Ink, A Journal for Advertisers—Fifty Years, 1888–1938*, July 28, 1938, 111, 370; Stephen Fox, *The Mirror Makers: A History of American Advertising and Its Creators* (New York: William Morrow and Co. Inc, 1984), 88.

16. *Printers' Ink: A Journal for Advertisers—Fifty Years, 1888–1938,* (July 28, 1938), 118.
17. T. J. Jackson Lears, *Fables of Abundance: A Cultural History of Advertising in America* (New York: Basic Books, 1994), 89–90; Pamela Walker Laird, *Advertising Progress: American Business and the Rise of Consumer Marketing* (Baltimore and London: The Johns Hopkins University Press, 1998), esp. chapters 5–7; Susan Strasser, *Satisfaction Guaranteed: The Making of the American Mass Market* (New York: Pantheon Books, 1989), esp. chapters 4–5. See also Michael Schudson, *Advertising: The Uneasy Persuasion* (New York: Basic Books, 1984); Roland Marchand, *Advertising the American Dream: Making Way for Modernity, 1920–1940* (Berkeley: University of California Press, 1985); Richard S. Tedlow, *New and Improved: The Story of Mass Marketing in America* (New York: Basic Books, 1990); Charles McGovern, *Sold American: Consumption and Citizenship, 1890–1945* (Chapel Hill: University of North Carolina Press, 2006).
18. Charles W. Hurd, "Different Uses of the Testimonial: Several Varieties of the Real Thing and a Few of the Imaginary Ones," *Printers' Ink* (August 28, 1913), 40.
19. My thanks to Charles McGovern for first pointing out this connection between trade characters and testimonials.
20. William G. Colgate, "'Pretty' Pictures in Copy Becoming Passé," *Printers' Ink* (September 15, 1910), 62, 64; Fox, *The Mirror Makers*, 67–69.
21. George H. Whitney, "The Personalities of Advertising Models: Woman's Antipathy to Certain Types a Real Factor," *Printers' Ink* (December 15, 1910), 12–13. L. B. Jones, "The Photograph in Display Advertising," *Printers' Ink* (May 4, 1910), 3. See also Elspeth H. Brown, "Rationalizing Consumption: Lejaren à Hiller and the Origins of American Advertising Photography, 1913–1924," *Enterprise & Society* 1 (December 2000): 715–738.
22. On the shift from the "reason why" to "soft sell" strategy, see Brown, "Rationalizing Consumption," 720–722; and Stephen Fox, *The Mirror Makers*, 74.
23. James W. Egbert, "What Makes a Good Testimonial: A Discussion of the Kinds of People Whose Names are Worth Having as Endorsements," *Printers' Ink* (October 12, 1911), 44, 46; Hurd, "Different Uses of the Testimonial," 34.
24. Benjamin McArthur, *Actors and American Culture, 1880–1920* (Philadelphia: Temple University Press, 1984).
25. Peiss, *Hope in a Jar*, 38.
26. Elsie de Wolfe, vol. 161, 20–21, Robinson Locke Collection, Billy Rose Theatre Collection, New York Public Library for the Performing Arts, Astor, Lenox and Tilden Foundations [hereafter RLC, BRTC]; Anna Held, vol. 264, 112, RLC, BRTC. "Gowns Seen on the Stage," *Harper's Bazar* (July 1913): 53–54; [Ad for *LHJ*] *The Delineator* (November 1913): 72.
27. Egbert, "What Makes a Good Testimonial," 44; Nowlan, "Warding Off Saturation Point by Changing Advertising Appeal," 27–28.
28. Egbert, "What Makes a Good Testimonial," 76–79; "Pianists' Endorsements," *Printers' Ink* (November 27, 1911), 30; Lynn G. Wright, "Giving References

for Your Product," *Printers' Ink* (April 20, 1911), 9–10; Egbert, "Making the Testimonial Worth More," *Printers' Ink* (November 23, 1911), 76.

29. "Chewing Gum," Box, 1, Folder 8; "Theater," Box 15, advertising cards, Warshaw, NMAH. See also Robert Jay, *The Trade Card in Nineteenth-Century America* (Columbia: University of Missouri Press, 1987).
30. According to stage legend, Aida Overton Walker met her future husband George Walker while posing for a cigarette advertisement. See http://www.si.umich.edu/chico/harlem/text/williams_walker.html. Accessed November 20, 2008. On the use of "exotic" Asian and Latina film actresses in cosmetics advertisements during the 1930s, see Sarah Berry, *Screen Style: Fashion and Femininity in 1930s Hollywood* (Minneapolis: University of Minnesota Press, 2000).
31. In 1916, ads for Pond's Vanishing Cream also began to include film stars. Peiss, *Hope in a Jar*, 126; "Free! Write for samples of these two creams today," Advertising Ephemera Collection, Emergence of Advertising On-Line Project, John W. Hartman Center for Sales, Advertising and Marketing History, Duke University Rare Book, Manuscript, and Special Collections Library [hereafter Hartman Center], http://library.duke.edu/digitalcollections/eaa.P0088/pg.1/ Accessed November 19, 2008.
32. On early cinema audiences, see Robert Sklar, *Movie Made America: A Cultural History of American Movies* (London: Random House, 1975); Kathryn H. Fuller, *At the Picture Show: Small-Town Audiences and the Creation of Movie Fan Culture* (Washington, DC: Smithsonian Institution Press, 1997); Lauren Rabinovitz, *For the Love of Pleasure: Women, Movies, and Culture in Turn-of-the-Century Chicago* (New Brunswick, NJ: Rutgers University Press, 1998); Shelley Stamp, *Movie-Struck Girls: Women and Motion Picture Culture After the Nickelodeon* (Princeton, NJ: Princeton University Press, 2000).
33. For more on the shift from "picture personalities" to stars, see Richard de Cordova, "The Emergence of the Star System in America," *Wide Angle* 6, 4 (1985): 10–11; de Cordova, *Picture Personalities: The Emergence of the Star System in America* (Champaign, IL: University of Illinois Press, 1990).
34. Laurence W. Griswold, "Value of a 'Star's' Name in Sales Plan: How Several Manufacturers Have Increased Consumer Interest by Featuring Products with the Names of Well-Known Actresses, Etc.," *Printers' Ink* (January 22, 1914), 144. On Rigaud's strategies for moving into American markets, see Peiss, *Hope in a Jar*, 98.
35. On Garden, see Susan Rutherford, "The Voice of Freedom: Images of the prima donna," in *The New Woman and Her Sisters: Feminism and the Theatre, 1850–1914*, ed. Viv Gardner and Susan Rutherford (Hertfordshire: Harvester Wheatsheaf, 1992): 95–114. See also M. Garden and L. Biancolli, *Mary Garden's Story* (London: Michael Joseph, 1952).
36. Charles W. Hurd, "Putting the Dramatic Punch into Window Display: Using the Stage Manager's Method," *Printers' Ink* (December 16, 1915), 60.
37. Griswold, "The Value of a 'Star's' Name," 143, 146.
38. Ibid., 143.

39. "Patent on a Name," *Printers' Ink* (February 6, 1908), 8.
40. McArthur, *Actors and American Culture*, 150–153.
41. "Patent on a Name," 8.
42. Illington Banes, "The Mad Search for Beauty," 956.
43. Diana Forbes-Robertson, *My Aunt Maxine: The Story of Maxine Elliott* (New York: The Viking Press, 1964), 181.
44. "Lillian Russell's Own Toilet Preparations [ad]," *Vanity Fair* (January 1914): 87.
45. "To the Women of America, by Lillian Russell [ad]," *Harper's Bazar* (April 1915): 69.
46. Parker Morell, *Lillian Russell: The Era of Plush* (Garden City, NY: Random House, 1943), 294–296; Armond Fields, *Lillian Russell: A Biography of "America's Beauty"* (Jefferson, NC: McFarland and Co., Inc. Publishers, 1999), 190.
47. See the essays by Slavishak and Moskowitz in this volume.
48. Griswold, "Value of a 'Star's' Name," 147.
49. Griswold, "Value of a 'Star's' Name," 147.
50. *Wood v. Lucy, Lady Duff-Gordon, 222 N.Y. 88, 118 N.E. 214 (1917)*, http://www.libfind.unl.edu/workslaw/lady_duff.html. Accessed November 19, 2008.
51. "Additional Note to *Wood v. Lucy, Lady Duff-Gordon*," 36, http://www.law.ucla.edu/students/academicinfo/coursepages/F99/100–5/Lucy.htm. See also "Sears-Roebuck's Latest Advertising Coup: Seeks to Wrest Fashion Prestige Away from New York Mail-order Houses," *Printers' Ink* (December 8, 1916), 7.
52. *Wood v. Lucy, Lady Duff-Gordon, 222 N.Y. 88, 118 N.E. 214 (1917).*
53. Fox, *The Mirror Makers*, 115; *Printer's Ink, A Journal for Advertisers—Fifty Years, 1888–1938*, July 28, 1938, 370. Today, celebrities are often required to sign endorsement contracts that specify that they may not publicly promote products from a competitor. In December 2007, *Desperate Housewives* actress Teri Hatcher was sued by skin care company Hydroderm, with which she had an endorsement deal, for apparently promoting a competitor's lip serum. "Desperately seeking payment: Teri Hatcher sued for £1 million over lip gloss endorsement deal," *Mail Online* (December 5, 2007). http://www.dailymail.co.uk/tvshowbiz/article-499855/Desperately-seeking-payment-Teri-Hatcher-sued-1million-lip-gloss-endorsement-deal.html. Accessed December 12, 2009.
54. The magazines I surveyed include *Vogue, Vanity Fair, Harper's Bazar, The Theatre Magazine, The Delineator,* and the *Ladies Home Journal* for the period 1911–1918.
55. Kathy Peiss uses the term "makeup" to refer to products such as rouge and tinted face powder that could dramatically alter appearance. See Peiss, *Hope in a Jar*, 53, 56.
56. Until 1915, *Vogue* was one of the few magazines to provide specific information about products such as rouge. See Richard Corson, *Fashions in Makeup, From Ancient to Modern Times* (London: Owen, 1972), 410; Peiss, *Hope in a Jar*, 50, 104–105, 123.

57. See Corson, *Fashions in Makeup*, 410; Peiss, *Hope in a Jar,* 105.
58. For those who continued to promote the notion that physical beauty was an indication of a pure and honest soul, see Sara A. Hubbard, *The Duty of Being Beautiful* (Chicago, 1908).
59. Peiss, *Hope in a Jar*, 59.
60. Peiss, *Hope in a Jar*, 42–43; On African-American beauty culture, see A'Lelia Bundles, *On Her Own Ground: The Life and Times of Madam C.J. Walker* (New York: Scribner, 2001); Maxine Leeds Craig, *Ain't I a Beauty Queen? Black Women, Beauty, and the Politics of Race* (New York: Oxford University Press, 2002); Julie A. Willett, *Permanent Waves: The Making of the American Beauty Shop* (New York and London: NYU Press, 2000); Noliwe M. Rooks, *Hair Raising: Beauty, Culture, and African American Women* (New Brunswick, NJ: Rutgers University Press, 1996); Julia Kirk Blackwelder, *Styling Jim Crow: African American Beauty Training During Segregation* (College Station: Texas A and M University Press, 2003).
61. Elsie Janis, "My Campaign for Good Looks," *The Delineator* (February 1911): 128.
62. Mary Garden, "My Working Theory of Beauty," *The Delineator* (March 1911): 230; Maxine Elliott, "Keeping Young and Fresh," *The Delineator* (April 1911): 337–338; Ellen Terry, "The Woman of Charm," *The Delineator* (May 1911): 428; Billie Burke, "My Simple Rules for Beauty," *The Delineator* (June 1911): 510; Christie MacDonald, "Good Complexions," *The Delineator* (September 1911): 204.
63. Unlike women's magazines, most daily newspapers were willing to give their female readers the detailed beauty advice they craved. See Peiss, *Hope in a Jar*, 50–51, 123.
64. Eleanor Schorer, "'Making Up' With Stage Stars—IV. Laurette Taylor," *The Evening World* (March 1913), Laurette Taylor, vol. 451, 86, RLC, BRTC; "'Making Up' with Stage Stars—X. Elsie Ferguson," *The New York World.* Elsie Ferguson, vol. 197, 65. RLC, BRTC. Eleanor Schorer, "'Making Up' With Stage Stars—VII. Jane Cowl," *The Evening World* (April 28, 1913), Jane Cowl, vol. 131, 99, RLC, BRTC.
65. See Peiss, *Hope in a Jar,* 55.
66. Billie Burke, Anna Pavlova, Frances Starr, and Maxine Elliott each endorsed more than one beauty product at the same time. See "The Face Beautiful" [ad for Crème Nerol], *Vogue* (October 15, 1911): 69; "Women Who Have the World at Their Feet Unite in Praise of Valaze" [ad for Helena Rubinstein], *Vanity Fair* (December 1915): 99; "For a Clear Complexion Maxine Elliott Toilet Soap," [ad] *The Theatre Magazine Advertiser* (June 1911): vi; "Free! Write for samples of these two creams" [ad for Pond's Cold Cream and Vanishing Cream], *The Ladies' Home Journal* (November 1916): 85; "Why your skin needs two creams," Advertising Ephemera Collection–Database # P0096, Emergence of Advertising On-Line Project, Hartman Center, http://library.duke.edu/digitalcollections/eaa.P0096/pg.1/ Accessed November 19, 2008.
67. Anna Held, "'Make-up'—on the Street and on the Stage: Hints for the Woman at Her Dressing-Table," *The Green Book Magazine* (February 1916), 331.

68. Anne Archbald, "A Plea for Make-up (No. 1)," *The Theatre Magazine* (April 1917): 238.
69. "The Face Beautiful and Créme Nerol," [ad] *Vogue* (October 15, 1911): 69. The Créme Nerol campaign ran for several years (I have tracked it as far as 1918) in the pages of *Vogue* and *Vanity Fair*, with the occasional new name appearing among the list of established stars.
70. Like Créme Nerol, most of these campaigns targeted society women, as the price of the products appearing in *Vogue, Harper's Bazar*, and other "class" magazines suggests.
71. See "Women Who Have the World at Their Feet Unite in Praise of Valaze" [ad for Helena Rubinstein], *Vanity Fair* (December 1915): 99; "Lillian Russell's Own Toilet Preparations," [ad] *Theatre Magazine Advertiser* (January 1914): 55.
72. "Le Secret Gaby Deslys" [ad], *The Theatre Magazine Advertiser* (June 1912): xix.
73. Peiss, *Hope In a Jar*, 121–122.
74. Peiss, *Hope in a Jar*, 126, 137–140; Fox, *The Mirror Makers*, 88, 90. Jennifer Scanlon offers a detailed account of Helen Landsdowne Resor and other female copywriters who worked for the J. Walter Thompson Company in the early twentieth century, and discusses their involvement in a number of key campaigns, including Pond's and Woodbury's Facial Soap. See "Advertising Women: The J. Walter Thompson Company Women's Editorial Department," *Inarticulate Longings:* The Ladies' Home Journal, *Gender, and the Promises of Consumer Culture* (New York: Routledge, 1995), 169–198.
75. Other prominent Pond's users included Mrs. Fiske, Julia Sanderson, Julie Opp, Rose Stahl, and Jane Cowl. "Send 4 cents for two weeks' supply. See for yourself what one application will do!" Advertising Ephemera Collection –Database # P0074, Emergence of Advertising On-Line Project, Hartman Center, http://library.duke.edu/digitalcollections/eaa.P0074/pg.1/ Accessed November 19, 2008.
76. Ellen Gartrell, "More about the Pond's Collection," Emergence of Advertising On-Line Project, Hartman Center, http://library.duke.edu/digitalcollections/eaa/ponds.html. Accessed November 19, 2008.
77. Peiss, *Hope in a Jar* 126, 137–140; Fox, *The Mirror Makers*, 88, 90; Scanlon, *Inarticulate Longings*, 169–198.
78. "Gleaming, soft, smooth skin (1915)," Emergence of Advertising On-Line Project, Database # P0072, Hartman Center, http://library.duke.edu/digitalcollections/eaa.P0072/pg.1/ Accessed November 19, 2008.
79. "What a man looks for in a Girl (1916)," Emergence of Advertising On-Line Project, Database # P0091, Hartman Center, http://library.duke.edu/digitalcollections/eaa.P0091/pg.1/ Accessed November 19, 2008.
80. "The charm every actress knows," [ad for Pond's vanishing Cream] *LHJ* (April 1916): 64.
81. Anna Held, "'Make-up'—on the Street and on the Stage," 133.

CHAPTER 6

"I AM KAY AND I PREFER MODERN": BRIDAL TESTIMONIALS AND THE RISE OF CONSUMER RITES, 1920S–1950S

VICKI HOWARD

Between the 1920s and the 1950s, the bride emerged as a central advertising figure, paralleling the rise of the American wedding industry.[1] Pictured in her long white gown and veil or as a newlywed, she appeared in promotions for products associated with women's roles and feminine identity, as well as in advertisements for goods that had little connection to weddings or marriage. Brides also featured in testimonial advertisements during the 1920s and 1930s. A woman about to marry or newly married provided a credible voice for the advertiser.[2] Indeed, bridal status itself brought a degree of authenticity to producers' claims. With the bride's combination of youth, innocence, and beauty, she offered the perfect psychological sell. As a future Mrs. Consumer, the bride was an ideal candidate for this type of advertising, able to share expertise in beauty products and household goods with readers who identified with her role as wife and future mother.

Like other testimonials, these ads employed elite women, drawing on their class status to sell the goods.[3] But by the early postwar period, with the rise of bridal magazines and a national wedding industry, the testifying bride took on a new form. Testimonials became a part of editorial advertising in bridal magazines, embedded in features that masked their ties to the producer. Unlike the debutantes of earlier testimonial campaigns examined here, later testimonial-type ads employing brides constructed a middle-class image. Accompanied by photographs and other identifying information, these "real women" invited consumers to follow them in a more subtle way than earlier testimonials had, simply by lauding bridal goods and services, rather than pushing a particular brand. These testimonials from ordinary women projected an image of modernity in which identity was the product of one's taste and consumer choices. Bridal testimonials contributed to the transformation of American wedding culture, helping to set a higher standard of consumption and promote new consumer rites, such as the gift registry and department store bridal salon. The changing bridal testimonial form, moreover, exemplified a major shift in the relationship between advertisers and consumers in the first half of the twentieth century as commercial culture permeated all avenues of American life.

BUILDING THE BUSINESS OF BRIDES

Although the bride today seems the perfect marketing tool, and has been so for more than half a century in the United States, in the nineteenth and early twentieth centuries it was not necessarily common sense to associate the woman in white with consumption and the world of goods. While some businesses, such as caterers and jewelers, had a wedding trade, weddings themselves were generally not widespread consumer rites. Before the twentieth century, most ordinary women did not marry in white, and many wore their wedding dress—their best dress—more than once after exchanging vows. Church ceremonies, which were generally considered to be more costly than civil ceremonies or home weddings, became increasingly popular over the course of the nineteenth century, but the ideal middle-class wedding reception was still supposed to be a private affair, celebrated among family and close friends in the bride's home. Single ring ceremonies, in which the bride alone received a ring, were the norm, and the bride's ring itself was not the brand-name, matching diamond engagement ring and wedding band set that spread in the 1930s and 1940s. Weddings were changing, however, as evinced by the writers, reformers, ministers, and even some businesses that expressed deep cultural ambivalence about consumer rites and the spending bride. In the decades after the Civil War, criticisms of wedding excesses fit into the growing concern over what historian Daniel Horowitz has called "the morality of spending." As the nation became increasingly industrial, urban, and immigrant, new commercial leisure practices came under attack by those who believed a simpler, more traditional way of life was slipping away. Proponents of Victorian genteel culture felt threatened in the face of an expanding world of goods and an emerging mass culture.[4] To elites, wedding rituals were supposed to be an immutable mark of civilization, something that, according to Edith Wharton, "belong[ed] to the dawn of history."[5]

At the turn of the century, a few merchants still felt the incongruity of the business of brides. Some expressed ambivalence about linking sentiment and commerce in advertisements directed specifically at brides. The department store trade journal, *Dry Goods Economist*, self-consciously noted the appropriateness of a bridal market: "Just now it may not be strictly within correct form to seek business from the prospectives." As if department stores were reluctant to make June brides, in their words, "a fair mark," trade writers encouraged them to target those about to marry. Merchants were concerned with being "dignified" when selling to brides. Trade writers warned them not to be too squeamish about marketing specifically to brides: "A little sentiment, however, 'is a dangerous thing' in business, and one must up to a certain point shut their eyes and take chances." They exhibited a similar concern for middle-class propriety and good form, advising "the merchant of refinement" to contact brides unobtrusively through letters. Retailers seemed to be aware that tracking brides by following engagement lists and writing personal appeals to obtain their business crossed some fine line of respectability.[6] At the same time, other trade articles suggested that businesses saw no conflict between commerce and romance. For example, one 1901 trade writer addressing the marketing of wedding silver to the June bride advised New York stores rather cynically not to get "behind in the race," but to "put out their grappling-irons in the shape of windows or ads, for this trade."[7] Others worked to reconcile the profit motive with the sentiments surrounding a wedding. Advice in the late 1920s on how to write letters soliciting bridal trade recommended that jewelers hide the "cold commercialism of the appeal." According to one 1929 trade article in *The Jewelers' Circular*, weddings were "sentiment and emotion and romance personified," and thus a sales pitch directed at brides could have "a most discordant sound."[8]

Brides needed a wide range of goods to establish a new household, and imagery that appealed to this need made sense. A bride hawking sewing machines or silverware might have seemed incongruous earlier in the nineteenth century, when women's proper sphere was believed to be in the home, not out in the public world of commerce and certainly not in the role as "saleswoman." By the late nineteenth and early twentieth centuries, however, she began to appear in such advertisements.[9] As a future wife and household consumer, the advertising bride reconciled this earlier conflict between public and private spheres. Increasingly, advertisers believed that women in general were well-suited to selling goods that fit their domestic role.[10]

In the 1920s, ambivalence about the bride/consumer faded and most critiques of the big wedding dissipated, and the commercialization of the wedding ceremony intensified as retailers and others discovered, or invented, the bridal market.[11] Although etiquette writers continued to warn prospective brides against wedding consumption that was out of proportion with their means, they too demonstrated an increased acceptance of consumer rites by including advice on choosing professional services, such as caterers, florists, and eventually, bridal consultants.[12] Even the religious aspect of a wedding—the church ceremony—became commercialized as jewelers began self-consciously including images of "famous churches" in their ads in order to "boost the sales of wedding rings."[13] As the formal white wedding with all the trimmings became a cultural ideal promoted by a wide range of businesses, the bride became a suitable spokeswoman for a consumer age. Getting her business meant getting the business of a new household and all the lifelong expenditures associated with it, as she formed brand loyalties and ties with particular merchants. According to one jewelers' trade article, "Beginning with the engagement ring, there is a constant string of events taking place that calls for his merchandise that does not end until the last anniversary of the wedding is celebrated."[14]

Advertising and merchandising campaigns that targeted brides were part of this larger shift toward marketing to women in the 1920s. Advertising trade articles in *Printer's Ink* and influential books, such as Christine Frederick's *Selling Mrs. Consumer* (1929) and Carl Naether's *Advertising to Women* (1928), gathered statistics on women's "buying power" and attempted to convince the industry that "selling meant selling to women."[15] With this new emphasis on marketing to women specifically, it is no wonder that the advertising bride became more prevalent as weddings were widely understood to be women's work.[16] Advertisers believed that women were "naturally" interested in luxury and beauty.[17] And typically women, not men, loved weddings. Bridal advertising imagery fit this interest and further encouraged the gendering of wedding consumption.

In addition to being the product of new ideas in marketing, the advertising bride also reflected contemporary gender ideology. Bridal imagery in advertising certainly conveyed a conservative cultural message—one that idealized female virginity and understood women's primary role as wife and potential mother. Demographics seemed to support this ideology; indeed, from the 1870s through the 1920s only 10 percent of all American women did not marry. The image of the bride was a deeply traditional one, signaling a connection with the past. She embodied values that resonated with many others besides those women about to marry. Weddings were shorthand for beliefs about marriage, beliefs that linked nationhood with heterosexuality, monogamy, and the nuclear family.[18]

Increasingly, however, other options including college, social work, and professional careers presented themselves to women; from the 1870s through the 1920s, between 40 and 60 percent of female college graduates did not marry.[19] Perhaps as white middle-class women took on a more public and seemingly emancipated modern role in society—driving automobiles, cutting their hair short, wearing new boyish fashions, divorcing more easily, experimenting sexually, and of course, voting—social prescriptions about the virgin bride seemed old-fashioned. The new bride-as-consumer fit these changing gender expectations and ideals. Though still traditional on the surface, the advertising bride also captured women's broader social role as a consumer—as someone who "voted" with her pocketbook. By the 1920s, bridal imagery was deemed suitable to advertise a broader range of goods, from such things as soap and beauty cream to cigarettes. In these ads, the bride's traditional, and historically noncommercial, image helped wash away any remaining ambivalence about advertising and the rise of a consumer culture.

TESTIFYING BRIDES

Given these developments, it is hardly surprising that the woman in white appeared specifically as a testimonial figure during this period. Such ads featured testimonials from women appearing at the point of marriage, or those recalling wedding memories and bridal images from the past. For example, a 1925 ad for Pond's Extract Co., included the Lady Diana Manners' wedding portrait in a testimonial that attributed her beauty to her use of the company's two-cream cleansing system. Part of a very successful J. Walter Thompson testimonial campaign using the endorsements of famous women, the Lady Manners ad ranked highest among a young readership, suggesting that bridal appeal worked well with an audience thinking about marriage in their future.[20] A portrait of a woman in her white bridal gown implicitly testified to the product's ability to keep a woman's skin youthful, as it supposedly was on her wedding day. A similar ad featuring the Duchess of Marlborough, formerly Gladys Deacon of Boston, used a portrait of "her Grace in the priceless gown of ivory lace she wore at her wedding."[21] Following a failed testimonial campaign that highlighted women of accomplishment, Pond's advertising agency, J. Walter Thompson, turned to American socialites or aristocrats such as Lady Manners or the Duchess of Marlborough to be their product spokeswomen. Endorsements by such elite and beautiful women helped Pond's compete with more expensive beauty treatments.[22] In a similar way, a Lux testimonial from the same year attested to the gentleness of the soap, with an image of an antique wedding veil and portrait of a bride: the "Princess Giambatistta Rospigliosi" testified that she used Lux to wash her great grandmother's rare lace wedding veil.[23] In each case, a noncommercial figure—the bride—was used for commercial purposes.

Generally, the women testifying that they successfully used such products were in fact not paid to do so. J. Walter Thompson's Women's Editorial Department did offer small sums to the college students they surveyed for a Woodbury's endorsement campaign, but they did so irregardless of whether the women used the product, suggesting an attempt at authenticity.[24] Surveys, however, revealed that consumers doubted the veracity of testimonials. Testimonial-style advertising needed to seem heartfelt and honest to work—a paid endorsement contradicted the idea that an individual truly used the product and found it effective. Perhaps advertisers instinctively turned the bride into a selling tool because references to a wedding or images of the product endorser in her wedding gown and veil added an element of reality to these ads. Readers who were married themselves, or who simply wanted to marry someday, would have been able to identify with the featured woman's experience and thus perhaps believe her claims about cream or soap. Still, the question of why an elite or wealthy figure would offer their services to an advertising agency must have hovered over such ads. One wealthy suffragist and feminist, Alva Belmont, endorsed Pond's Cold Cream in the mid-1920s for a $1000 donation to a feminist cause (though the donation was not mentioned in the testimonial ad produced by the Women's Editorial Department at the J. Walter Thompson's agency). Others responded to private beauty contests run by the ad agency, as in a Woodbury contest in the late 1920s that drew on Junior League branches to find the ideal Woodbury beauty in a variety of categories, such as bride, wife, or business girl.[25]

Bridal testimonials changed over the next two decades, perhaps signaling a shift in advertisers' understanding of their audience. One example from the 1930s suggests that the advertising form took itself less seriously by this time, or at least advertisers knew that readers were more sophisticated and able to read different levels of meaning in an ad. A 1939 testimonial for Ivory Soap titled "Matron-of-Honor Shocks Bride!" noted that marriage was "not all moonlight and roses," something the bride would find out when she got rough hands from dishwashing. The matron-of-honor's playful observation about marriage suggested that a decline in romance was routine as women's everyday responsibilities wore away the glamour of the wedding and the wedding night. The accompanying image of a bride with her mouth gaping open in disbelief and one soft hand (before they were ruined by wifely duties) held up to her face in horror was certainly meant to have a humorous appeal, as was perhaps the idea that Ivory Soap could save a marriage. Not all bridal testimonial figures in the 1930s worked this way; others stuck to basics, as in the assertion by one "lovely Toronto Bride" that she has "always used Palmolive."[26] In the 1940s, one bridal testimonial campaign for Woodbury soap worked in both ways, making a traditional class appeal but also including some humor and sexually suggestive language that provided a more modern tone. These Woodbury facial soap ads in magazines such as *Ladies' Home Journal* and *McCall's* used title copy such as "Another Woodbury Deb Marries," and "She's Another Woodbury Marrying Deb!" Ad copy subtly linked the product with sexual fulfillment, as well as the more overt goal of finding a husband, asserting in no uncertain terms that "Woodbury helps you *score*, girls" (emphasis in original: see figure 6.2).[27] A Woodbury campaign in the early 1950s, however, used wedding night sexuality more subtly. In a large photo format, instead of the storyboard style of the 1940s, one 1953 bride testified to the product's ability to produce beautiful skin: "'Let your own mirror show you' says Mrs. William P. Helburn, another lovely Woodbury bride." The way this bride posed with her mirror in a lacy peignoir, her wedding ring in the foreground, conveys the bride's sexuality and her feeling of satisfaction; whether this satisfaction derives from the soap or her married state is left for the individual reader to decide (see figure 6.1).

Testimonial ads during all three decades drew on prescribed ideals of class, gender, and race. Ads for soaps or creams used the cultural ideal that all brides are beautiful, suggesting that their product maintained the youth and beauty of a woman on her wedding day. And most brides, if these ads were to be believed, were wealthy and white. Ads for household products thus worked by erasing the more mundane reality of most women's lives—the fact of endless loads of laundry and dishes—by having privileged upper-class brides provide the product testimonial, women who likely did not do their own household chores. Women in Woodbury soap testimonial ads from the late 1940s, for example, were southern belles, with nicknames like "Kappy" or "Calise." One "Woodbury deb" descended from a "proud Virginia family." The grooms and male members of the bride's family always held prominent positions, such as the grandfather of Caroline Louise Chauvenet (Calise), allegedly called the "father of United States Naval Academy." The women's status in these testimonials came not only from their class position, but from their ability "to *score*" or capture the right man, one who would guarantee them continued socioeconomic success. And of course, ads emphasized that this ability came from the women's use of the advertised product.[28]

The 1940s Woodbury testimonial campaign also featured white women with very pale skin, linking their whiteness with the cleanliness and purity of soap. As if to highlight their product's properties and the whiteness of the women using the soap, one Woodbury ad used photo insets of African Americans in stereotypical roles. The 1949 testimonial of southern bride, Katherine Ellison, pictured her and her groom in a photo inset with a black child, seemingly gratuitously speaking in "dialect" and posed as a waiter in a chef's hat (see figure 6.2). The 1949 testimonial of southern bride, Calise,

WOODBURY
"Let your own mirror show you..." SAYS MRS. WILLIAM P. HELBURN, ANOTHER LOVELY WOODBURY BRIDE
New way to beautiful skin!
New Woodbury Soap enriched with 7 Face Cream Oils
You know that fine oils and emollients are used in expensive face creams. Now, these very *same* ingredients are blended right into every cake of New Woodbury Soap. That means your complexion can be really, thoroughly, soap-and-water clean – and be exquisitely soft as well! These gentle face cream oils are intended to help *replace* the natural oils you usually wash away . . . oils your skin *needs* to stay young-looking. That's so important—especially to dry skin! In the bath, too, you'll love the gentle, soothing luxury-lather of the New Woodbury Soap and the thorough way it cleanses. You'll be delighted with its new sea-spray green color and delicate fragrance.
You'll recognize it immediately in its new blue and white wrapper with the picture of the lovely lady and her mirror. Whether you use it in facial or big bath size, you'll find that New Woodbury Soap gives you the *cleanest, most radiant complexion of your life!*
Now better than ever! "Woodbury Soap for the skin you love to touch!"
164

Figure 6.1 "New way to beautiful skin!" 1953. A bride's testimonial allowed advertisers to use sex to sell their product within the safe context of marriage.

Source: Author's collection.

featured a photo inset taken at the plantation where the bride was born. Accompanying the couple is "Aunt Cloe," an elderly African-American woman in a kerchief who had looked after the bride and had helped her "bloom," along with Woodbury soap. Presented as a black mammy, she worked as "the other," signifying the racial and class superiority of the

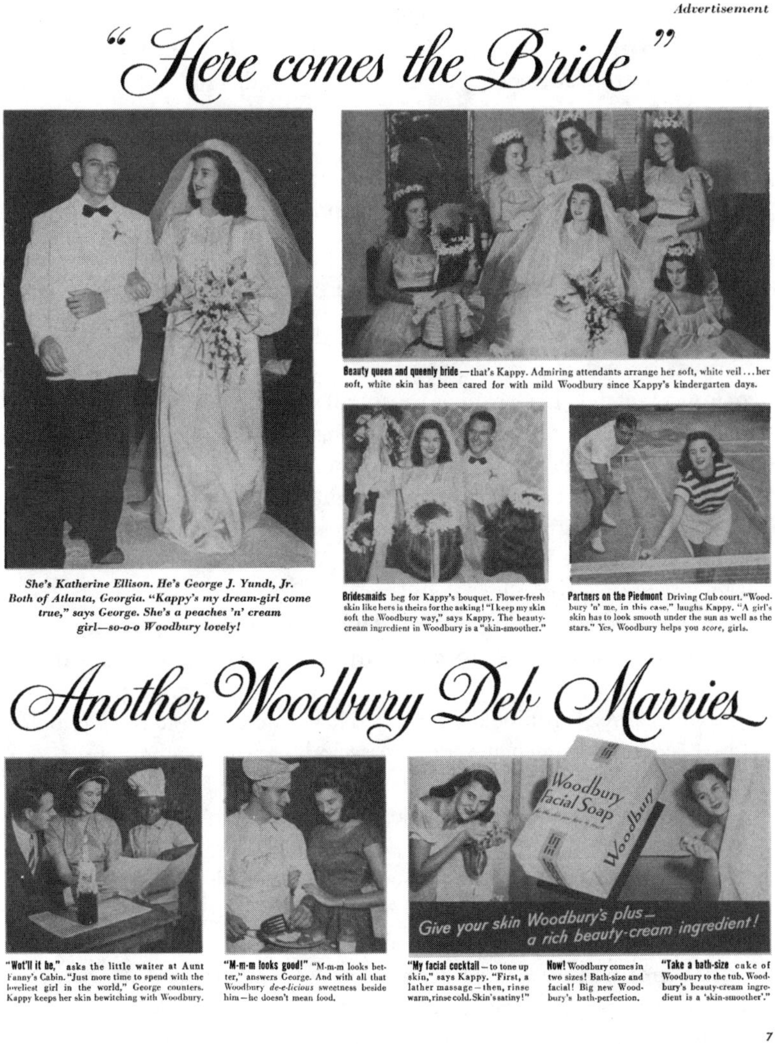
Advertisement
"Here comes the Bride"
She's Katherine Ellison. He's George J. Yundt, Jr. Both of Atlanta, Georgia. "Kappy's my dream-girl come true," says George. She's a peaches 'n' cream girl—so-o-o Woodbury lovely!
Beauty queen and queenly bride—that's Kappy. Admiring attendants arrange her soft, white veil...her soft, white skin has been cared for with mild Woodbury since Kappy's kindergarten days.
Bridesmaids beg for Kappy's bouquet. Flower-fresh skin like hers is theirs for the asking! "I keep my skin soft the Woodbury way," says Kappy. The beauty-cream ingredient in Woodbury is a "skin-smoother."
Partners on the Piedmont Driving Club court. "Woodbury 'n' me, in this case," laughs Kappy. "A girl's skin has to look smooth under the sun as well as the stars." Yes, Woodbury helps you score, girls.
Another Woodbury Deb Marries
Woodbury Facial Soap
Woodbury
Give your skin Woodbury's plus—
a rich beauty-cream ingredient!
"Wot'll it be," asks the little waiter at Aunt Fanny's Cabin. "Just more time to spend with the loveliest girl in the world," George counters. Kappy keeps her skin bewitching with Woodbury.
"M-m-m looks good!" "M-m-m looks better," answers George. And with all that Woodbury de-e-licious sweetness beside him—he doesn't mean food.
"My facial cocktail—to tone up skin," says Kappy. "First, a lather massage—then, rinse warm, rinse cold. Skin's satiny!"
Now! Woodbury comes in two sizes! Bath-size and facial! Big new Woodbury's bath-perfection.
"Take a bath-size cake of Woodbury to the tub. Woodbury's beauty-cream ingredient is a 'skin-smoother'."
7

Figure 6.2 "Another Woodbury Deb Marries," 1949. Woodbury testimonial advertisements linked the whiteness and purity of the youthful bride with their soap product.

Source: Author's collection.

white figures in the photo. The Woodbury bride engaged in leisure activities and appeared as a consumer, not as a worker like the black woman in the ad. Such a leisurely image elevated the status of the testifying bride, a status that consumers were supposed to emulate by purchasing Woodbury soap. The close association between whiteness and weddings also worked in these bridal testimonials. Woodbury bride Kappy, or Katherine Ellison, appeared in her gown surrounded by her white bridesmaids. The ad copy described how the "admiring attendants arrange[d] her soft, white veil . . . her soft white skin has been cared for with mild Woodbury soap since Kappy's kindergarten days."[29] By pairing the whiteness of her wedding veil with the description of her skin, the ad linked the product with the purity and youth associated with the virgin bride—and her privileged racial status.[30]

Bridal Magazine Testimonials

Bridal testimonials, such as those found in the Pond's and Woodbury Soap campaigns, were not targeted specifically at women about to marry, but were instead intended to have a broad appeal among women who "naturally" were interested in weddings and everything surrounding them. With the rise of a wedding industry, the bridal testimonial became part of a more narrowly defined market segment in publications such as *Bride's*, which started in 1934 as a free-controlled circulation magazine, and *Modern Bride*, which first appeared on the newsstands in 1949. As advertising publications first and foremost, they consolidated and expanded the wedding-related advice, information, and advertising that had long been a staple of women's magazines. Part of a general shift toward market segmentation and advertising-driven publications, bridal magazines gave advertisers a "must-buy" market unlike any before. Testimonials published here would be read by that highly lucrative market—women about to marry and set up a new household.

Bride's magazine in particular helped centralize and professionalize the wedding industry, conducting market research, participating in national advertising, and establishing networks with mass and specialty retailers. *Bride's* became the linchpin for a growing industry by hosting bridal clinics for department stores, which in turn helped spread wedding salons and gift registries across the country.[31] Advertisements, which were responsible for the magazine's heft, promoted department store salons and gift registries, household goods, and, of course, wedding gown designs. Although advertising dominated their pages, these magazines also sought to project an image of service. They presented themselves as sources of information and advice for women about to marry.

To cover their stark commercial orientation, bridal magazines, like other women's magazines, employed editorial advertising. Editorial advertising was a form of covert advertising in which regular articles, columns, or feature pieces promoted a variety of professional wedding services and goods for setting up a new household. This was something like the advertising trade's use of "editorial copy" or "puffing" in the 1920s. Roland Marchand and Ellen Gruber Garvey have shown how ads employing this trick tried to compete with popular features in magazines and newspapers by imitating their layout and pictures. These ads were often camouflaged as editorial features. In the *Ladies' Home Journal*, for example, ads and editorial matter were scarcely distinguishable, as in the Crisco ad that featured copious text and separate headlines, such as "Every Woman is Interested in This," or "A Scientific Discovery Which will Affect Every Kitchen in America." As Jennifer Scanlon has argued in her book on the *Ladies' Home Journal*, through the "integration of advertising into the magazine's text and hence into the magazine's message," advertisers "effectively merged women's roles as magazine readers and primary consumers."[32]

Testimonial advertising worked well in this form, emerging in a new way as editorial advertisements through a series of *Modern Bride* articles in the mid-1950s featuring a "real life bride." In these so-called articles, the bride herself became a sophisticated marketing tool. In turn, she gained the status of having her nuptials and household planning upheld as a model for women to follow. (It is unknown whether the women in these articles received discounts, kickbacks, or any sort of payment for their story, or even if they were real women, though from the photographs and background information on the women included in the articles it appears that they were.) Unlike the earlier bridal testimonials that employed elite women, these real-life brides were not society women or celebrities. Women in these ads were young and attractive, nevertheless, with the sort of everyday glamour idealized in 1950s consumer culture. Posed smiling in their fashionable New Look outfits with gloves and hat, these well-coifed real-life brides represented a femininity that was at once idealized and yet accessible. In magazines with the primary function of selling goods and services to those about to marry, these women's stories helped mask the stark commercial goals of the publications. Other magazines, such as *True Story*, generated reader interest through the "real life" account, and perhaps bridal magazines sought to have that appeal as well. In any event, such articles helped the publishers disguise the fact that what was being purchased when a bride bought a magazine was simply a bunch of ads intended to make her spend more money on her wedding.

"Real life" bridal testimonials promoted the commercial goals of different areas of the wedding industry, such as department stores. These features took the reader through a woman's wedding story and plans for her future home by way of promoting a particular retailer. In keeping with bridal magazines' efforts to develop the department store wedding business and form networks with particular businesses, engaged women in testimonial-style articles praised a major retailer in the city where they lived. Each of these articles began their photograph series with an image of the engaged woman posed in front of the store's sign or logo. However, unlike earlier testimonial ads that tried to connect the brand with the woman promoting it, these testimonial-style articles incorporated their promotions very gracefully and naturally so that it appeared to the reader that they were simply looking at an informational article.[33] When Brooklyn's Abraham and Straus received a lengthy hidden testimonial from Margaret Regan in 1955, for example, she and her husband were described as coming from "old Brooklyn families." Since the bride was already a regular customer at the department store, according to the article, "it was logical" for her to register at their bridal salon and use the store's consultant for help with the wedding plans, bridal apparel, and reception.[34] Photos accompanying the article allowed the reader to shop alongside the couple as they visited the store's luggage, carpet, draperies, hardware, and silverware departments. The reader learned that "the silverware department at Abraham & Straus was full of temptations." The bride was transformed into a future Mrs. Consumer before the reader's eyes when a photo depicted Margaret "absorbed in china, pots, pans and hollow ware ... items she had been only marginally interested in before."[35] Similarly, another "real life bride" testimonial-style article followed a Minneapolis bride, Virginia Ecklund, through Dayton's department store, photographing her as she surveyed glassware, tried on a wedding gown in the store's bridal salon, and examined lamps, lingerie, and small appliances.[36]

Bridal testimonial-style articles also promoted brand-name goods, though unlike traditional testimonials, these editorial advertisements detailed a wide selection of house wares needed by the bride. An early version of the "real life bride" series ran in the first issue of *Modern Bride* in 1949. Presenting itself as a gift guide, this article featured a number of brides with varying tastes and different married futures, largely indicated by their future husband's professional status. Each of the profiled brides introduced herself and described her situation. Her brief statement was followed by detailed information, prices, and store location for brand-name goods that would fit her future home. Instead of pushing one brand or one type of item, this advertising article gave the reader the plush material outlines of different levels of well-appointed homes, with images of Wedgwood china, International silver-plated coffee services, folding gin rummy tables, French Provincial lamps, maple coffee tables, and mahogany tea wagons. In these covert advertisements, the bride was likely not a "real life" person, as suggested by the sketchy photograph of a partial face that accompanied each promotion and lack of a last name. The article, moreover, slotted each women into a type that would likely appeal to different segments of the magazine's readership. Thus, readers were told that "I am Kay and I prefer modern," or that "I am Ann and I'll be a campus wife until John gets his degree in engineering."[37]

Modern Bride magazine defined these testifying brides in a way that allowed them to become target markets, each with their own styles and product needs. Bridal testimonial-style features thus promoted specific brands or designers associated with or available at the department store. The "real life bride" series would do the same thing as this earlier 1949 version, only in a more subtle, sophisticated way. Reading about Virginia Ecklund, for example, we learn that she loved modeling her new clothes at Dayton's, and we are told that she purchased a "handmade Regina Brenner silk peignoir." Other goods she purchased at Dayton's are fit into the narrative by name, such as the Dorothy Gray "Wedgwood" cosmetic kit she bought as a gift for each of her seven bridal attendants.[38] Similarly, the "real life bride" shopping at Brooklyn's Abraham and Straus testified for a host of fashions, from her Maurer design wedding dress to her trousseau clothes by "Junior Sophisticates."[39]

Such editorial ads did more than just promote particular stores and brands: they also naturalized the use of professional bridal services, contributing to the commercialization of American weddings. Not surprisingly, the women who told their story all had "a big formal wedding."[40] These articles were covert ads for the department store bridal business overall. They played on the idea that an approaching wedding date set off an exhausting department store shopping frenzy as a couple searched for things for their new home. Through these stories, the bridal magazine helped department stores expand the goods "needed" to set up a new home. "Real life brides" appeared using gift registries and preprinted forms that told them what they needed to register for, or buy for, their future home. Real-life brides like Virginia Ecklund testified to the usefulness of Dayton's bridal services. As "no tyro in the kitchen," when appliance shopping Ecklund stated that she needed the guidance from the "will need, must buy" list that Dayton's provided.[41] She felt she needed the help the store provided, as, according to the article, Dayton's "understood" the different problems that newlyweds faced when setting up their home. Her particular problem was that she and her husband, Harry, were going to have to live in temporary quarters for awhile after their marriage until he finished graduate school. Dayton's bridal consultant advised her to focus on lamps, pictures, and linens that would make the transition to her permanent home. As she traveled from the store's "first floor to the seventh floor and back down to the third floor and then up to the sixth" she was able to complete everything she needed to do before the wedding.[42] In another "real life bride" installment from a later issue of *Modern Bride*, professional bridal services appeared in the background for each woman featured.[43] Such articles spread the idea that a wedding would simply not be a wedding without the gown and all the new household goods provided by the department store—conveniently all under one roof.

Editorial advertisements like the "real life bride" series highlighted the prominent role that department stores played in the rise of a wedding industry. Stores like Dayton's allowed a bride to complete all her shopping efficiently, registering for gifts, purchasing household items, selecting a wedding gown, and even making wedding and honeymoon plans. When magazines like *Modern Bride* agreed to run articles like these, which were really masked advertisements for particular stores, they furthered the important networks forged between mass retailers and bridal magazines in the 1930s. From its inception in 1934, *Bride's* magazine had developed a relationship with mass retailers behind the scenes beyond selling advertising space to different stores. Various campaigns promoted department store bridal merchandising, sponsoring store promotions and providing tie-in advertising articles on the events across the country. In 1939, for example, it first ran a contest for its readers that tied into department store promotions for household goods. "The Home for Two" contest, advertised in *Bride's*, took place at Altman's and at Carson Pirie Scott and Company. Each department store tagged merchandise for the contest, and supplied each contestant with a floor plan, sketches of furniture, and instructed the contestant to choose furnishings for their ideal home. The winners, who were written up in the magazine, had their choices displayed in a special apartment constructed at the store.[44] Such contests fostered store loyalty among new couples at the same time as they linked marriage to a consumer ethic. Bridal testimonials promoted stores in much the same way, showing the loyalty of individual women to their town's or city's major retailers. Assuming that the brides and their stories were "real," these articles made a credible case for the importance of department stores in the business of getting married.

Marketing Bridal Types

Testimonial-style editorial advertisements tried to capture a larger readership and market by featuring the different "types" of women who marry. By the 1950s, a range of prefabricated bridal identities emerged in editorial advertising articles in both *Bride's* and *Modern Bride*. Such testimonials offered readers a range of consumer types with which women could identify or emulate: from the small-town girl to the campus wife to the career woman. On some level, editors must have been responding to what they perceived as consumer demand in that they devised a range of female types that might cover a broad spectrum of the readership. Usually delineated by the budget available to the bride, they reflected class identities, while cautiously avoiding the use of the term. Types ranged from the society bride to the solidly middle-class bride to the bride on a budget. All were white, and none were working-class, likely reflecting the publication's primary function of selling advertising space and its need to deliver a readership with attractive purchasing power. Editorial advertising articles like "Trousseau for Audrey" and "Trousseau for Ricki" in *Bride's* magazine, and "I am Joyce" and "I am Kay" in *Modern Bride*, for example, presented women with different budgets, tastes, and needs. Pictured with the furniture, home décor, china, and silver they bought or requested as wedding gifts, these white women and their testimonials appeared as ordinary brides—types that were supposed to represent the range of individuals that made up the magazine's readership. They emphasized women's role as consumer, in keeping with the magazine's function as an advertising publication. Although other personal details emerged, the women's interests focused on entertaining and decorating, not surprising in an article that ultimately intended to sell china, silver, glassware, and furniture. For example, Kay, who was married to "Phil," worked outside the home and "love[d] city life." The feature did not discuss her career in more detail, however, but instead emphasized traditionally feminine concerns: because she worked, she needed her "apartment to be as streamlined as possible for causal and easy entertaining."[45] In "I Am Susan," readers were briefly introduced to a "small-town girl," who married an attorney and lived in a Cape Cod house in a new suburb. The piece emphasized her domestic focus and signaled that children were going to be in her future. On the surface, such details were seemingly provided for general interest of the reader, but in fact were meant to plug the goods pictured below Susan's photograph and biographical blurb. For example, Susan liked the Early American style and such things as hooked rugs, maple pieces, and copper pans, because "children are more comfortable with that."[46] Ultimately, each of these women mirrored the limited gender roles prescribed for women in the postwar era. Thinly veiled advertisements, articles such as these defined the parameters of women's identity in as much as they offered up ideals against which readers could evaluate their own consumer realities.[47]

While at a distance it is clear that these covert testimonials from "real life brides" served the commercial goals of the industry and its advertisers, the question remains whether readers at the time were influenced by the consumer information in these articles. Were readers also white and middle and upper-middle class, like the brides depicted in the magazines? Did readers identify with these brides and have bigger, more expensive weddings as a result? Did they turn to department stores and their experts to help them emulate the elaborate material world outlined in bridal magazines? According to the market research sponsored by the bridal magazine industry, the advertisements in these publications worked. Many readers were convinced by "real life brides" to frequent particular stores or follow the dictates of the wedding industry. In the late 1950s, for the first time bridal magazines conducted national market research that provided advertisers with basic demographic information about their readership. In 1958, *Bride's* sponsored the first representative study using random sampling methods. The study sampled 3,800 brides from marriage license registrations in fifty sample counties that covered both rural and urban areas. To eliminate bias due to nonrespondents, a certain number of nonresponding brides were interviewed in person or by telephone.[48] This early study helped advertisers and bridal magazines define their target audience more precisely than ever before in order to reach them more effectively. In the process of researching this bridal market, publications like *Bride's* and *Modern Bride* rationalized and standardized the wedding process, turning the men and women who married and set up house into consumers for increasing numbers of markets.

The consumer message of *Bride's* magazine reached a relatively well-off group, which as a whole had a higher percentage of participation in the industry and conformity with the white wedding ideal—much like the "real life brides" depicted in *Modern Bride*'s testimonial-style series. The market analysis from 1958 found that of the 1,254 marriage licensees interviewed for the study, 349, or 28 percent, identified themselves as buyers of *Bride's* magazine. These readers were mainly middle-class women employed in white-collar, professional, and technical fields and had a higher medium annual income when combined with their future husbands' than the general population. A dual-income family meant increased purchasing power, but it could also mean that the bride had more control over the couple's future consumer decisions, something good for advertisers in *Bride's*. Readers of the magazine also used gift registries at a higher rate than the rest of the bridal market in the United States, suggesting that perhaps editorial advertisements promoting the new service worked. They also received a higher percentage of certain wedding gifts, such as silver, fine china, crystal, earthenware, glass stemware, and plastic dinnerware, indicating that their participation in gift registry or their reading of *Bride's* resulted in a standardization of gifts. Readers also spent more on honeymoons than other American brides. Such statistics would have helped *Bride's* magazine sell advertising space in the late 1950s, as the figures suggest that businesses would reach a relatively well-to-do market, one where there was the potential to gain the consumer loyalty of brides as they furnished their home and began establishing brand preferences. In addition, advertisers were able to reach others as the magazine passed to the bride's family members and friends.[49]

White "real life brides" mirrored the mainstream image of women in postwar popular culture. Well-heeled, domestically oriented, and consumerist, the advertising bride promoted a limited gender identity rooted in materialism. Other identities were not visible. Even though the readership of bridal magazines reflected some of the diversity of the nation, it did not appear in the testimonial-style articles or advertisements. The racial identity of the "types" or of the "real life brides," and of women in bridal magazines as a whole, was consistently white through the 1950s. Even though the publications had readers of color, and brides and grooms from a variety of racial backgrounds had weddings with all the trimmings, attitudes changed slowly in these publications. With very few exceptions, the couples featured were white, though one 1962 *Modern Bride* issue featured an interracial marriage of a white American lieutenant and a Japanese-American woman. Until the late 1960s, African-American brides were completely absent, with blacks only appearing as servant figures in advertisements, and then too, rarely.[50] Through this absence, bridal advertisements, the "real life bride" series, and other features like it racialized the "white wedding" tradition.[51] Such cultural texts provided an ideal against which readers would judge their own celebrations and plans for married life, and this ideal had a gendered, race, and class component.

Conclusion

In keeping with the larger commercial goals of bridal magazines and the wedding industry as a whole, the ideal advertising bride could well afford to have the lucrative formal white wedding with all the trimmings. Spending big on a wedding also became more culturally acceptable. Bridal testimonials in the 1920s and 1930s and later editorial testimonial-style advertisements clearly linked marriage and commerce. While the older style of bridal testimonial ad in which a prominent woman gave her name to products like Pond's or Lux did not survive, bridal testimonial-style editorial ads heralded a new level of commercialization in the American wedding and a cultural celebration of Mrs. Consumer. At the beginning of the twenty-first century, more people than ever before choose to have a big wedding. In 2005, the average cost of a wedding passed $30,000. With numbers like these, it is not surprising that weddings today are a 70 billion dollar industry and an important part of the economy.[52] By telling her story and promoting different goods and services, the advertising bride contributed to this transformation, legitimizing the alliance of romance and commerce.

Notes

1. This essay comes out of research I conducted originally for my doctoral dissertation at University of Texas at Austin, "American Weddings: Gender, Consumption and the Business of Brides" (2000). Since then, I have published *Brides, Inc. American Weddings and the Business of Brides* (Philadelphia: University of Pennsylvania Press, 2006). Some material from Chapter 3 of that book is reprinted here by permission of the University of Pennsylvania Press. In recent years, many scholars and journalists have published books on weddings, though my work remains the only one focused historically on the

businesses behind the growth of the commercialized contemporary American wedding culture. For other scholarly treatments of the white wedding and related bridal rituals, see Cele Otnes and Elizabeth Pleck, *Cinderella Dreams: The Allure of the Lavish Wedding* (Berkeley: University of California Press, 2003); Beth Montemurro, *Something Old, Something Bold: Bridal Showers and Bachelorette Parties* (New Brunswick, NJ: Rutgers University Press, 2006); Katherine Jellison, *It's Our Day: America's Love Affair with the White Wedding, 1945–2005* (Lawrence: University of Kansas Press, 2008). An earlier sociological critique of the subject is Chrys Ingraham's *White Weddings: Romancing Heterosexuality in Popular Culture* (New York: Routledge, 1999).

2. Roland Marchand has argued that testimonials by public figures were considered more credible than those messages delivered by the producer or his sales representative. *Advertising the American Dream: Making Way for Modernity, 1920–1940* (Berkeley: University of California Press, 1985), 112.
3. On cosmetics testimonials by society women, see Kathy Peiss, *Hope in a Jar* (New York: Metropolitan Books, 1998), 64.
4. Daniel Horowitz, *The Morality of Spending: Attitudes toward the Consumer Society in America, 1875–1940* (Baltimore: The Johns Hopkins University Press, 1985), 68–69; On the rise of "consumer rites" and the critiques of wedding consumption, see Chapter 1 in Howard, *Brides, Inc.* On changing ring traditions and the jewelry industry, see Chapter 2 in *Brides, Inc.*
5. Edith Wharton, *Age of Innocence: Complete Text with Introduction, Historical Contexts, Critical Essays*, ed. Carol J. Singley (Boston: Houghton Mifflin Company, 2000), 154.
6. "June Brides a Fair Mark," *Dry Goods Economist* (June 8, 1901), 43; "Cheap Tableware Fairly Active," *Dry Goods Economist* (May 18, 1901), 15.
7. "Silverware," *Dry Goods Economist* (June 8, 1901), 42. This section has been taken with permission from Howard, *Brides Inc.*, Chapter 1.
8. "Advertising and Selling Suggestions for June," *The Jewelers' Circular* (May 16, 1929), 45.
9. "Domestic Sewing Machine," 1882, Baker Library, Harvard Business School, Historical Collections. http://via.harvard.edu. Accessed January 7, 2009. "Silver Plate that Wears," 1915 Ad for 1847 Rogers Bros., N. W. Ayer Advertising Agency Records, Archives Center, National Museum of American History, Behring Center, Smithsonian Institution, Washington, DC.
10. For example, see Bruce Bliven, "The Woman Advertiser and Manufacturer," *Printers' Ink* (February 20, 1919), 17; Also, see "Are Women Best Sellers of Products for Housekeepers," *Printers' Ink* (January 6, 1921), 35.
11. For example, see Jane Grant, "Purveyors to the Bride," *Saturday Evening Post* (September 5, 1925), 23, 89.
12. For critiques of costly weddings, see Edith Ordway, *The Etiquette of To-Day* (New York: George Sully and Company, Inc., 1913), 198, 200. For a discussion of etiquette books and consumer rites, see Howard, *Brides, Inc.*, Chapter 3.

13. D. G. Baird, "Famous Churches in Advertisements Boost the Sales of Wedding Rings," *Printers' Ink* (July 8, 1920), 57.
14. "Selling More Gifts for the June Bride," *The Jewelers' Circular* (May 11, 1927), 117.
15. For a discussion of the link forged between consumption and women's role in the advertising industry, see Kenon Breazeale, "In Spite of Women: Esquire Magazine and the Construction of the Male Consumer," in *The Gender and Consumer Culture Reader*, ed. Jennifer Scanlon (New York: New York University Press, 2000), 228.
16. Vicki Howard, "American Weddings: Gender, Consumption, and the Business of Brides" (Ph.D. diss., University of Texas at Austin, 2000), 262, also Chapter 5.
17. Bruce Barton, "Handling 1,000 Men Working on Commission," *Printers' Ink* (February 4, 1915), 6.
18. For a history of the social construction of marriage, see Nancy Cott, *Public Vows: A History of Marriage and the Nation* (Cambridge, MA: Harvard University Press, 2000).
19. For these statistics, see Carroll Smith-Rosenberg, *Disorderly Conduct: Visions of Gender in Victorian America* (New York: Oxford University Press), 1985, 253.
20. On the readership for the different endorsements, see Jennifer Scanlon, *Inarticulate Longings: The Ladies' Home Journal, Gender, and the Promises of Consumer Culture* (New York: Routledge, 1995), 219. The J. Walter Thompson's decision to solicit testimonials from society women to promote Pond's Extract Co. represented an important departure from their previous use of theatre and film actresses in the 1910s and early 1920s. For more on the earlier campaign, see Marlis Schweitzer's essay in this volume.
21. Image of ad in Scanlon, *Inarticulate Longings*, 218.
22. Peiss, *Hope in a Jar*, 136–137.
23. Emergence of Advertising in America, 1850–1920, Lever Brothers' Lux Soap (Flakes), Ad# L0081, 1925. Advertising Ephemera Collection—Database #A0160, Emergence of Advertising On-Line Project. John W. Hartman Center for Sales, Advertising and Marketing History, Duke University Rare Book, Manuscript, and Special Collections Library. http://library.duke.edu/digitalcollections/eaa/ Accessed January 7, 2009.
24. Scanlon, *Inarticulate Longings*, 209.
25. Ibid., 217, 192, 211.
26. Ad*Access: Beauty and Hygiene: Ad# BH0835, 1939; Ad# BH1041, 1936.
27. Ad*Access: Beauty and Hygiene, Ad# BH1336, 1949; Ad# BH1338, 1949; "Here comes the Bride," 1949, Ad Access: Beauty and Hygiene: Soaps: 1940, Ad#BH1336.
28. Ad*Access: Beauty & Hygiene, Ad# BH1336, 1949; Ad# BH1338, 1949; "Here comes the Bride," 1949, Ad Access: Beauty and Hygiene: Soaps: 1940, Ad#BH1336.
29. Ad*Access: Beauty and Hygiene, Ad# BH1336, 1949.

30. For a discussion of soap and the racialization of domesticity, see Anne McClintock, "Soft-Soaping Empire: Commodity Racism and Imperial Advertising," in *The Gender and Consumer Culture Reader*, 129–152.
31. *The Bride's Magazine* (hereafter cited as *Bride's Magazine*) started "a long form-sheet" gift registry that standardized the process. "The Retailer-Happy as the Bride," *Sales Management* (May 1, 1950), 8. This section draws on *Brides Inc.* Chapter 3.
32. Marchand, *Advertising the American Dream*, 103. On "puffing," see Ellen Gruber Garvey, *The Adman in the Parlor: Magazines and the Gendering of Consumer Culture, 1880s to 1910s* (New York: Oxford University Press, 1996), 94–95.On editorial advertising in the *Ladies' Home Journal*, see Scanlon, *Inarticulate Longings*, 201–202. Quote from page 202.
33. "Real life bride... Virginia Ecklund of Minneapolis," *Modern Bride* (Fall 1955), 174. "Real Life Bride, Introducing Margaret Regan of Brooklyn, N.Y.," *Modern Bride* (Spring 1955), 149.
34. Quotes from "Margaret Regan," *Modern Bride*, 149.
35. Ibid., 152.
36. "Virginia Ecklund," *Modern Bride*, 174–179.
37. "I am Kay," *Modern Bride* (Fall 1949), 69; "I am Ann," *Modern Bride* (Fall 1949), 70. Also see "I am Joyce," *Modern Bride* (Fall 1949), 68 and "I am Susan," *Modern Bride* (Fall 1949), 71. The J. Walter Thompson agency, interestingly, had categorized women into four categories in the 1920s: housewife, club woman, society woman, and business woman. See Scanlon, *Inarticulate Longings*, 192.
38. Quotes from "Virginia Ecklund," 176.
39. Quotes from "Margaret Regan," 150–151.
40. "Katherine Jones met Bud Davies," *Modern Bride* (Winter 1955–1956), 86.
41. Quotes from "Virginia Ecklund," 176.
42. Quotes from "Virginia Ecklund," 179.
43. "Joanne Youngblood met Bill Harrah," *Modern Bride* (Winter 1955–1956), 67; "Katherine Jones met Bud Davies," 87.
44. "Domestic Trousseau is Upper-Bracket Promotion," *Department Store Economist* (May 10, 1939), 16.; Also, see *Bride's* Spring 1939 and Autumn 1939 issues. This section draws on *Brides Inc.*, Chapter 3.
45. "I am Kay," *Modern Bride* (Fall 1949), 69.
46. "I Am Susan," *Modern Bride* (Fall 1949), 71.
47. "Trousseau for Audrey," *Bride's Magazine* (Winter 1954), 94. Also see "Wedding-Day fashions they prefer," *Bride's Magazine* (Autumn 1959), 146–148; "I am Joyce," *Modern Bride* (Fall 1949), 68; "I am Kay," 69.
48. *Bride's* first study was *The Bridal Market: An Authoritative New Study* (Philadelphia: National Analysts Inc., 1958); for references to studies by *Modern Bride*, see "Traditional or Modern: Stainless Steel Bridal Promotions go Year-round," *Merchandising Week* (October 24, 1966,) 26; See also *Modern Bride*'s *A Study of Bridal Market Retail Spending* (New York: Ziff-Davis Publishing Company, Inc., 1975).

49. *The Bridal Market: An Authoritative New Study*, 8–13, 16–17, 24, 31. This paragraph draws on *Brides Inc.*, Chapter 3.
50. Adele Bahn, "Changes and Continuities," 150, 141; Robert E. Weems, Jr., *Desegregating the Dollar* (New York: New York University, 1998), 70–71.
51. For a discussion of whiteness and the contemporary wedding industry, see Ingraham, *White Weddings*.
52. The wedding industry provides its own figures, which are used by bridal magazines to attract advertisers. For the 70 billion dollar figure, see http://web.archive.org/web/20050110084004/http://www.condenet.com/press/condenet/wedding.html; see also, "The May Department Stores Company and The Knot Announce Marketing Alliance," http://web.archive.org/web/20060324173125/http://www.theknot.com/02.25.02.shtml. For the $30,000 figure, see http://web.archive.org/web/20020416000318/http://www.entrepreneur.com/article/0,4621,290139,00.html and http://web.archive.org/web/20050524155343/http://money.cnn.com/2005/05/20/pf/weddings/ All accessed January 7, 2009.

CHAPTER 7

"Dear Friend": Charles Atlas, American Masculinity, and the Bodybuilding Testimonial, 1894–1944

Dominique Padurano

"Dear Friend: Just a line to let you know I am enjoying the best of health," Charles Atlas wrote to his bodybuilding mentor, Earle Liederman, in 1920. "I often think back of [*sic*] the days when this was not the case," he continued. Readers of *Physical Culture* magazine, where the letter was published in an advertisement for Liederman's strength-building course, were likely as familiar with the tale of transformation described in the text as was Atlas himself. The testimonial—of which a photograph of Atlas' nude body played an integral part—followed the well-worn patterns of a genre that had been established during the nineteenth century, and yet was offered as proof that Liederman's exercise system worked. By the time Atlas cofounded his own mail-order fitness lessons company, Charles Atlas, Ltd. in 1929, testimonials of transformation had become a staple of bodybuilding advertising. Atlas and his business partner, Charles Roman, actively solicited their customers' personal stories of physical metamorphoses and regularly featured them in the company's own advertisements during the 1930s and 1940s.

For the advertiser, the potential benefit of testimonial advertisements was clear. Relying on young men's claims that Dynamic Tension (DT), Atlas' twelve-week course, was effective, Charles Atlas, Ltd. hoped to lure more customers into the fold. DT was an exercise program based on isometric contractions in which the user would use the weight and force of his own body in order to build muscle tone. Consisting entirely of explanatory words and images, DT could be marketed more inexpensively than the courses of Atlas' competitors because no weights, pulleys, or other gadgets needed to be sent through the mail. By late 1929, the fact that DT consisted of a few sheets of paper was a crucial component in its success, but potential clients still needed to be courted to send away for the program in the first place. As the United States entered the Great Depression, the virtue of the "common man" began to be hailed from all corners of American cultural life; advertising was no exception.[1] But what was it that motivated the young consumers of DT to document their metamorphoses in words and images, and then to send such intimate information about their bodies to Atlas? Some, it seems, longed for a personal connection with Atlas, whose avuncular tone throughout the pages of DT may have convinced them that such a relationship was possible. Other, perhaps more savvy, customers recognized their testimonials as potentially remunerative for their teacher and hoped for a piece of the pie. Having witnessed Atlas' own start as an unknown but well-built amateur in Liederman's 1920 ad and elsewhere in the physical culture press between 1914 and 1929, Atlas' students during the 1930s and 1940s hoped to capitalize similarly upon their physical transformations. Several even offered to trade words and images of their bodies for an appearance in DT ads and a recommendation of their bodies from Atlas himself—a testimonial *quid pro quo* of sorts—just as Liederman had done for Atlas in 1920. While most of the authors of bodybuilding testimonials were not as explicit about their wishes for future fame and fortune, such letters lay bare the core of all such narratives of physical metamorphosis. Implicit in the bodybuilding testimonial was a concomitant social transformation that was at least as significant (if not more so) to the writer as the changing contours of his body.

The narrative of social transformation that marked the testimonies of Charles Atlas' students was hardly new. As a budding fitness entrepreneur in the 1920s, Atlas himself frequently framed his own evolution into a successful American businessman against the backdrop of his increasing health and strength. This model, pioneered by the first modern bodybuilder, the European Eugen Sandow, quickly took root at the turn of the twentieth century in the United States, where narratives of social transformation had long held sway over the American imagination. John Bunyan, Benjamin Franklin, and Horatio Alger, for example, narrated real and fictional stories of change in works that would become staples of the American canon.[2] While the peregrination of Christian, the hero of Bunyan's *Pilgrim's Progress*, might, at first, seem at odds with the ascent of Alger's Ragged Dick through the bourgeois world of industrializing New York City, their ultimate destination was, in fact, identical. Their voyages facilitated a metamorphosis of the self into an exemplar of manhood for their respective times. One of the lessons that Benjamin Franklin learned as a boy from *Pilgrim's Progress* was that the seventeenth-century path to ideal manhood lay in a spiritual rebirth. By the late eighteenth and early nineteenth centuries, Franklin's own *Autobiography* documented his adult attempts to "arriv[e] at moral Perfection," a process that he hoped would help cultivate in others "virtuous and *manly* minds" [my emphasis].[3] A century after Franklin's death, the tenacity and upward social mobility of Alger's Ragged Dick would serve as a model of self-improvement for boys hoping to become men during the Gilded Age. For centuries, then, transformation narratives occupied a seminal place in the American imagination, often illustrating the path to ideal manhood according to the dominant values of the time.

By the early twentieth century, that path had begun to acquire a physical component. The Christian piety of *Pilgrim's Progress* had long since ceased to function as an essential marker of American masculinity.[4] Even the secular virtue and "moral Perfection" described by Franklin—along with such related attributes as "duty," "honor," and "integrity"—were less and less culturally relevant to Americans' notions of "manhood" by the twentieth century. As cultural historian Warren Susman noted, around the end of the nineteenth century, Americans began to value "personality" over "character."[5] Though Susman's seminal article did not treat these as specifically gendered terms, I would argue that the shift he described in fact corresponded to an evolution in Americans' masculine ideal. In *Manliness and Civilization*, historian Gail Bederman built upon Susman's work by defining the nineteenth-century ideal as encapsulated in the term "manhood," and the twentieth-century standard as "masculinity."[6] The turn away from manliness and character was gradual and never wholly complete—indeed, remnants of the discourse of character as a distinguishing characteristic of manhood remain extant even today. Nevertheless, around the turn of the twentieth century a distinct shift took place. Americans—especially men—strove to become, as Susman has written, "attractive," "stunning," "glowing," and "forceful"—characteristics that conjure up a distinct corporeal quality. The field of bodybuilding, which emerged at the same moment as "personality" began to usurp the place of "character" in Americans' definition of the ideal man, both manifested and responded to this new embrace of the body as a vital signifier of masculine identity.

Likewise, the bodybuilding testimonial, comprised of text and photograph, both extended and departed from the long tradition of the American transformation narrative. On the one hand, it borrowed from (and greatly simplified) the "before-and-after" format characteristic of the older stories.

Moreover, its authors were often upwardly socially mobile young men who staked claims upon an ideal masculine identity through their bodies and their narratives. In the case of Charles Atlas and many of his students, bodybuilding testimonials provided a format in which immigrant and ethnic men could assert their masculinity *and* their American identity at the same time. On the other hand, testimonial advertisements used by Charles Atlas, Ltd. turned men's narratives of physical and social metamorphoses into selling tools, commodifying the stories, men's bodies, and the men themselves. In the world of "personality," the bodybuilding testimonial showcased the authors' attainment of ideal masculinity while implicitly acknowledging that twentieth-century "success" would be possible only within the marketplace and with the help of other men.

The first section of this essay will trace the inception and evolution of the genre of the bodybuilding testimonial, from its founding by Eugen Sandow to its development in Bernarr Macfadden's *Physical Culture* magazine. By presenting the "body beautiful" as obtainable by anyone, early bodybuilders implicitly defined the activity as a meritocracy. Within this meritocratic community, testimonials functioned in two ways. First, the texts and photographs, consciously constructed as "before-and-after" stories, placed bodybuilders' consumer products squarely within the American tradition of transformation narratives. This rhetorical move endeavored to make bodybuilding more palatable to a public unfamiliar, and often uncomfortable, with the sexualization and commodification of men's bodies that bodybuilding promoted. Moreover, framing testimonials in the template of American transformation narratives allowed immigrant and ethnic men a mode of assimilation during a time when educational and other professional doors often were closed to them.

The life and career of Charles Atlas—born Angelo Siciliano in Calabria, Italy, in 1892—illustrates how one immigrant bodybuilder used the narrative framework established by his predecessors to construct his own biography and public persona. The second section of this essay investigates how Atlas used the genre to present his own life story and, through it, to sell his body to the American public during the early 1920s. From 1920 through 1922, Atlas experimented with the transformation narrative in a variety of formats. He offered his own testimonial to others' fitness products, and published his autobiography in *Physical Culture* after winning its editor's "Most Handsome Man" contest. A master of the bodybuilding testimonial, Atlas then utilized the genre extensively to sell his mail-order fitness course, Dynamic Tension, during the 1930s and 1940s.

The last section of this essay will analyze how, why, and to what effect Charles Atlas, Ltd. used testimonials during the 1930s and 1940s.

The ubiquity of men with surnames from Southern and Eastern Europe in Dynamic Tension ads during the Great Depression and World War II suggests that the company's techniques were successful in drawing other immigrants and ethnics into its fold. During these decades, a number of advertisers across the country stopped relying on expert advice to sell products and instead extolled the opinion of the common man. Testimonial advertising thus was an important technique among all marketers during the Great Depression and World War II. Having already been defined as a meritocracy, bodybuilding during this period continued to showcase transformation narratives by the common man through testimonial ads. During years when many doubted the viability of the American dream, Atlas' testimonial advertisements helped convince some consumers that transforming oneself into a newer, improved version was not only still possible but also available to them all, if only they were prepared to sweat for it.

"I Was a Puny Lad": Eugen Sandow, Bernarr Macfadden, and the Establishment of the Bodybuilding Testimonial Genre, 1894–1920

Three years after his first appearance before American audiences at the 1893 World Columbian Exposition in Chicago, the Prussian strongman Eugen Sandow established the basic framework of the bodybuilding testimonial in an interview in *The New York Times.* "I was a puny lad," Sandow recalled, "and my desire to improve myself physically was inspired by a view of the grand works of sculpture that I saw when my father took me through the art galleries of Rome."[7] Whether such an Italian sojourn actually took place is subject to question; so, too, are the "facts" of much of the performer's life. Born Friedrich Wilhelm Müller in Königsberg on April 2, 1867, by the time he reached the United States twenty-six years later, this fruit peddler's son frequently told the tale of his childhood frailty. A biography published in 1894, for example, claimed, "Up to his fifteenth year, indeed, young Eugen was of slight build and rather delicate constitution."[8] The pictures that made his adult body famous, though, contradicted that inauspicious start, thus rendering his alleged physical transformation all the more remarkable. Later amateur and professional bodybuilders, including Charles Atlas, would reiterate tales of their own youthful debility, so that it soon became the standard introduction of the emerging genre of the bodybuilding testimonial.

The genre's second chapter, the transformation itself, highlighted the meritocratic nature of the metamorphosis in order to best convince the reader that he, too, could perform similar feats. Once again, Eugen Sandow's own biography established the testimonial's template. By 1919, after spending more than three decades traveling throughout Europe and the United States as a strongman and the epitome of the body beautiful, Sandow emphasized the meritocratic nature of his youthful physical transformation:

> I had not obtained my own health and strength by accident. I was, indeed, on the other hand, a delicate child. But I had proved in my own body that if the attainment and maintenance of health was not an exact science, it was governed by natural, and therefore, exact laws, and was, consequently, obtainable by all.[9]

Asserting that the acquisition of a body such as his was not limited to an elite few allowed Sandow to more effectively hawk various exercise courses and equipment. After all, if his body were the result only of superior genes, who would buy Sandow's products, let alone spend time trying to replicate his success?[10] Testifying to his own youthful physical frailty, Sandow helped convince the consuming public that a well-conditioned body was in the reach of everybody, an essential step in the formation of the fitness industry.

In his careful use of photography, though, Eugen Sandow ensured that the bodybuilding testimonial would become a tribute to the teller's social evolution as much as his corporeal transformation. The title of Sandow's 1904 book, *Body-building, or Man in the Making* (which was the first published appearance of the term), perfectly expressed the goal of bodybuilding—the self-conscious and joint re-creation of one's physical and social selves.[11] As historians Roberta Park, John Kasson, and others have noted, nineteenth-century athletes such as boxers often posed for the camera surrounded by props that conjured up Greco-Roman antiquity in the hopes that the association with "high culture" would mitigate the questionable practice of appearing unclothed in photographs.[12] Likewise, bodybuilders from Sandow to Atlas often cited their first glimpse of classical statuary as the catalyst that inspired them to transform their own immature bodies into those of muscular men. Often, the same bodybuilders made a handsome income from the sale of images of their nude bodies as the Farnese Hercules, Polyclitus' Spear Bearer, Mercury, the Dying Slave, or, simply, the Atlas of Greek myth.[13]

As important as such photographs were in the process of legitimizing the field of early bodybuilding, however, pictures of the men dressed to the nines were equally vital in establishing the individuals' reputations as respectable. Sandow, for instance, often had himself photographed as a "gentleman" and even arrived in the United States boasting an aristocratic family line, calling himself "Count" in the American press.[14] In what would soon become standard practice in the field of bodybuilding, Sandow also changed his name from Müller to an Anglicized version of his mother's Russian surname, Sandov.[15] The adoption of a name that had a less ethnic ring to it and, often, an association with strength and/or classicism, would be replicated by several professional bodybuilders during the first three decades of the twentieth century: Siciliano became Atlas, for example, and Max Unger became Lionel Strongfort. Choosing English-sounding names often comprised the final step in the bodybuilder's social transformation, serving as the public testament to his changed self.

While Eugen Sandow forged the template of the bodybuilding testimonial during the 1890s, Bernarr Macfadden's *Physical Culture* provided one important venue in which the testimonial would evolve into a genre over the course of the following two decades. Born Bernard Adolphus MacFadden, the publisher's early life (or, at least, his accounts of it) followed a similar path as that laid out by Sandow, only one year his elder: sickly childhood, classical epiphany, physical metamorphosis followed by name change. (According to his biographer, Robert Ernst, he changed the spelling of his surname to be more memorable, and that of his first name to more closely echo a tiger's roar.[16]) After a peripatetic youth during which he saw Sandow perform in Chicago in 1893, Macfadden followed the steps of his European idol by touring the stages of Great Britain as a strength performer and classical model.[17] In 1899, Macfadden settled in New York and began publishing the monthly magazine, *Physical Culture*, in which he edited a column entitled, "The Virtues of Our Methods Proven." A glorified "Letters to the Editor" forum, "Virtues" showcased letters and photographs from male and female readers who followed the advice in *Physical Culture* and gained health, strength, or beauty. Readers' autobiographies of physical rejuvenation echoed the "before-and-after" narrative established by Sandow at the turn of the century. J. C. Olden, for example, wrote to Macfadden in 1909, "Your exercises have been of inestimable value to me. When I started taking your course I had been a constant sufferer from nervous dyspepsia for five months.... But a few days after taking your exercises I was entirely relieved."[18] Other letters regaled fellow readers with stories of how a new diet had also changed the authors' bodies and lives.

Readers' testimonies of the benefits of the physical culture life also took photographic form, especially when their transformations were primarily muscular. Mirroring the poses of Macfadden himself, which he—like Sandow before him—sold for profit in postcard form, some readers, like fifteen-year-old Robert Snyder, sent to the editor snapshots of their "well-developed physique" along with their written testimonies of muscular metamorphoses. "Enclosed are photographs of myself," Snyder's letter of 1912 began, "showing the development I have attained by practicing the methods advocated in your magazine."[19] Month after month, year after year, physical culture enthusiasts and budding bodybuilders imbibed the visual and textual formulae of testimonials published in *Physical Culture.*

Some of those aspiring bodybuilders went on to comprise a cadre of fitness entrepreneurs during the 1920s, a decade that historians have dubbed the Golden Age of Sports in the United States.[20] For example, physical culture entrepreneur Antone Matysek, who sold a variety of bodybuilding products during the 1920s, from photographs of his own physique to a mail-order fitness course, was a reader of *Physical Culture* during the 1910s. While still an amateur bodybuilder, Matysek wrote to Macfadden, "It is now about four years ago since I first bought *Physical Culture* magazine. I was then in pretty bad physical condition." Published in the November 1913 "Virtues of Our Methods Proven" column, Matysek's letter continued, "After reading your magazine over, I started to exercise and in about two months I built myself up to normal weight." As if to prove his own assessment that, "I have developed myself into a strong man," Matysek concluded his letter promising, "Enclosed you will find my latest photograph."[21] Clearly, amateur fitness enthusiasts during the 1910s read and learned from the narratives of transformation that Sandow, Macfadden, and others used to legitimate their "methods" and, thus, to sell future issues of *Physical Culture.* Some amateurs, like Matysek, went on in the 1920s to become professionals, utilizing the genre to which they had contributed in order to market their own fitness products.

Though Charles Atlas never sent Macfadden the story of his own physical transformation, he certainly was familiar with *Physical Culture* magazine during the 1910s, and thus he most likely understood the ubiquitous role of the testimonial within it. He appeared as a model in the magazine at least twice before 1920. In November 1914, a young Atlas epitomized "man" in the illustration for the front cover's question, "Are you a Man or a Weakling?" He also demonstrated the proper way to massage one's own body for the article, "Massage at Home." As in the case of his contemporary Matysek, young Atlas used Macfadden's *Physical Culture* as a primer not only for learning useful exercises but also for understanding how to narrate his metamorphosis after successfully performing those exercises and changing his body.[22]

By the 1920s, many of the young amateurs who modeled for and wrote into *Physical Culture* during their teens had formed physical culture businesses of their own. They continued their relationships with the magazine, but during this decade they used it instead as an important venue in which to cultivate their own customer bases. Antone Matysek, for example, regularly advertised as a physical culture "director" in *Physical Culture* during the 1920s. The decade that witnessed enormous growth and maturation in the field of modern advertising also gave birth to the proliferation of professional physical culturists. In this highly competitive environment, bodybuilding testimonials helped fitness entrepreneurs assert the superiority of their products. Since consumption of bodybuilding products was predicated upon the ability of anybody to change his physical form, testimonials were essential to prove the meritocratic nature of the field in order to convince young men to spend their money. Entrepreneurs thus increasingly looked to their clients to provide them with narratives of their physical progress in order to sell courses. In the process, some customers recognized the potential value of their own words and photographs. Rather than simply help a magazine editor hawk more magazines, a gifted student's story and pictures might aid his teacher in selling more courses or barbells in a field now rife with competition. In return, the testimonial giver could use the national exposure he garnered by appearing in a *Physical Culture* advertisement as a springboard to a potentially lucrative career in the business.

Charles Atlas' appearance in Earle Liederman's 1920 advertisement, "The Most Powerful Back in the World," functioned in precisely this manner. An industry leader during the 1920s, Liederman boasted, "my files are crowded with photographs and letters of commendation from my thousands of satisfied pupils." Beneath that sentence, a photograph of Atlas, nude and reclining, appeared above the caption, "READ WHAT ONE OF OUR LEADING STRONG MEN SAYS." "It was by following your guidance and the course which you laid out for me," Atlas wrote, "that I have acquired the wonderful physique which I now enjoy." In the same published letter, then twenty-seven-year-old Atlas wrote that he was "devoting [his] entire time to this profession [strong man]." As a relative newcomer to the intensely competitive—and visual—world of fitness entrepreneurship, Atlas needed to acquaint consumers with the aesthetic merits of his body if he ever hoped to build his own clientele in the future. The large nude photograph of Atlas in the bottom left-hand corner of the advertisement did just that. Combined with his written testimonial, the image of Atlas' trim, muscular body helped Liederman sell courses at the same time that it enabled Atlas to present himself in the tradition of successful bodybuilders since Sandow.[23]

In 1920, Charles Atlas was poised to embark on a lifelong career in bodybuilding that would soon eclipse that of his mentor, Liederman. By the mid-1930s, he had nearly cleared the once-competitive field of rivals. Though his mastery and creative interpretation of the testimonial genre was not the only technique that enabled Charles Atlas, Ltd. to achieve industry dominance, it was certainly one important weapon in the fledging company's advertising arsenal. The next section will examine closely Charles Atlas' autobiographical transformation narratives, published both in article and advertisement form during the 1920s, 1930s, and early 1940s. Subtle changes in these narratives document how Atlas incorporated the template first established by Sandow in order to frame his own metamorphosis as a feat of social and physical change. At the same time, he was careful to paint that change as not so remarkable as to be impossible to be replicated by others. Highlighting the meritocratic nature of his transformation, Atlas opened the door to imitators and, of course, to thousands of consumers of his Dynamic Tension course.

"My Real Name Is Angelo Siciliano, But I Am Best Known as Charlie Atlas": Charles Atlas and the Bodybuilding Testimonial, 1921–1942

In November and December 1921, Charles Atlas had the perfect opportunity to acquaint potential consumers with his body and with his life story, which he crafted to resemble the autobiography of Eugen Sandow in several respects. *Physical Culture* published the two-part story, "Building the Physique of a 'Greek God,'" after Atlas took first prize in the magazine's "World's Most Handsome Man" contest earlier that year. Given the article's title and its author's stage name, it is unsurprising that antiquity took center stage in Atlas' autobiography. Photographs depicted him as Polyclitus' Spear Bearer and in a pose reminiscent of the Laocoön. More importantly, he set the site of his conversion to physical culture in the ancient sculpture galleries of the Brooklyn Museum. During a school field trip to the museum when he was sixteen years old, Atlas alleged, "[w]hile the other boys were wandering about looking at other things, I remained studying the magnificent bodies of Hercules, the Dying Gladiator, the Wrestlers, the Discus Thrower, the Boxer and the rest of the splendid specimens of manhood." Claiming that he "couldn't believe that such men had ever really existed," Atlas asked his teacher whether mere mortals could ever hope to achieve such "physical perfection." Mr. Davenport, the teacher at the Italian Settlement School, responded, "Most anybody can be strong.... Anyone who is willing to work for it can obtain the same muscular development."[24]

With the sport of bodybuilding framed as a meritocracy of muscle, Atlas continued to craft his autobiography as a self-made journey to strength. Mr. Davenport supposedly sent young Atlas to the YMCA to learn the rudiments of physical culture, and although the teenager was "amazed and delighted with what [he] saw," Atlas claimed that he "was too poor to join.... " With tenacity recalling Ben Franklin or Ragged Dick, Atlas claimed that he "was too much in earnest to be turned from [his] purpose on that account," so he "went home and made [him]self a bar bell with a stick and two stones.... " Using the homemade barbell and practicing "faithfully" other exercises that he had learned at the YMCA, Atlas "felt [him]self growing stronger perceptibly... [a]nd... the admiration [his] strength excited spurred [him] on to greater efforts." Physical transformation complete, Atlas then described the social and economic benefits that he derived from his newly developed strength. He helped move a stalled automobile; performed as a strong man on Coney Island; and posed as an artist's model, claiming, "I am known among artists as the Greek God; and I don't know of anything that gives me more pleasure, for I think the Greek God as shown in the old sculptures is so splendid to look at that to be likened to one is the highest compliment that could be paid me."[25] Indeed, Atlas had come full circle: little Angelo had turned himself into the ancient sculpture that had inspired his metamorphosis in the first place.

While "Building the Physique of a 'Greek God'" functions on the surface as a story documenting Atlas's journey from child to strong man, its subtexts describe parallel transformations and offer insights into the appeal of the genre to future customers of Dynamic Tension. Most importantly, in the hands of Atlas, the autobiographical bodybuilding narrative also became the tale of his transformation from immigrant to American. He first described his birth "in beautiful Calabria," and his life as a boy, "healthy and happy, with no thought but of eating, sleeping and playing." Atlas recalled that, "[i]n 1905, when I was eleven years old, my father brought his family to this country," and he stated, "[t]hat is when my life really began." Despite his allegedly happy childhood in southern Italy, Atlas chose to designate the start of his "real" life as the moment he arrived in the United States. He enrolled in the Italian Settlement School in downtown Brooklyn "to learn English and to be set in the way of becoming an American citizen." The next scene in the narrative focused upon the school trip to the Brooklyn Museum, and since Atlas never returned to the theme of his immigrant origins in the article, the reader might infer that his conversion to physical culture in the ancient sculpture gallery also marked his transformation into an American.

The article's silences, however, testify even more strongly to that cultural metamorphosis. The changes that Atlas made to the actual facts of his early life also bear witness to his growing awareness that in the culture of the marketplace, one's image counted more than truth. For example, Atlas transformed significantly the circumstances of his own childhood in "Building the Physique." Since the late nineteenth century, Americans had come to expect that childhood would be a time of life distinct from adulthood, unblemished by work in the market. Angelo Siciliano, however, had been apprenticed to a shoemaker at age six; his early experiences were so traumatic—and so far from the "happy" and carefree life he strove to depict in *Physical Culture*—that his adult son recalled that Atlas had held a lifelong contempt for Italy, and chose to never return to the land of his birth.[26] Moreover, while an intact, nuclear family might have been emerging as the

American ideal, young Angelo emigrated from Italy with his mother only, and lived for his first couple of years in the United States with his mother's brother, not with his own father. In fact, his mother's distinct surname—Fiorelli, not Siciliano—suggests that his parents may have been estranged or perhaps had never married at all.[27] By contrast, Atlas bolstered the altered story of his own childhood with a photograph of himself with his wife and young son in the December installment of the article. Though the majority of the photographs accompanying the text depict Atlas in poses mimicking ancient sculptures or illustrating various exercises, the top photograph on the first page of the November installment showed Atlas, looking directly at the camera in a three-quarters pose, dressed in a three-piece suit and tie. Both photographs, underscoring his status as a respectable American, complemented the "transformation" of the facts of his early life, helping to shape him into an ideal American as much as did his stated goals of "learn[ing] English" and "becoming an American citizen."

These accomplishments notwithstanding, in 1921, Atlas' social transformation was still incomplete. The most remarkable evidence of the unfinished nature of Atlas' evolution into an American was the article's byline: "Angelo Siciliano (Chas. Atlas)." Indeed, during the following year, Atlas continued to be known in *Physical Culture* by both his Italian surname and his American stage names. In the magazine's "Body Beautiful" feature from May 1922, for example, an artistic rendering of Atlas was accompanied by a caption identifying the model as "Charles Siciliano (Atlas)." This version of Atlas' name was repeated in captions describing photographs of Atlas in the June, July, and September issues of the same year. While the variety of names by which Atlas appeared in *Physical Culture* could have been the result of poor fact-checking, it seems more likely that, at the very least, Atlas regularly went by both sets of names during the early 1920s. In fact, Atlas himself stated on the first page of the November 1921 installment of "Building the Physique": "My real name is Angelo Siciliano, but I am best known as Charlie Atlas, which is my professional name."[28] Such duality suggests that while he had incorporated some aspects of the bodybuilding testimonial genre to describe his physical and social transformations, the process of Atlas' Americanization might not have kept pace with his remarkable metamorphosis in muscle.

The unfinished nature of Angelo Siciliano's journey to becoming Charles Atlas in 1921–1922 becomes even more apparent in light of biographical narratives published about him two decades later. In 1942, both *The Saturday Evening Post* and *The New Yorker* ran feature articles on Atlas, who, by this time, was widely recognized as the undisputed leader in the field of physical fitness. Both pieces tweak the account of his life that he had given to *Physical Culture* in 1921; not surprisingly, the new versions fit more comfortably within the bodybuilding testimonial genre than had the old. For example, in 1921, Atlas had written, "I was never sickly but on the contrary was rather strong" as a child. In, "You, Too, Can Be a New Man," the *Post* article of February 1942, however, Atlas claimed, "Up till the age of seventeen... I was a ninety-seven-pound-runt. I was skinny, pale, nervous and weak." The author, Maurice Zolotow, went on to chronicle how thin Angelo "was attacked by one of the neighborhood bullies" and then physically punished by his uncle "for getting into fights." At that moment, Atlas recalled that he had promised himself, "that I would never allow any man on this earth to hurt me again." Long gone was the conversion to physical culture in the antiquities gallery of the Brooklyn Museum—not to mention his 1921 characterization of his boyhood health as strong. Instead, the Zolotow article dramatized the change by painting Atlas as a weak, helpless boy, much as Eugen Sandow had done in his own autobiography fifty years earlier.

Robert Taylor's piece in the *New Yorker* the previous month—titled, "I Was Once a 97-Pound Weakling"—painted a similar picture of young Angelo's "spindly" body, "wan face," and "attitude of listless dejection." Nevertheless, this magazine, aimed at a sophisticated, urbane audience, retained the Brooklyn Museum story as the site of Angelo's adoption of physical culture. Taylor's portrait blamed Brooklyn itself for the boy's debility: "Up to the time the family came to this country, Angelo had been a normally husky child, thriving on the spaghetti-and-citrus diet of his homeland, but once in Brooklyn he began to sicken." Taylor alleged that it was this weakness that caused young Angelo to stop in the classical sculpture galleries: "exhausted by the trip" to the museum, he "subsided on a stone bench" which offered a prime view of "an object that changed the whole course of his life... a gigantic statue of Hercules...." Dramatizing his eventual physical metamorphosis in both the *Post* and *New Yorker* pieces by claiming childhood frailty, Atlas crafted a life story that fitted more neatly into the bodybuilding testimonial genre than had the 1921 version in *Physical Culture.*

Nevertheless, the journey that Atlas took during the twenty years since the first publication of his autobiography went beyond fudging the details of his early health. The differences between the accounts of Atlas' early life published in *The New Yorker* in January 1942, and those that appeared a month later in *The Saturday Evening Post*, suggest that Atlas' shifts had less to do with the vagaries of memory than with a conscious intent to shape his public persona to capture the attention of distinct audiences. Atlas may have gambled that readers of the highbrow *New Yorker* might have been moved by a story of Greco-Roman culture influencing the course of a young, immigrant boy's life, while *The Saturday Evening Post*'s working-class audience might have identified more strongly with a tale recounting an underdog's comeback from routine beatings by neighborhood bullies.[29] In this explicit re-crafting of his own autobiography, Charles Atlas showed in 1942 that his metamorphosis into an American businessman was complete. The 1921 deviation from Atlas' Italian childhood might have been intended to obscure details of his life that did not fit squarely into the American ideal during a period of intense nativism. Yet, the misrepresentation of several incidents in Atlas' life that he condoned in the 1942 articles is perhaps even more striking because the facts contradict not only the narrative of two decades earlier but also each other. It is therefore plausible to infer that Atlas intended to consciously strike a chord within the distinct audiences reading each account.[30] The poor, (possibly) scrawny Italian boy had not only changed the contours of his body but also become a savvy American entrepreneur.

But what happened in the meantime, or at least in between the 1921 and 1942 articles, and what role did the bodybuilding testimonial play in that journey? Atlas announced his didactic intent in the first paragraph of "Building the Physique of a 'Greek God,'": "if the telling of my story will induce others to make the best of themselves I can at least feel that I have been of some use in the world."[31] Like Benjamin Franklin more than a century earlier, Atlas hoped that the story of his own metamorphosis might inspire young men to model their own journeys of transformation after his own. It was not until the 1930s, however, that Atlas, with the help of his business partner, Charles Roman, understood the latent commercial power in such tales, and used testimonials of transformation to attract new customers.

During the 1920s, Charles Atlas struggled in business, experimenting with a variety of commercial ventures and continuing to profit from appearing in testimonials for others' products. "Building the Physique" was published on the heels of Atlas' first victory in the "Most Handsome Man" contest sponsored by Bernarr Macfadden in 1921. Along with the $1000 prize money from that competition, Atlas used another $1000 he won the next year in *Physical Culture*'s "Most Perfectly Developed Man" contest to found his first mail-order fitness lessons company late in 1922.[32] Atlas' advertisements for his first course strongly resembled those of other physical culture entrepreneurs of the time. Usually occupying a single, narrow column, they featured a small image of Atlas at the top of the vertical band, followed by copious text in a tiny font. During the mid-1920s, Atlas also opened and operated a gym in midtown Manhattan, and a summer camp for children in the Catskill Mountains in upstate New York.[33] It was perhaps the financial strain caused by his multiple business ventures (not to mention his own shortcomings as a businessman) that prompted him to continue offering endorsements of various fitness products during these years, such as his 1926 endorsement of the Battle Creek "Health Builder" in *Physical Culture.* Though such appearances for other companies' products were infrequent, they kept Atlas' name current in the physical culture press during the competitive 1920s. Unfortunately, they were neither frequent nor remunerative enough to keep Atlas himself out of bankruptcy court several times between 1926 and 1929.[34]

Nevertheless, Charles Atlas' appearances in testimonial advertisements did increase his familiarity with a genre that he would exploit fully with the advent of his second mail-order fitness company, Charles Atlas, Ltd., which he cofounded with advertising executive Charles P. Roman in 1929. The following section traces how Atlas put to use for his own company in the 1930s and 1940s the knowledge of testimonials that he had garnered during the 1920s by offering his own endorsements for a variety of fitness entrepreneurs and products. During these two decades, Roman transformed the alleged story of Atlas' own metamorphosis from 97-pound weakling into the longest-running advertisement in American history, "The Insult that Made a Man Out of 'Mac.' "[35] "The Insult" not only mastered the crucial elements of the bodybuilding testimonial, erasing any evidence of the protagonist's healthy childhood, it also translated the testimonial genre into visual form. "Continuity copy"—or advertisements in comic strip form—appeared during the 1930s, the same decade during which visual culture, such as movies, fan magazines, and comic books, began to occupy a more prominent place in American popular culture than ever before.[36] Converting the tale of Atlas' life from article to comic strip also enabled Charles Atlas, Ltd. to capture the attention and desire of a new generation of younger consumers, who were particularly drawn to the intensely visual story that so closely mirrored their own experiences during puberty and adolescence. The company then tapped these boys and young men for their own tales of transformation to build the Dynamic Tension dynasty.

"You Can Have a Body Like Mine!": Charles Atlas, Ltd. and the Bodybuilding Testimonial, 1932–1944

The August 1932 issue of *Physical Culture* featured "The Insult That Made a Man Out of 'Mac' " for the first time. Its protagonist wore a sleeveless beach shirt and Grace, the girl he tried to impress, donned a one-piece bathing suit instead of a bikini, but the main elements of the ad differ little from its more famous, postwar descendants on the back covers of comic books. "Mac," a "sickly," "97-pound," "scare-crow," sits peacefully on a beach blanket with the alluring brunette, while the "beach bully" kicks sand in their faces. Though Mac tries to protest, the bully threatens that he would "smash [Mac's] face—only [he was] so skinny [that he] might [have] dr[ied] up and blow[n] away." Though Grace assuages Mac's emasculated ego two panels later, her body language—arms raised and head turned submissively toward the bully—suggest that her true feelings lay with his nemesis. Indeed, when

Mac attempts to call on Grace at her home in the following panel, she rebuffs him. "[S]ick and tired of being a scarecrow," Mac sends for Charles Atlas' exercises and in the next panel, admires himself in the mirror, marveling, "It didn't take Atlas long to do this for me! Look at those muscles bulge out NOW!" Physically transformed, Mac heads to the beach for revenge, and punches the bully, who had been showing off to Grace and Mac's "crowd." In the final panel of the ad, the girls clasp their hands in wonder, and Grace returns her affection to Mac, gushing, "Oh Mac! You ARE a real man after all!" In keeping with the template of the bodybuilding testimonial, Mac's story culminates with his rise in social status as a result of his improved physique.

Charles Atlas, Ltd. associated its namesake with "Mac" in a variety of ways, implying that the fictional metamorphosis of the comic strip figure was true, and therefore able to be replicated. At the bottom left-hand corner, a photograph of Atlas, shown from head-to-chest, bulging biceps crossed over prominent pectorals, anchored visually the entire advertisement. Next to Atlas' head, words in bold print explained his connection to Mac: "The 97-lb. Weakling Who Became 'The World's Most Perfectly Developed Man.'" The text—greatly reduced in quantity relative to Atlas' ads of the 1920s—echoed the testimonial of transformation in the visual story of Mac above: "They used to think there wasn't much hope for me. . . . Then I discovered *Dynamic-Tension.* It gave me the body that twice won the title, 'The World's Most Perfectly Developed Man.'" Just as he had done for Earle Liederman in 1920, Atlas used his own narrative and photograph—now accompanied by a comic strip—to entice potential customers to send for his course. "Now I make you this amazing offer. *At my own risk* I'll give you PROOF *in just 7 days* that my same method can make you over into a NEW MAN of giant power and energy" [emphasis in original]. In even smaller font beneath this offer, Atlas boasted the social benefits that clients could expect as a result of their new bodies. "[T]he prettiest girls, the best jobs," would suddenly be within reach of the "confident, powerful HE-M[E]N" who practiced Dynamic Tension.

While it is impossible to discover exactly how effective such advertisements and testimonials were in garnering the attention of Charles Atlas, Ltd.'s intended audience, several pieces of evidence suggest that Atlas' newest testimonial may have at least played a part in his ascending fortunes during the 1930s. First, the fact that Atlas *stopped* appearing in bankruptcy court during the 1930s, after having made several appearances there during the previous decade, suggests that, despite the onset of the Great Depression, Charles Atlas, Ltd. was, at the very least, surviving the tough times. Indeed, when other bodybuilders' advertisements petered off during the early 1930s and eventually stopped altogether by the middle of the decade, Atlas' advertisements continued to appear more frequently and larger than ever before. Earle Liederman, Atlas' erstwhile mentor, for example, attributed his own business' collapse to the economic climate of the Depression.[37] Second, the attention paid by the Federal Trade Commission to Charles Atlas, Ltd. throughout the 1930s also implies Atlas' growing stature in the field (and the widespread perception of his unethical marketing techniques).[38] There would have been little need to investigate an advertiser whose product was not being bought. The increased attention paid to Atlas in the press outside the bodybuilding community during the 1930s—in publications ranging from the national men's magazine, *Esquire*, to syndicated pieces in local newspapers like the Ashtabula, Ohio *Star-Beacon*—also suggests that Atlas' courses were being sold in large quantities and with a broad geographical reach. Soon, Charles Atlas became a celebrity, appearing with comedian Lew Lehr in a movie sketch, visiting Jack Dempsey's radio program as a featured guest, and performing for President Franklin D. Roosevelt at his Waldorf Astoria 1936 birthday bash. While testimonial advertisements certainly did not account for Atlas' meteoric rise during the early years of the Great Depression, neither can they be discounted entirely from the formula for his success.[39]

Perhaps the most convincing piece of evidence pointing to the efficacy of Charles Atlas, Ltd.'s testimonial advertisements, in particular, during the 1930s, is the frequency with which students of Dynamic Tension offered their own testimonials of transformation to their teacher. Though some students clearly expected a professional endorsement of their bodies to boost their own fledging careers in show business, many students wrote to Atlas to affirm their new selves. Like the writers to Macfadden's "Virtues of Our Methods Proven," column in *Physical Culture* during the 1910s, many DT users expected to remain amateur bodybuilders but simply enjoyed the opportunity of identifying with Atlas by likening their own lives to his. Charles Atlas, Ltd. clearly encouraged this process of identification, soliciting students' letters several times throughout the text of the twelve-week Dynamic Tension course. For example, Lesson Two from the 1931 course opens with the paragraph, "Dear Student: How was that first week of exercise? I have already received letters from some fellows who enrolled with you saying that they see the muscles of their chest 'standing out.' Keep up the good work."[40] Seven years later, Atlas modified this paragraph to actively encourage students to send him their testimonies: "Dear Friend: How was that first week of exercise? I usually receive letters by this time telling me that the chest muscles are already beginning to 'stand out.' Let me hear from you."[41] Having premised the entire worth of his course upon the dream of self-transformation, Atlas encouraged students to look for evidence of that metamorphosis in the contours of their bodies.

One way that Charles Atlas, Ltd. was able to convince young men to reveal intimate details about their bodies to a corporate entity was by shifting the overall tone of the course and its advertisements to a more familiar one than had been employed during the 1920s. As historian of American advertising Roland Marchand has pointed out, many other advertisers during the Great Depression sought to convey sympathy with the "common man," rather than to maintain its aura of expertise and technical know-how that had held resonance during the tail end of the Progressive Era, with its emphasis on scientific expertise.[42] In the field of physical culture, entrepreneurs such as Charles Atlas routinely prefaced their names with the title "Prof[essor]." throughout the 1910s and 1920s.[43] However, by the early 1930s, Atlas had dropped the prefix "Professor," and changed his lessons' salutation from "Dear Student" to "Dear Friend." Gone, too, were photographs of Atlas dressed up as Greco-Roman statuary, a potential association with highbrow culture that may have contradicted the company's new emphasis on the common man. Instead, photographs from the 1930s show Atlas on the beach or removed from any background at all, the latter technique also handy for highlighting the contours of his muscles against the white page. All of these subtle shifts helped to construct Atlas as a "regular Joe," an avuncular persona only slightly more knowledgeable than the students whose testimonials he sought in the 1930s, and to reiterate the meritocratic nature of their shared undertaking.

Atlas' folksy appeal to his students to send them written and photographic testimonials of their muscular metamorphoses worked. Young men from around the world sent their teacher heartfelt notes of thanks and meticulous records of their growing bodies throughout the 1930s and 1940s, often expecting that they would be used as testimonials. As early as 1923, C. Mutschler wrote, "Dear Mr. Atlas: ... You may depend on me to highly recommend your Course to all my friends. ... I am sending you some pictures of myself, which you are at liberty to use in any way you may desire. ..."[44]

Another student from the 1920s, Andrew Gioseffi, wrote:

> Dear Mr. Atlas
>
> After completing your course in physical culter [*sic*] I am sending you a few of my photographs to show you the wonderfull [*sic*] results that I have have received ~~thre~~ threw [*sic*] faithfully following you intructions [*sic*] you may use any of my photographs in your literatures if you which [*sic*].
>
> Your [*sic*] Very Truly
> Andrew Gioseffi[45]

In 1937, Albino Anzolut reported from the Bronx that he was "afraid of nobody I fell [*sic*] 100 pro [*sic*] cent A Million tanks [*sic*] to you best Wishes your freind [*sic*] Albino." Lenn Otto described his transformation to Atlas in 1939: "…I feel quite a different man [as] from Mars full of pep, courage, vitality and strength."[46] In 1942, John P. Foy recalled, "I completed your P.C. course back in the year 1930, twelve years ago, and am still exercising every day, and my abdominal muscles now have that familiar 'washboard' appearance and am feeling strong and vigorous at the age of 45."[47] Students of all ages responded heartily to Atlas' request for their written testimonials from the 1920s through the 1940s.

No one responded with more vigor to Atlas' solicitation of student letters, perhaps, than Patrick J. Rohan, an English customer who wrote to Atlas no fewer than five times in 1937 and 1938. His first letter was peppered with health and dietary questions, and reports on his progress. "I am more than delighted to inform you that after a short month of exercise on your splendid course, I have achieved remarkable results.…In one month I gained 30 lbs…in weight, four and a half inches…on my normal chest measurement, 1 ¾ inches around neck." After signing the letter only with the initials, "P.J.R.," Rohan included the postscript, "Thanks Mr. Atlas. I hope to join the Police now." Ordering Atlas' course sometimes elicited embarrassment among DT students; this may have been the reason Rohan signed off with his initials only.[48] Rohan's next letter, signed "P.J. Rohan," reported on his professional progress, and perhaps his concomitant lessened sense of shame over having had to enroll in Dynamic Tension. "The Chief of Police of Norfolk has agreed to take me on as a Police Officer for the new Year.…Never had such a happy time before in life." Rohan implicitly attributed his new social and economic success to his physical transformation: "Thank you for helping me to develop my body into a master piece.…I can now…face the day with confidence and can look the world in the face.…" The closing of Rohan's fourth letter—"P.J. Rohan, Constable"—underscores the extent to which his sense of self was tied to his professional standing, an achievement he attributed to his changed body. This 1938 letter also demonstrates that Rohan had begun to consider his body and his word an endorsement of Dynamic Tension:

> I think I told you before that I took up your course privately. I told no one about it. As months, very short months passed, I joined the Police, and still I clung to your advice and am doing so and shall for so for ever [*sic*]. I got too big for my collar and tunic. My officers and Sergeant were interested in the cause, and I told them out of love for you Mr. Atlas, that you were the good man that helped to build me into a masterpiece.

Rohan's final letter, written to Atlas later the same year, opened, "While I look back on the three months I have spent following your instructions,

I now realize that they have been the happiest of my life." Rohan then went on to recount a story recalling Mac's winning back Grace's affection in "The Insult That Made a Man Out of 'Mac'":

> I am ever so happy and no wonder as I am blessed with health, strength, happiness, a good job as a Police Officer and the company of a very nice young lady. I was taking particulars from her a month ago about an offence [*sic*], which I intended to report her for. I asked her what was the date, as I was not quite sure. "Oh," she said, "we shall make the date for next Monday the third." We smiled. I cautioned her and she is very friendly with me now. She says I'm her best. With Thanks, From P. J. Rohan.

Rohan's letters from 1937 and 1938 indicate that some students of DT took their teacher's request for letters of their progress quite seriously, and that many internalized the links that Atlas and his predecessors had forged between a man's body and his place in the world. Charting his physical metamorphosis alongside his acquisition of a "prett[y] girl" and a "[good] job" promised by Atlas in advertisements like "The Insult," Rohan's letters testify to the ability of others to do the same.[49]

Notwithstanding Rohan's "very nice young lady," the subtext of his letters suggests that Charles Atlas, Ltd.'s testimonial advertisements may have also elicited homoerotic feelings within the potential customer, encouraging him to purchase Dynamic Tension as a way to enter a homosocial community, or even as a pornographic pleasure. Before Rohan told his superiors about Dynamic Tension "out of love" for Atlas, for example, he also inquired about intimate details of his teacher's life, perhaps inspired by the course's newly familiar tone. "Could I call in, see and speak to you in your London home whenever I visit the Metropolis?" the officer from Norfolk asked Atlas. "Will you permit me to regard you as one of my best friend [*sic*] May I ask are you married?"[50] While the admiration for Atlas' body that Rohan expressed may or may not have been an expression of homoerotic desire, some men during the interwar period clearly purchased physical culture products—replete, as they were, with photographs of scantily-clad or nude, muscular men—as pornography. "R.S.," wrote to Atlas on January 13, 1934, complaining that his order of photographs did not reveal enough of Atlas' body:

> Dear. Ser. I. Don't. Like. None. of. the. pose Thees, are. no. nude. pose I. want. [naked] pose. no. clothe. full. front. view. [private] expose. I. see. such. pose. as_ you. send. in. the. phicical. culture. every. month. i. want. no. clothe. around. [private] full. front. view. if. not. send. money. back. and. take. out. postage.[51]

Though R. S.'s letter is highly atypical, the homoerotic sentiments that it expressed may not have been. As George Chauncey has shown, homosexuality was developing into an identity distinct from heterosexuality during this time. Chauncey estimates that by 1940, homosexual acts were no longer compatible with a masculine identity (which was, by its very nature, heterosexual), and they were effectively "closeted."[52] Courses such as DT may have provided men who sexually desired other men with a means of arousal as well as a virtual community when older venues, such as saloons and parks, were increasingly surveilled as homosexuality became criminalized and pathologized. Charles Atlas, Ltd. may have captured the "gay market" with its frequent use of testimonials, which depended so heavily on the photographs of its young, svelte consumers.[53]

The letters of other students from the 1930s and 1940s suggest that many testimonial writers recognized the potential appeal of their stories to other young men seeking similar transformations in their bodies and in their lives. Letters that accompanied their photographic narratives of transformation suggest that such students offered their stories in an implicit *quid pro quo* for a shot at fame and fortune. For instance, William Goldstein wrote to Atlas in 1936, "...During a recent visit at your office, I gave you a group of snapshots....In equivalence to money, I would like you to use one or two of these poses and, give me a good write up, as your prize pupil of 1936...." Recognizing that his photographs might "bring [Atlas] many pupils," Goldstein hoped that Atlas' "write up" would help propel him further "on the road to great success, stage or movies, perhaps...."[54] Like Goldstein, Herman Weinsoff, a soldier in World War II, also recognized and highlighted the supposed advantages that his teacher's company would accrue by publishing his photographic testimonial:

> Dear Mr. Roman,
>
> ...I wish you would give me some action on the proposed pictures of Chas. Atlas and myself. An article on the muscle building game, showing photographs of the movement's foremost instructor and chief pupil would be magniloquent for a magazine of the "PIC" or "PEEK" variety. Most people read the advertisements and say BUNK. Here is your chance to put forth an elucidating article showing the SOME wonderful results that have been obtained. The photo's [*sic*] would create interest. Or, a picture story for "Physical Culture" publication showing C. Atlas and pupil in a series of poses and at play....I am getting in excellent condition, and also acquiring a heavy tan.
>
> Expecting a return reply, I remain,
> Impetuously yours,
> Herman Weinsoff
> BEST BUILDT [*sic*] MAN IN AFRICA[55]

DT students who potentially had seen Charles Atlas appearing in testimonials for Earle Liederman and others during the early 1920s in *Physical Culture* attempted to copy their teacher's methods and, hopefully, replicate his success throughout the later 1920s, 1930s, and 1940s.

Like Angelo Siciliano, many of these students were ethnic or immigrant Americans. Names like Gioseffi, Anzolut, Goldstein, and Weinsoff were common among the ranks of Dynamic Tension students during the interwar years. Potentially barred from attaining material success through professions like law, medicine, or business due to their limited educations, lack of social networking opportunities, and religious or ethnic discrimination, such young men may have been drawn to careers such as bodybuilding or acting in which bodies counted more than bank accounts and hustle amounted to more than Harvard. Thus, as Charles Atlas' own notoriety grew during the 1930s, the insistence with which students pursued him for their own chances for similar success increased in frequency and intensity. Many surely hoped to replicate the transformation that their teacher had effectuated during the 1910s—from alleged 97-pound weakling to "the world's most handsome man," and implicitly, from reviled Italian immigrant Angelo Siciliano to powerful, successful, American man of personality, Charles Atlas.

Some of the testimonial writers did eventually get their wish. A Carl Mutchler (probably the same author of the 1923 letter to Atlas signed, "C. Mutschler"), appeared in a two-paged promotional brochure from 1931 entitled, "Everlasting Strength and Health." Mut[s]chler's photograph appeared along with those of fourteen other muscular men, flexing and posing for the camera in boxing trunks, "g-strings," or nothing at all. Above the photographs of (German-American?) Mut[s]chler, (Jewish-American?) Leo Becker, and (Italian-American?) David Bonaco, loomed the title, " 'Glorify God In Your Bodies' Says the Bible," while the plea "Let Me Train You As I Did This Group of Huskies" hovered atop pictures of men from around the world on the following page. Men's countries of origin were listed in parentheses beneath their names; men like "Luis Garnica (Brazil)," "Cheng Liang Sing (China)," and "M. Tia (Siam)" were presented alongside Americans with names both foreign-sounding (e.g., "Clevio Massimo (New York)" and "F. G. Diorio (Massachusetts)") and potentially native-born (e.g., "J. W. Livingston (Georgia)"). One dark-skinned man, the famous Indian bodybuilder, K. V. Iyer, was given special prominence on page 33 by being the only figure represented outside a picture frame, the contours of his muscular body highlighted against the blank white background of the page. Like most of Atlas' testimonial advertisements, this spread portrays Dynamic Tension enthusiasts—regardless of race, ethnicity, or nationality—as equals. All appear more or less in the nude, without the traditional indicators of wealth and status that clothing, jewelry, and other accessories might connote.

Though some men face the camera and others' backs are toward it, and some look directly into the lens while others' faces point away from it, such poses were most likely chosen to highlight the most muscular part of each student's body, not to efface any particular student's individuality. Like Atlas' embrace of continuity copy and his rejection of the title, "Professor," "This Group of Huskies" embraces the virtues of the common man.

In the process, Atlas and his students helped change Americans' notions of who or what the "common man" might be or look like. Benjamin Franklin had written his autobiography to guide other young men like him: white, Protestant fellows most likely born in the British North American colonies (or later, the United States). Written before the late nineteenth-century wave of immigration, Horatio Alger's tales were also likely intended for native-born, young white men. After Congress had closed the door to virtually all Southern and Eastern Europeans with the 1924 National Origins Act, however, young men who looked like Atlas or who had names like Massimo were slightly less threatening to old stock Americans, who had earlier feared that the influence of their own kind would dwindle when faced with the fecundity of the immigrant population. By the onset of the Great Depression, ethnic and old stock Americans shared together the pain and fear of economic chaos. Certainly, ethnic heroes during this period did not supplant Anglo-Saxons—one need only recall the popularity of John Steinbeck's Joad family, or Margaret Mitchell's Scarlett O'Hara, to understand the enduring appeal of native-born underdogs.

Nevertheless, American culture made way for an increasingly diverse cast of characters to find its place among the ranks of the "common man." Indeed, Scarlett's father was Irish-born, and Pietro DiDonato's *Christ in Concrete* shared Book-of-the-Month Club status with Steinbeck's *The Grapes of Wrath* in 1939. And though Henry Ford brought Steinbeck's classic to the silver screen the following year, it was Sicilian-born Frank Capra who memorialized the "common man" for Depression-era Americans in classics like *Mr. Smith Goes To Washington* (1939). The enormous allure of the gangster picture during these years perhaps best epitomizes the extent to which Americans of the 1930s embraced immigrant and ethnic men as "common man" archetypes. As Scarface and Little Caesar flaunted their disobedience to traditional authority figures and lived the good life, Depression-era audiences cheered. Real-life ethnics like Charles Atlas and his students needed to operate within the boundaries of the law, but nevertheless benefited from this larger cultural acceptance of immigrants and ethnics, especially as bearers of the "common man" mantle. The "Glorify God"/"This Group of Huskies" illustration demonstrates the extent to which ethnics—brown-, yellow-, olive-, or white-skinned, might be united with all others by his meritocratic metamorphosis to the brotherhood of muscles. Their photographs, which Atlas most likely had solicited while they were students enrolled in the Dynamic Tension course, stood as testaments to the feasibility of a similar transformation among the uninitiated viewer contemplating buying the course.

The undated promotional pamphlet, "Here's Living Proof That I Build Power-Muscled He-Man Bodies," (figures 7.1 and 7.2) likewise showcases a

Figure 7.1 "Here's Living Proof That I Build Power-Muscled He-Man Bodies" advertisement.
Source: Author's collection.

pan-ethnic collection of muscular men attesting to the transformative powers of Dynamic Tension. Hector Romero, Sidney Loev, Charles Kraus, and, on the reverse side, J. Chiovitti, Phil Santillo, Paul Krolok, Louis Garbarini, T. Kelczewski, and W. Goldstein, flex and pose for the camera, all under the watchful gaze of Atlas himself. Like Atlas, dressed in his trademark leopard-skin briefs, the students' bodies are almost bare, shorn even of their body hair. Their written comments add textual confirmation to the stories that their muscular physiques imply. "I thought you would be interested in results at the end of a WEEK," C. S. Withrow from West Virginia wrote. "Arm relaxed, 1½" more. Forearm 7/8 ", wrist ½", chest normal 2 ½", weight 4 pounds increase." Marine Michael S. Worch testified, "I am enclosing a picture showing what your Dynamic Tension course has done for me. I've been asked hundreds of times how I came to be built so well. I was proud to say the answer is Charles Atlas!" Hawaiian Jacob Man perhaps epitomized the men's comments, relating, "I am very well pleased with your wonderful course of body building. I have a great number of friends now. I feel like a real man, as compared to a few years ago." In this pan-ethnic community in which status was built on the accumulation of muscle rather than capital,

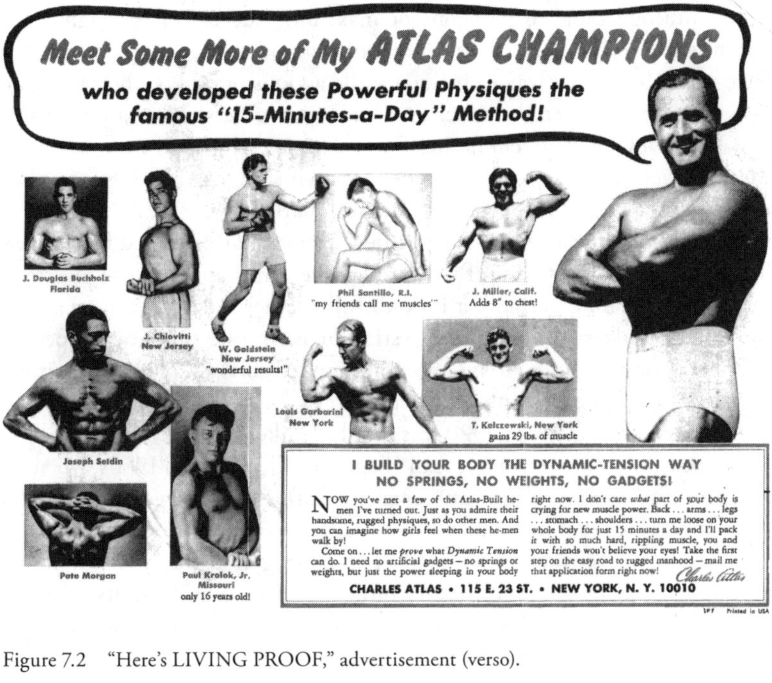

Figure 7.2 "Here's LIVING PROOF," advertisement (verso).

Source: Author's collection.

the authors of these testimonials appeared to revel in the social transformations that their physical metamorphoses helped accomplish.

Or, at least, this is one potential reading of the advertisements, "Here's Living Proof," "Group of Huskies," and the scores of testimonial ads that Charles Atlas, Ltd. ran during the 1930s and 1940s. Seen collectively and from afar, however, each man's individuality was less important than the sum to which his muscles added a part. Indeed, in these and other testimonial advertisements, the men who offered their written and photographic narratives of transformation ultimately bolstered the celebrity of the only man who appeared in the ads again and again and again. Ever after his death in 1972, Charles Atlas' image continued to serve as a symbol of eternal youth and vigor, exuding the concept of personality that was so essential for masculine success in the twentieth century. Meanwhile, who would ever hear again from Carl Mutchler, Leo Becker, David Bonaco, or William Goldstein? By appearing alongside Atlas in an advertisement, the students had reasoned that their own abilities to win friends would be enhanced, thus cultivating their personalities and their status as "real he-men." Nevertheless, by treating their bodies as commodities, exchanging them—or at least, images of and statements about their bodies—"[i]n equivalence to money," these men helped to promote standards of ideal masculinity that would have been unrecognizable to paragons of masculine success of the eighteenth and nineteenth centuries. While Benjamin Franklin and Ragged Dick may have used charm as a way to influence the actions of others, their ultimate goal was control over their "selves"—and over others. Herman Weinsoff and William Goldstein, emulating Eugen Sandow and Charles Atlas before them, however, quickly packaged the muscular shells of their selves in photographic form, and shipped them off to Charles Atlas, Ltd. hoping for a shot at future fame and fortune. While they may have received the proverbial fifteen minutes' worth of the former when they appeared in advertisements for Dynamic Tension, it is doubtful whether they ever reaped any of the latter—at least through their testimonials. By the time they appeared in the DT ads, Charles Atlas, Ltd. commanded so firm a lead in the field of mail-order fitness lessons, that a spin-off of the type that Atlas had engineered from Liederman in 1920 was highly unlikely.

Indeed, Atlas' luster did not really begin to fade until the 1960s, when no amount of testimony could counteract the influence of larger cultural and structural forces that denigrated the muscular yet naturalistic aesthetic that Atlas' body had always represented. The androgynous body of the hippy began to steal his spotlight, while professional bodybuilders like Arnold Schwarzenegger adopted a chemically enhanced, hyper-muscular physique that left the margins and entered the mainstream of the sport in the late 1960s and 1970s. Nevertheless, the legacy of Charles Atlas remains a vital part of American culture. First, Atlas played an important role in linking men's bodies to their social status. Though he was hardly the only physical culture entrepreneur to do so, the ubiquity of Dynamic Tension in the American market of the 1930s and 1940s ensured that his was a dominant voice encouraging that development. Second, Charles Atlas, Ltd.'s frequent use of testimonials in its advertisements of these years helped establish a practice that is now standard in the industry. Moreover, by narrating his own autobiography as a testimonial of physical and cultural transformation, Atlas modeled new ways of becoming an American man to thousands of ethnics and immigrants during the interwar period. His company provided a cultural space for young men to lay claim to their own American masculine identity when it published their testimonials. Though they allowed their bodies, thoughts, and words to become useful commodities in the process, these young men also seem to have profited emotionally, physically, and socially, at least according to the journeys they describe in their letters and photographs. During a period in which a steady job was often difficult to obtain, Atlas' course—and the testimonials that helped sell it—provided many men with alternatives for making themselves into American men.

NOTES

I would like to thank the editors of this volume, the anonymous readers, Stacy Sewell, and Rocco Marinaccio for their helpful readings of earlier versions of this article. I would also like to thank Jeffrey Hogue and Cynthia Soroka of Charles Atlas, Ltd. for their gracious hosting during the research stage of this project.

1. One need think only of the popularity of Charlie Chaplin, gangster films, or John Steinbeck's *The Grapes of Wrath* as examples of this trend. For a full discussion of the rhetoric of the common man in American culture during the 1930s, see Robert S. McElvaine, *The Great Depression, 1929–1941* (New York: Three Rivers Press, 1993), esp. chapter 9. For its manifestation in American advertising during the decade, see Roland Marchand, *Advertising the American Dream: Making Way for Modernity, 1920–1940* (Berkeley: University of California Press, 1985).
2. See, for example, John Bunyan, *The Pilgrim's Progress*, ed. N. H. Keeble (Oxford: Oxford University Press, 1998); Horatio Alger, *Ragged Dick, or, Street Life in New York with the Boot-Blacks*, ed. Alan Trachtenberg (New York: Penguin, 1990); Benjamin Franklin, *The Autobiography of Benjamin Franklin*, ed. Louis P. Masur, The Bedford Series in History and Culture (Boston: Bedford/St. Martin's Press, 1993).
3. Franklin, *The Autobiography of Benjamin Franklin*, 35–36, 82, 89.
4. E. Anthony Rotundo, *American Manhood: Transformations in Masculinity from the Revolution to the Modern Era* (New York: Basic Books, 1993). Moreover, as Ann Douglas has shown, Christianity became the purview of

women throughout the nineteenth century. See Douglas, *The Feminization of American Culture* (New York: Knopf, 1977).

5. Warren I. Susman, "'Personality' and the Making of Twentieth-Century Culture," *Culture as History: The Transformation of American Society in the Twentieth Century* (Washington, DC: Smithsonian Institution Press, 2003), 271–285.
6. Gail Bederman, *Manliness and Civilization: A Cultural History of Gender and Race in the United States, 1880–1917* (Chicago and London: University of Chicago Press, 1995).
7. "How Men May Acquire Strength," *New York Times*, March 1, 1896, 9. In his biography of Sandow, David Chapman recounts a similarly told recollection of Sandow's inspiration; see David L. Chapman, *Sandow the Magnificent: Eugen Sandow and the Beginnings of Bodybuilding* (Urbana and Chicago: University of Illinois Press, 1994), 5. In *Houdini, Tarzan, and the Perfect Man: The White Male Body and the Challenge of Modernity in America* (New York: Hill and Wang, 2001), John F. Kasson corroborates this "almost certainly inauthentic" autobiography of Sandow; see 30–32.
8. For the claim that Sandow's father was a greengrocer, see Chapman, *Sandow the Magnificent*, 5. Eugene Sandow, *Sandow on Physical Training; A Study in the Perfect Type of the Human Form* (New York: J. Selwin Tait and Sons, 1894), 23.
9. Eugen Sandow, *Life is Movement: The Physical Reconstruction and Regeneration of the People (A Diseaseless World)* (London: Gale and Polden, 1919), 8.
10. Though Sandow, his contemporaries, and later bodybuilders asserted the ability of any man to change his physique through diet and exercise, they also argued for a Lamarckian-inspired version of genetic transmission. The belief in the inheritance of acquired characteristics became particularly apparent after World War I. In *Life as Movement*, for example, Sandow claimed that "scientific physical movement" could catalyze "the conscious evolution of new and better cells" (v) and bemoaned that while there were "laws, acts, regulations and restrictions.... for the breeding and health preservation of horses and cattle," there were none of the same for "the breeding and bringing-up of the children upon whom the whole future of a country depends..." (84). Similarly, in 1942, Charles "Atlas [saw] little hope for the future unless we mend[ed] our bodily habits.... 'Feet will disappear in 500 years unless American walk more.'" Atlas also claimed that far from "carrying physical culture to extremes..., All I want is to build a perfect race, a country of perfect human masterpieces." See Maurice Zolotow, "You, Too, Can Be a New Man," *The Saturday Evening Post* (February 7, 1942), 62. Though such rhetoric paralleled eugenics thought during the interwar period, it is important to point out that while Atlas, Sandow, and Macfadden—who trained a group of Mussolini's cadets in 1931—embraced the cult of the body beautiful that was also championed by fascists of the same period, they never endorsed its tragic corollary undertaken in the death camps of Nazi Germany. For Macfadden's six months with the Italian cadets, see Thomas B. Morgan, *Italian Physical Culture Demonstration* (New York: Macfadden Book Company, 1932).

Moreover, the open presence of Jewish students among the rosters of Atlas' best students—not to mention that Atlas' business partner, Charles Roman, was a Jew—suggests that neither Atlas nor his company harbored the anti-Semitism that was promoted by the fascist states that, nevertheless, may have shared their dreams of a perfect physical future.

11. Oxford English Dictionary, "bodybuilding" page, http://dictionary.oed.com.proxy.libraries.rutgers.edu/cgi/entry/50024425/50024425se59?single=1&query_type=word&queryword=bodybuilding&first=1&max_to_show=10&hilite=50024425se59, accessed December 22, 2006. A note about terms: I use "weightlifter" and "weightlifting" to refer to those athletes and the sport concerned primarily with strength and with the amount of weight they could lift; the appearance of their bodies was of secondary importance to these men. I use "bodybuilder" and "bodybuilding" to refer to those men and the sport concerned primarily with the body's aesthetic qualities rather than with the amount of weight they can lift. Finally, "physical culture" (and "physical culturist") refers to a way of life predicated upon physical fitness (and those who followed that way of life), and includes bodybuilding and weightlifting under its more general umbrella.
12. For early bodybuilders' use of classicism as a way to perform publicly while wearing scarcely any clothing, see Kasson, *Houdini, Tarzan, and the Perfect Man*, 33; and Roberta J. Park, "Healthy, Moral, and Strong: Educational Views of Exercise and Athletics in Nineteenth-Century America," in *Fitness in American Culture*, ed. Harvey Green (Amherst: University of Massachusetts Press, 1989), 123–168.
13. Sandow posed as the Farnese Hercules in *Life is Movement* (500). Macfadden toured Great Britain in the mid-1890s performing as classical "tableaux vivants" (living paintings); a photograph of him posing as Mercury is in the collection of the Library of Congress. F. W. Guerin, "Nude male, Prof. B. A. McFadden, full-length portrait, standing on one foot on pedestal, facing right, wearing a fig leaf," 1893, http://memory.loc.gov/cgi-bin/query/D?ils:2:./temp/~pp_6lOD::@@@mdb=app,grabill,lomax,pan,wtc,ils,vv,gottscho,detr,bbcards,prok,nclc,fsa. Accessed December 13, 2008. Atlas posed as Polyclitus' Spear Bearer in the November 1921 issue of *Physical Culture* (37); as the Apollo Belvedere in the September 1922 issue of *Physical Culture* (19); and as the mythological Atlas on the front cover of his promotional brochure, "Secrets of Everlasting Health and Strength," from 1929 onward. (From 1923 to 1929, the same brochure was titled, "Secrets of Muscular Power and Beauty," and a copy may be found at Roger Filary and Gil Waldron, "Sandow and the Golden Age of Iron Men," http://www.sandowplus.co.uk/Competition/Atlas/SMPB/smpb01.htm. Accessed December 13, 2008.) A photograph of Atlas as the Dying Slave has been published in George Butler, Charles Gaines, and Charles Roman, *Yours In Perfect Manhood: The Most Effective Fitness Program Ever Devised* (New York: Simon and Schuster, 1982), 43.
14. Article 13—No Title, *New York Times* (July 18, 1893), 9. "Attila Against Sandow," *New York Times* (July 25, 1893), 9.

15. Chapman, *Sandow the Magnificent*, 4–6.
16. Robert Ernst, *Weakness is a Crime: The Life of Bernarr Macfadden* (Syracuse, NY: Syracuse University Press, 1991), 18.
17. Ernst, *Weakness is a Crime*, 4–10; William R. Hunt, *Body Love: The Amazing Career of Bernarr Macfadden* (Bowling Green, OH: Bowling Green State University Popular Press, 1989), ch. 2.
18. J. C. Olden, "The Virtues of Our Methods Proven," *Physical Culture* (October 1909), 370.
19. "Souvenir Post Cards of the Editor" advertisement, *Physical Culture* (October 1909), 371. Robert B. Snyder, Jr., "The Virtues of Our Methods Proven," *Physical Culture* (July 1912), 109.
20. Elliott J. Gorn and Warren Goldstein, *A Brief History of American Sports* (Urbana and Chicago: University of Illinois Press, 2004), 194, caption.
21. Antone J. Matysek, "The Virtues of Our Methods Proven," *Physical Culture* (November 1913), 544.
22. *Physical Culture* (British version), (November 1914), front cover; Carl Easton Williams, "Massage at Home," undated article found in Charles Atlas Scrapbook, Todd-McLean Physical Culture Collection (hereafter TMPCC); though the date of article is uncertain, given Siciliano's youth, it had to be pre-1920.
23. Earle Liederman, "The Most Powerful Back in the World," advertisement, *Physical Culture* (October 1920), 79. To appreciate the myth-making aspect of the bodybuilding testimonial, one needs only note that in this advertisement Atlas notes that his health was not always good, while in the *Physical Culture* piece of the following year (discussed in the following paragraph of this piece), he claims to have enjoyed a healthful childhood.
24. Angelo Siciliano (Chas. Atlas), "Building the Physique of a 'Greek God,'" *Physical Culture* (November 1921), 37.
25. Ibid., 38, 39, 103, 104.
26. Telephone interview with Charles Atlas, Jr., December 1, 2005, author in El Paso, Texas, interviewee in Santa Monica, California.
27. Angelo Siciliano emigrated from Italy with "Francesca Fiorelli," who listed him as her son on the ship manifest of the S.S. Lahn. See Statue of Liberty-Ellis Island Foundation, Inc., database at http://www.ellisisland.org/search/shipManifest.asp?MID=20253634410256587904&FNM=ANGELO&LNM=SICILIANO&PLNM=SICILIANO&CGD=M&bSYR=1891&bEYR=1893&first_kind=1&last_kind=0&RF=2&pID=102496090403&. Accessed December 15, 2008. The same Francesca Fiorelli is listed as Angelo Siciliano's mother on his marriage certificate; see Municipal Archives of the City of New York, King's County, Marriage License of Angelo Siciliano and Margaret Cassano, January 13, 1918.
28. Siciliano (Atlas), "Building the Physique," (November 1921), 36.
29. For the audience of *The New Yorker* in the 1930s, see, for example, Theodore Peterson, *Magazines in the Twentieth Century* (Urbana: University of Illinois Press, 1975), 260–261; and John Tebbel and Mary Ellen Zuckerman, *The Magazine in America: 1741–1990* (New York: Oxford University Press,

1991), 219–220. For the characterization of the *Post's* audience as "blue-collar" in the 1920s and 1930s, see Tebbel and Zuckerman, 175.

30. Marchand argues that advertisers spent enormous sums of money to "strike only those notes that would evoke a positive resonance" in their audience and to "associat[e] their selling messages with the values and attitudes already held by their audience." While he acknowledges that it is impossible to document the precise effects of advertisements upon audiences of consumers, Marchand asserts that "it may be possible to argue that ads actually surpass most other recorded communications as a basis for *plausible inference* about popular attitudes and values," given the investment that advertisers have made in identifying and tapping into those values. Marchand, *Advertising the American Dream*, xix (emphasis in original).
31. Siciliano (Atlas), "Building the Physique" (November 1921), 36.
32. Though the advertisements for both contests, which appeared monthly in *Physical Culture* during 1921 and 1922, stated that the first-prize winner would take home $1000, it is possible that this prize money was actually split between the top three winners. See Earle Liederman to Ottley Coulter, February 25, 1968, TMPCC: Ottley Coulter Collection, Folder of Correspondence between Liederman and Ottley Coulter.
33. For photographic evidence of Atlas' gym and summer camp, see Smithsonian Institution, National Museum of American History, Charles Atlas Collection (hereafter NMAH/CAC), Unprocessed boxes 9–11. For written information about "Camp Atlas," see Sullivan County, *Sullivan County, New York*, Travel brochure, 1926; Jerry Cowle, "As I Did It," *Sports Illustrated*, June 11, 1979, M6+; and, Butler et al., 63. For references to the gym, see Butler et al., 63; and, untitled photograph of Atlas leading a fitness class from around this period, NMAH/CAC, Unprocessed boxes 9–11.
34. Both friends and family seem to agree on Atlas' ineptitude as a businessman: interview with Charles Atlas, Jr., and telephone interview with Ronald P. Roman (son of Atlas' business partner, Charles P. Roman), July 14, 2004, interviewee in Miami Beach, Florida, and author in Belmar, New Jersey. The *New York Times* also documented a string of Atlas' appearances in bankruptcy court during the late 1920s: "Business Records," *New York Times*, October 15, 1926, 40; and "Business Records," *New York Times*, January 15, 1929, 55. For testimonial, see Sanitarium Equipment Co., "HEALTH in 15 Minutes a day!" advertisement, *Physical Culture* (November 1926), 105.
35. Sam Danna, "The 97-Pound Weakling Who Became the 'World's Most Perfectly Developed Man,'" *Iron Game History* (September 1996): 3–4.
36. See Marchand, *Advertising the American Dream*, for the increased visuality of 1930s advertisements and of Depression-era culture in general, as well as for the emergence of continuity copy that decade.
37. Earle Liederman to Ottley Coulter, February 25, 1968, TMPCC.
38. In 1931 and 1938, Charles Atlas, Ltd. was accused of false and misleading advertising by claiming, for example, that he could guarantee a physique such as his own to men who practiced DT for just fifteen minutes a day. Atlas' 1936 appearance in front of the FTC also raised questions about the

veracity of his claims about DT, but this time in the context of a suit that he himself brought against competitor Robert Hoffman. For a fuller discussion of the 1936 hearings, see Dominique Padurano, "Building American Men: Charles Atlas and the Business of Bodies, 1892–1945" (Ph.D. diss., Rutgers University, 2007). For transcripts of the hearings themselves, see National Archives Records Administration (NARA), Record Group (RG) 122, Docket Numbers 1952, 2542, and 3308.

39. "Muscle Business," *Fortune*, XVII, Number 1, 1938, 10+; "Backstage with Esquire," *Esquire*, October 1936, 28+; "Sports Briefs," *Star-Beacon* (Ashtabula, OH), October 10, 1936, NMAH/CAC, Unprocessed boxes 9–11. For Atlas in Lew Lehr sketch, see "Lew Lehr Indorses [*sic*] Crusade for Shorts for Office Girls," Charles Atlas, Ltd. (hereafter referred to as CAL), Harrington Park, New Jersey. For photographs and transcript of Atlas on Jack Dempsey radio program on New York's WMAC on Friday, May 15, 1936, see NMAH/CAC, Unprocessed boxes 9–11. For Atlas' performance as the figure of "Health" at FDR's birthday party, see "National Affairs: The Presidency," *Time* (February 10, 1936), 11. In chapter four of my dissertation, I attribute Charles Atlas' rise during the 1930s largely to the company's increasingly visual advertisements and their ability to adapt to the visual culture that emerged during the decade.
40. NARA, RG 122, Docket 1952, Box 1317, Folder 1, Lesson 2, p. 1.
41. NARA, RG 122, Docket 3308, Box 2496, Lesson 2, p. 1.
42. See Marchand, *Advertising the American Dream*, 288, for the Depression-era tendency of advertisers to try and convey sympathy with the common man.
43. See, for example, "Professor Charles Atlas" advertisement in the October1923 issue of *Physical Culture* (86).
44. C. Mutschler to Charles Atlas, 1923, CAL.
45. A. G. to Charles Atlas, ca. 1920s, CAL, Flat File Q. (Although it is undated, given the tank-top style swim or body suit that the man, presumably the letter-writer, wears in the photograph appearing on the reverse side of the postcard on which the letter is written, I estimate that the letter was written sometime during the 1920s. By the 1930s, even amateur bodybuilders were regularly photographed with bare torsos.)
46. Lenn Otto to Charles Atlas, April 20, 1939, CAL.
47. John P. Foy to Charles Atlas, 1942, CAL.
48. In "Brown Paper Wrapper" *Some Freaks* (New York: Viking, 1989), David Mamet artfully describes the shame that many boys in postwar America felt in wanting a better physique.
49. Letters of Patrick J. Rohan to Charles Atlas, Norfolk, England, 1937 and 1938, CAL.
50. Patrick John Rohan to Charles Atlas, Norfolk, England, 1938, CAL.
51. "R. S." to Charles Atlas, Florida, January 13, 1934, CAL. All punctuation and spelling are presented as printed in penciled box letters on original. The words in brackets represent words whose exact letters I was unable to make out, but, given the context of the sentence and the letters of the word that *were* legible, represent my best guesses.

52. George Chauncey, *Gay New York: Gender, Urban Culture, and the Making of the Gay Male World, 1890–1940* (New York: Basic Books, 1994).
53. For more on the homoeroticism of bodybuilding in general and in the career of Atlas, in particular, see Padurano, ch. 4.
54. William Goldstein to Charles Atlas, Perth Amboy, NJ, February 15, 1937, CAL, Archival Box 1.
55. Herman Weinsoff to Charles Roman, Bronx, NY, April 22, 1941, CAL, Archival Box 1. The word "some" was included above the rest of the written line, as if the writer had gone back to add it after having written the rest of the sentence or the letter. It is unclear why Weinsoff designated himself the "BEST BUILDT [*sic*] MAN IN AFRICA," when he had not yet left the Bronx for military service. It is possible, however, that given the fact that the first line of Weinsoff's letter to Roman reads, "I write in some haste as my first draft appeal for deferrment [*sic*] has just been rejected.," that he anticipated soon serving in Africa.

CHAPTER 8

"For Us, By Us": Hip-Hop Fashion, Commodity Blackness and the Culture of Emulation

Mary Rizzo

Clothing is arguably the primary method by which individuals and groups publicly construct their identities. On a daily basis, we must decide what to wear and most of us are savvy, to some degree, about the symbolic meaning of the clothes we choose. We often seek, subconsciously or purposefully, to emulate an image, a person, or a way of life through the way we dress. While fashion, with its associations of excess, aesthetics and decoration, has long been seen as a concern for women, it is obvious that men—as designers, as consumers, and as endorsers—are part of the fashion industry as well. Although the menswear market is highly differentiated, ranging from couture tuxedos to sportswear, its most spectacular success in the late twentieth century has been in the niche known as "urban wear." A loose term, urban wear can be generally defined as those styles derived from the hip-hop subculture of the 1980s and 1990s and which have, since that time, become popular across age, race and geography.

One of the most successful and long-standing companies producing urban wear is FUBU, whose targeted marketing campaigns use African-American celebrities, primarily rapper LL Cool J, as endorsers. Begun in 1992 by four African-American men living in Queens, New York, FUBU distinguished itself from other companies producing urban wear because the founders were themselves part of the hip-hop subculture and were producing mainly for other participants in that subculture. As Daymond John, FUBU's CEO, explained in 1999, he and his friends started FUBU because "major companies really were not selling to the African-American market,"[1] suggesting a desire to address the perceived historic disinterest fashion companies have exhibited in appealing specifically to African Americans.

Yet, in the space of a few years FUBU shifted from explicitly focusing on a particular niche to arguing that its brand should not necessarily be associated with the African-American market. In 2002 FUBU's President of Marketing Leslie Short complained, "I don't understand when clothing became a color issue... What we do and what we've always done is young men's clothing, and if FUBU is urban, then what is DKNY, Nautica, Diesel?"[2] Her assertion suggests two movements. On one hand, it positions FUBU as the equal of these more established companies. On the other, it obfuscates clothing's symbolic role. Racial associations had no more disappeared from the young men's clothing market in the late 1990s than had class. But what happened in the period between FUBU's founding and Short's quote was the spread of hip-hop out of its original urban context and into the global marketplace. While business writers, such as Leon Wynter, interpreted hip-hop's increasing popularity with white, Asian, and Latino youth as a sign that racial difference had become less important in contemporary America, this essay argues that race is only obscured in the global popularization of hip-hop fashion. Instead, in order to understand the distinction between the two statements it is necessary to examine how hip-hop fashion producers, including FUBU, as well as larger companies like Tommy Hilfiger, used their marketing, especially testimonials and endorsements, to produce visual representations that connected upper-class white culture to urban black culture through fashion advertising. Hip-hop fashion ads do not sell baseball caps and baggy jeans, but commodified racial and gender identities. Using celebrity endorsements and iconic visual imagery, these ads attest to the possibility of self-transformation through emulation.

The culture of emulation created through hip-hop fashion begins with the striking remixing of clothing items associated with economically divergent lifestyles. For example, a typical hip-hop men's outfit might pair an expensive ski jacket with hiking boots, oversized jeans, and a bandanna.[3] While the ski jacket and hiking boots are items designed for use in outdoors environments usually connected with leisure, privilege, and whiteness, oversized jeans and bandannas are common elements of urban fashion, particularly worn by youth of color. These combinations are not merely comprehensible through the lens of class or race or gender, but all three, simultaneously. While scholars have argued that marginalized groups have utilized bricolage as a means of parodying the powerful, in the case of hip-hop fashion parody is not the goal. Instead, urban youth creatively combined items that were available to them as well as those that had been given meaning through popular culture. Through such bricolage the producers of hip-hop style (which, in its earliest days were youth involved in the subculture and which now include fashion companies designing for this market) created a hybrid style that is, in Eric Lott's words, a "racial fantasy" of both urban, lower-class black masculinity and white, upper-class culture. In this essay, I chart the development of hip-hop fashion through the 1980s and 1990s, showing the dialectic relationship between the hip-hop subculture and the wider fashion culture. In particular, I analyze a Tommy Hilfiger advertisement as representative of the use of images of upper-class America by mass fashion producers to sell commodified elite whiteness to the hip-hop market.

I then turn to FUBU, a company founded to produce for the urban hip-hop market. FUBU's marketing campaigns utilize both celebrity endorsements to assert the brand's connection with a confrontational, urban masculinity and the founders' success story as a testimonial for the reality of the American Dream. In addition to examining FUBU's advertising and marketing campaigns, I interviewed FUBU CEO Daymond John in 2005 about the issue of emulation. What becomes clear is that hip-hop fashion, even more than its music, offers consumers the choice of which identities they would like to embody. Although by the early 2000s, FUBU asserted the lack of a clear racial identity for its clothing, it was ignoring the complicated racial politics of hip-hop fashion. Not simply a vision of black masculinity, FUBU, like DKNY, Nautica, and Diesel, was also selling a vision of white masculinity, identities that are only given meaning in relation to each other. Hip-hop fashion is a lens into this mutual construction during a historic moment of consumer capitalism and identity-play.

Hip-Hop Fashion: Remix

Hip-hop was born in New York City's South Bronx in the mid-1970s. This subculture, which included music, dance, art, and fashion, was fundamentally shaped by the hegemonic crises of this era, which included the Watergate scandal, U.S. defeat in Vietnam, the oil crisis, the Iran hostage crisis, and, especially, "stagflation." Cities, especially New York, were particularly hard hit by the urban riots of the late 1960s and white flight to the suburbs, and nearly suffered complete economic collapse. These intense difficulties accounted for the deep frustrations many Americans—people of color and white ethnics, progressives, and conservatives—felt about the state of the American nation both abroad and at home and fed the conservative political victories of the 1970s and 1980s.

Unsurprisingly, urban people of color, geographically isolated in inner cities, had few resources to contend with macro economic shifts.[4] Yet while the two major subcultures affecting mainstream popular culture in this era—punk and disco—tended to either reject society or focus on glamorous surfaces,[5] youth of color in New York created hip-hop as an aesthetic practice that incorporated the cultural practices of the African diaspora, especially the Caribbean, into African-American popular music such as funk and soul music. In this way hip-hop spoke back "to the realities of displacement, disillusion, and despair created by the austerity economy of post-industrial capitalism."[6] Hip-hoppers ultimately established a subculture that both criticized and fantasized about the larger culture it differentiated itself from. These parallel emotions—critique and fantasy—suggest the contradictory impulses of "love and theft" that characterized blackface minstrelsy in the nineteenth century. As Eric Lott has written, "It appears that during this stretch of American cultural history the intercourse between racial cultures was at once so attractive and so threatening as to require a cultural marker or visible sign of cultural interaction."[7]More than one hundred years later, a similar visible sign was required as the Civil Rights Movement slowed and a globalized youth culture began. Hip-hop fashion came to be a "visible sign of cultural interaction," as clothing identified with hip-hop became popular with white and suburban youth.

Like other spectacular subcultures,[8] hip-hoppers adopted a recognizable style by adapting common fashion items and remixing them to create new, often jarring combinations. For example, beginning in the mid 1980s, hip-hoppers wore their jeans in extra-large sizes and paired these with sneakers with untied laces, two styles unacceptable to middle-class models of proper dress. As hip-hop, especially rap music, became more popular outside of its original geographic context, its fashions spread as well. Two events, in particular, helped to bring rap fully into the larger youth culture, with critical effects on the development of hip-hop fashion.

In 1985, rap group Run DMC made hip-hop history with "Walk This Way," their cover of a song by rock group Aerosmith proving that rap could be widely popular. They were also important figures in the spread of an athleticized hip-hop style focused on brand names. While early hip-hop fashion of the late 1970s and early 1980s was similar to the popular styles of the era (tight, dark blue jeans and leather jackets), the popularity of break dancing shifted the style to include more athletically inspired clothing such as brand name tracksuits, sweatshirts, and sneakers. Rappers, like Run DMC, became some of the first hip-hop fashion endorsers as many utilized specific brand names, especially haute couture labels like Louis Vuitton and Gucci, as well as more accessible brands like Tommy Hilfiger, in their songs.[9] Perhaps the most influential moment of brand-naming came when producer Russell Simmons, the head of Run DMC's label Def Jam Records and the brother of Reverend Run, a member of the group, invited representatives of the Adidas athletic shoe company to a Run DMC concert. The group began their song, "My Adidas," which included lines such as: "I wear my Adidas when I rock the beat/on stage, front page every show I go/it's Adidas on my feet high top or low/My Adidas." Throughout the audience, fans held up their Adidas sneakers, preferably shell-toes, waving them in unison with the song. With no urging from corporations, rappers had voluntarily positioned themselves as brand endorsers. Fashion executives simply had to find ways to seize on the burgeoning popularity of hip-hop to promote their brands without alienating their consumer base.

The second event spread rap music worldwide. In 1989 MTV debuted Yo! MTV Raps, a program on the popular cable television network solely devoted to rap music. This legitimated rap as a form of music that, while still subcultural, could have resonance far afield from its original urban context. Furthermore, it distributed rap in a *visual* format, creating a recognizable and increasingly standardized style to accompany the music. This style extended from clothing into body language as well, as rappers tended to displays of aggressive masculinity such as scowling, hostile hand gestures, and physical violence or the threat of it in videos that emphasized the ghetto environment that spawned hip-hop.

Aggressive masculinity and inner-city life were central to rap's most controversial subgenre, gangsta rap. Gangsta rap burst into general knowledge with the release of Los Angeles group NWA's (Niggaz with Attitude) 1991 album *Straight Outta Compton*, and it became immediately controversial. Public outcry included concern about lyrics as well as the spread of gangsta fashions, both of which were cited as encouraging gang violence.[10] Gangsta rappers such as Ice Cube argued that gangsta rappers were merely "underground street reporters" telling it "how we see it, nothing more, nothing less," suggesting that the gangsta rapper's authenticity was proven by his personal experiences with ghetto life.[11] While some gangsta rappers had been involved in gang activity, Ice Cube's words dismiss the cultural precedents that informed gangsta rap as well as the creation of fictional persona by rappers. As Robin D. G. Kelley shows, gangsta rap follows in a long tradition of black outlaw characters derived from the blues, 1970s pimp narratives, and blaxploitation films. At the same time, gangsta rappers were also influenced by white cultural forms like mafia movies such as *The Godfather* and *Scarface*, suggesting that the personal experiences of gangsta rappers were reimagined through the lenses available in popular culture. Portrayed as authentic slices of ghetto life, the first-person narratives of gangsta rap utilized the combination of personal experience and generic familiarity to create a highly profitable music that came to be particularly, though not exclusively, popular with young suburban men looking to emulate a lifestyle of danger. Perhaps surprisingly, it was with the popularity of gangsta rap that "preppy," or elite, white styles fully entered into the hip-hop fashion lexicon.

The aggregate effect of the gangsta look was to distinguish the hip-hop subculture and to emphasize the authority of the wearer through the construction of a particular body type that was clearly stylized, though not according to accepted rules. This places hip-hop fashion within the long tradition of black men utilizing clothing and style to construct eye-catching public identities. Once as extravagant as women's clothes, men's clothing became increasingly standardized in the nineteenth century with the rise of industrial capitalism and its need for sober, rational managers. Instead, as Thorstein Veblen argues, wives became the locus of conspicuous consumption. White men who were interested in clothing were, therefore, emasculated and likely to be seen as effeminate or homosexual. However, African-American men since slavery have used style and a concern with bodily presentation as a means of constructing a positive masculine identity and to express resistance to white society. As Shane White and Graham White show, when slaves were brought to the United States they were "quickly clothed in European garb and made to conform to European concepts of decency."[12] Yet while slaves were heavily policed they found ways, such as by wearing bright, clashing colors or by combining the cast-off finery of their masters with daily homespun clothing, to alter their dress to demonstrate their disaffiliation from Euro-American society. Understanding the challenge that these actions posed, those in power reacted in a variety of ways, from violence at the recognition that slaves were dressing above their station to head-shaking at African-American obsession with clothing.

Nineteenth-century African-American dandies used clothing similarly. As Richard J. Powell argues "the black dandy's striking, audacious appearance on America's street corners disrupted the white majority's false notions of social order, racial homogeneity, and cultural superiority."[13] Additionally, famous black abolitionists such as Frederick Douglass dressed in a dandy style as well, critiquing the precepts and ideology of slavery through both their words and their personae. While these styles may have had counterparts among white America, they were particularly meaningful within a black community that had been defined as uncivilized. Furthermore, they had specific gender connotations. Through slavery and reconstruction, black men had been systematically robbed of the markers of masculinity. Through style the black male reclaimed his body as aesthetically pleasing, the defining characteristic of the dandy, rather than merely suited for laboring.

Later black activists married the dandy's interest in clothing with a powerful black masculinity. Male members of the Black Panther Party for Self Defense, for example, dressed in nearly identical fitted leather jackets, dark trousers, and berets, giving them a uniform and contained appearance that suggested a high level of interest in clothing and style. Through their clothing, their ever-present weapons, and their refusal to back down in conflicts with the police, the Black Panthers linked attention to fashion to a powerful black urban masculinity connected to, but distinct from, the earlier Civil Rights Movement.

Unlike the Black Panthers, hip-hoppers wore their clothes oversized in order to construct a different, though related, defiant style. Oversized jeans, for example, were worn pulled down far enough to show the wearer's underwear. This style was said to have derived from badly fitted prison uniforms, which were baggy and dropped below the waist, giving rise to the term "saggin' and baggin'" to describe someone wearing these styles. Hugely baggy pants have to be pulled up often and are antithetical to middle-class models of proper dress, suggesting the wearer has removed himself, or accepted his removal, from the legitimate economy as well as the rules of middle-class success. At the same time that these styles demonstrate an aversion to middle-class ideals, they also construct a larger-than-life male body. Each element in the gangsta wardrobe added physical bulk to the wearer. Swathed in yards of denim and padded in ski jackets, the bodies of these young men were made to seem large and physically intimidating as they claimed more space in public areas.[14] These clothes also necessitated certain kinds of bodily movements. It is difficult to run while wearing oversized pants, causing the wearer to adopt a slower gait that suggested a sense of ownership over the streets. Physical intimidation was reinforced by the logos on these clothes, which included sports teams with names that suggested violence, such as the Raiders, a kind of endorsement unplanned for by those teams.

Surprisingly, black men's long-standing interest in fashion had not resulted in the larger fashion industry seeking them as consumers. Instead, most corporate fashion designers have been wary of linking their brands with black culture for fear of alienating white buyers, whose patronage is considered necessary for profitability. Carl Jones, a founder of Cross Colours, argued that large fashion companies ignored the ethnic market, especially in the realm of advertising: "They never used Black male fit models or Black male models in their advertisements, yet their customer was the Black male . . . It wasn't even discussed or even important until they saw it could be profitable."[15] What has occurred with hip-hop fashion, however, is that clothing that was seen as connoting urban black culture began to be sold by small and large companies to the black market and was then successfully mass marketed to both blacks and whites, becoming, essentially, mainstream fashion.[16] Rather than embracing these roots, hip-hop fashion is sold as "urban wear" or "urban fashion." Hip-hop producer and fashion designer Russell Simmons has decried the use of this term, recognizing that "urban" is a code word for "black" that also slyly evokes the aura of the "urban" as an exoticized lower-class realm of danger. Simmons, looking for more mainstream acceptance, calls the clothing he designs simply "classic."[17]

Simmons' description of hip-hop clothing as classic is more than rhetoric. Hip-hop fashion has often been inspired by what is best described as preppy style—khaki pants, hiking boots, ski jackets, and logos. While hip-hoppers, as I have argued, reinterpret them in innovative ways, the fact that they are emulating styles that most clearly connote a version of upper-class whiteness suggests that a particular sort of racial fantasy is being expressed in hip-hop style. Before fashion companies began producing specifically for the hip-hop market, hip-hoppers tended to buy clothing by companies such as Polo Ralph Lauren and Tommy Hilfiger, both of which utilized imagery that referenced highly idealized visions of an elite America. For example, this advertisement (see figure 8.1) for Hilfiger's fragrance "Tommy" appeared several times in *The Source: The Magazine of Hip Hop, Politics and Culture*, the major hip-hop–oriented magazine, in the late 1990s. While this is not an advertisement for clothing, specifically, it is exemplary of Hilfiger's larger advertising campaigns. The ad depicts a group of two white men and a white woman lounging with two black men and a black woman in front of an idyllic looking barn that is a less-than-subtle reference to the Kennedy residence in Hyannisport.

With an equal mix of black and white models, the American flag waving in the background and the words "real american" beneath, the image is clearly meant to evoke a fantasy multicultural nation where there is diversity without conflict. As Lisa Lowe suggests, an image like this unifies "the diversity of the United States through the integration of differences as *cultural* equivalents abstracted from the histories of racial inequality unresolved in the economic and political domains."[18] Particularly important is the sense of intimacy conveyed in the ad, suggesting that the nation is constructed through a horizontal comradeship that is best expressed through personal relationships. The models in this ad lounge together, touch each other casually, and laugh and smile with ease, suggesting security and privilege. They have no need to fight for a place in society, it is assumed. Hilfiger has explained that his clothing is supposed to reference "a more New England, outdoorsy, and classic campus look that I knew would last."[19] The preppy New England that is pictured is far removed from the reality of most youth of color. As a fantasy, however, it suggests a world of secure privilege, which may explain its popularity. Yet its placement in *The Source* suggests that Hilfiger is directly appealing to the hip-hop subculture even though the ad's imagery seems out of place in a magazine devoted to hip-hop and urban America. However, knowing how hip-hop fashion remixed Hilfiger's clothing in new combinations, the ad begins to make sense: it is the explicit visualization of the upscale lifestyle that had been borrowed in developing a recognizable hip-hop style.

Figure 8.1 Advertisement for Tommy, Tommy Hilfiger's fragrance.
Source: *The Source*: *The Magazine for Hip Hop, Culture and Politics* (November 1998).

FUBU: For Us, By Us—Emulation and Lifestyle Marketing

A very different kind of ad appeared in the February 1996 issue of the same magazine (figure 8.2). Unlike the Hilfiger ad, this early FUBU print ad does not attempt to create a narrative or encourage the viewer to place himself

Figure 8.2 FUBU advertisement featuring LL Cool J.

Source: *The Source*: *The Magazine for Hip Hop, Culture and Politics* (February 1996).

within the ad's implied story. Instead, it focuses the viewer's complete attention on popular rapper LL Cool J, who would be well known to the readers of *The Source*. Cool J, wearing a FUBU hat and jacket, is posed to emphasize the FUBU logo, which appears four times. With no discernible background and little further detail, this advertisement trades on Cool J's notoriety and persona as a respected, noncontroversial rapper. As CEO Daymond John explains, "We had just started to do shirts, and we decided we needed LL to wear one in a magazine, to get some more exposure and to seem more legit than we were."[20] Cool J's endorsement would increase the visibility of the brand without losing the connection with the music and culture that had originally inspired the founders. Having this image appear in a magazine would further give the fledgling company legitimacy, as magazine advertising continues to be a primary method of marketing clothing. This advertisement utilizes the aura of LL Cool J as a representative of hip-hop authenticity and black masculinity to create an implicit testimonial for the product and demonstrates the main marketing method utilized by FUBU, which has relied on celebrity endorsements as well as the testimonials of the founders.

Where other hip-hop fashion companies have perished, FUBU has thrived, garnering a number of awards for the founders, including an Essence Award (1999) and an Ernst and Young New York Entrepreneur of the Year Award (2003). Perhaps most interesting, and a major clue to FUBU's success, is the award the company received in 1999: *Brandweek's* Marketer of the Year. Yet at the outset, the four friends started FUBU with no experience in the fashion industry. Their main goal was to appeal to the hip-hop subculture while also reinterpreting upscale clothing elements common to the style. Daymond John explained that he "was looking to create a line that had all the elements of design but was interpreted for the purpose of wearing it in the street." While Gortex ski jackets were popular with urban hip-hoppers, they were also extremely expensive—generally costing several hundred dollars. John argued that hip-hoppers "didn't need to really be spending $800 because we weren't going skiing in it most likely. But we liked the design aspect of it so I wanted to make something like that for about one-third the cost with the same amount of flair and style in it."[21] With the goal of combining upscale designs with an urban flair, the four partners created FUBU, an acronym meaning "for us, by us." Since its inception, FUBU has been one of the success stories of the hip-hop fashion industry and has recently moved beyond menswear, producing boys' and women's clothes, footwear, bags, and accessories.[22] In addition to being sold in most major department stores in the United States, FUBU also has freestanding stores in Australia, England, France, Mexico, Saudi Arabia, and so on. In fact, some of its fastest growth has been in France, Korea, and Japan.

FUBU's marketing strategy has been to position the brand as a lifestyle that is linked with a version of hip-hop authenticity that a cross section of young consumers can emulate. As John has explained, "We're a company... we're expanding into a lifestyle. It's hard enough to be a brand but it's even ten times harder to be a lifestyle."[23] Clothing brands, according to marketing researchers Lan Nguyen Chaplin and Deborah Roedder John, are seen by young people as more meaningful in expressing their self-image than most other types of commodities. As they mature, youth become increasingly sophisticated in describing the character of all brands and, especially, clothing. For example, in Chaplin and Roedder's research, a seventh-grade girl did not see FUBU as representing her since "it's really for urban boys—you know the type that wear real baggy pants and talk slang."[24] While FUBU may try to extend their brand with tuxedoes and suits, they are still strongly associated with hip-hop street style. As John speculated, "I'm not certain now, but I believe we have the number two best rented and sold tuxedo in the country. I can say that all I want, but people will still think of FUBU as just baggy jeans."[25] However, seeing FUBU as "just baggy jeans" may be critical in giving it the stamp of authenticity that has become a critical concept in hip-hop since its commercialization in the early 1980s.

FUBU long eschewed traditional advertising, using a targeted approach that emphasized its street credibility through links with the urban hip-hop community. Even in 1998, FUBU was only spending $400,000 on advertising (which represented an increase of $150,000 over the previous year), and all its advertisements were produced in-house.[26] While FUBU has utilized a variety of marketing techniques, the most long-standing and successful has been its use of testimonials and celebrity endorsements to create an aspirational lifestyle brand.[27] As marketer Bernd H. Schmitt notes, the distinction between the marketing of the past and today is that currently "marketers . . . need to be sensitive to lifestyle trends—or even better, become drivers of lifestyle trends—and make sure that our brands are associated, in fact, form part of the lifestyle."[28] For hip-hop fashion, these lifestyles are linked with aspirational brands, or high-priced, easily identified items that represent a lifestyle that is above the status of the purchaser.[29] Consumption, especially of fashion items, becomes a public method of compensating for a lack of economic and social power.[30] This is part of a long history of subcultures using " 'flashy' clothes . . . in the art of impression management" which defies "the assumption that to be poor one necessarily has to 'show' it."[31]

However, FUBU works as an aspirational brand on two different levels, which gives it the power to be widely marketed. First, FUBU connects itself to hip-hop as the source of its credibility through celebrity endorsements and marketing. In this way, FUBU makes "hip hop" a lifestyle to be aspired to. Consumers are asked to emulate celebrity endorsers through a brand that becomes the gateway to hip-hop authenticity. A critical aspect of FUBU's long-standing success is the fact that it has not utilized marginal or hardcore rappers as endorsers, instead focusing on celebrities who are both associated with hip-hop, but also widely acceptable and recognizable, such as the brand's main spokesperson LL Cool J, who was an early rap celebrity but who widened his appeal through starring in a television show and in a number of movies. Second, FUBU uses the "rags to riches" story of the founders to mark the brand as the quintessential American success story of upward mobility. These parallel strategies not only define FUBU's marketing plan, but that of most of the hip-hop fashion industry, which blithely combines images of scowling rappers with status items and American imagery. While wealthy rappers have likely left the urban ghetto behind, they must continually demonstrate their connections to it to prove their authenticity. The FUBU founders and other hip-hop fashion designers, such as Sean Combs, do the same, while other mainstream fashion designers are able to remain successful on the merits of their designs. Combs, who gained notoriety as a producer and rapper, has changed his name several times (from "Puff Daddy" to "P. Diddy," and most recently to a more straightforward "Diddy") to construct multiple identities that are differentiated but still connected to each other and to hip-hop. He has utilized this name recognition, like numerous other rappers, to launch a clothing brand, Sean John, in 1998. While Sean John is a FUBU competitor, Combs has tended to focus his attention on a more upscale market. In fact, Combs was named Menswear Designer of the Year by the Council of Fashion Designers of America in 2004.[32] While distinct in this way, both Combs and the FUBU founders express a central quality of hip-hop—a desire for success married to a need to prove connection with the urban black community.

Linking these two strategies for FUBU is its name and ubiquitous logo. Logos have been a long-standing aspect of hip-hop style since the early 1980s. For FUBU CEO Daymond John, logos are signals that the consumer is being asked to emulate another person or lifestyle. As he said, "emulation is most of the reason why any successful high-end or mid-tier fashion line works. Other than that we could all just wear T-shirts and basic jeans with no logos on them. But once you see a logo, they're trying to emulate something to an extent."[33] For John the logo is the differentiation between a basic clothing item and one with the possibility of being used in terms of emulation, as the logo is laden with the brand's meaning that the consumer will hopefully want to embody. In this case, the brand's endorser becomes critical in constructing the logo as something that can be emulated and embodied by a consumer. Additionally, the logo is also a means of developing and maintaining subcultural boundaries, as "insiders" know which logos to wear and which to eschew. For example, FUBU's acronym stands for "for us, by us," yet it is often misinterpreted as "for you, by you," demonstrating ignorance of the subculture's symbols.

"For us, by us," however, is also key to the success of the brand as representative of hip-hop credibility. Daymond John explained in our interview that he created FUBU in part to develop less expensive versions of popular street styles. These styles were defined as "hip hop" through being worn by neighborhood youth involved in hip-hop culture. However, this stylistic appropriation was often at odds with the image that the companies producing the clothing wanted to portray, as hip-hoppers practiced bricolage with items familiar to them. When asked to explain the derivation of the FUBU name, John began by expressing frustration with most clothing companies in the late 1980s and early 1990s. Timberland, which manufactures hiking boots, earned particular critique when its president said in 1993, "One of the things that young inner city kids are telling us right now is that Timberland and the 'gangster' look, the street kid look, are compatible visions. Okay, you're welcome to that, but it's not what we intended the product for."[34] More than a decade later, John placed this issue at the heart of FUBU's creation:

> The acronym came to be... when the reports came out of Timberland that they didn't make boots for drug dealers and I was a hard-working gentleman who was not a drug dealer and I used to support Timberland extensively—I used to buy three or four pairs of Timberlands a month—I was insulted at that statement. And I felt that everybody else applying to the market had no idea of the market. It wasn't necessarily a color thing... but it was Versace, an Italian gentleman from Italy, it was Timberland guys who live in the woods in Vermont... it wasn't people who understood this new uprising culture, whether it be hip hop, R&B or just Generation Y. For us by us, was in the sense of we were designing for ourselves now.[35]

As John suggests, FUBU's goal was to emphasize its unique connection to the hip-hop subculture through the knowledge and cultural affiliations of the founders. While others could profit from the hip-hop market without truly comprehending it, FUBU was tied to it, as represented in the acronym. "We represent hip-hop," says Daymond John, "And the people who buy our clothes know that we're 'down,' they know that we don't just make clothes, we wear the clothes and we are part of the culture."[36] While the "for us" is mutable, depending on the consumer, the "by us" always remains the founders, who represent hip-hop through their urban roots in the subculture. In this way, the name FUBU helps to call a specific community into being, allowing it to be closely associated with a hip-hop lifestyle. While the name was the first part of FUBU's marketing strategy, it was given localized meaning through other techniques, including painting the logo on New York stores' metal security doors, offering FUBU wearers in New York tickets to events, producing hip-hop CDs, and, especially, getting FUBU clothing worn by celebrities.

A list of FUBU's endorsers includes the Wayans Brothers, Will Smith, Brandy, and Lennox Lewis.[37] FUBU's press kit further notes that "the music industry's hottest directors, such as Hype Williams, David LaChapelle, and Chris Robertson have featured the collection in their videos" and that a number of musicians, such as "50 Cent, Queen Latifah, Janet Jackson, Will Smith, Busta Rhymes, Sean Puffy Combs, Christina Aguilera... and N'SYNC," wear FUBU.[38] More than simply building ad campaigns around celebrities, FUBU's tactic has been to encourage important members of the music industry to wear the brand, knowing that having these people seen in the clothing is critical to FUBU's image. As the list above shows, FUBU has associated itself with a variety of celebrities, some of whom are involved in hip-hop, such as 50 Cent and Queen Latifah, some of whom are pop musicians, like Christina Aguilera and N'SYNC, and some of whom are athletes, like Lennox Lewis. This suggests that FUBU is trying to maintain its connections with hip-hop while also broadening its appeal. As John claims, "we feel that we're the Levis of the current age." It is extremely difficult to tread this line. Even John admits that "there were times when we became too mainstream and it's just something you face."[39] In the hypercompetitive youth fashion market, hip-hop clothing companies have a great deal to lose if they are perceived as conventional.

Celebrity endorsers also become guides to self-transformation for the consumer. A celebrity wearing the clothing in an advertisement or music video suggests that the product is part of that celebrity's persona, which implies that the consumer who buys this product is also purchasing a means of recreating that persona. The celebrity occupies a contradictory position in such an ad as he becomes both a recognizable individual and the representative of a lifestyle that can be emulated by millions. The product mirrors this contradiction as it becomes a marker of a singular, authentic identity and the gateway to a community of users/believers who are imbued with the reflected glory of the celebrity as endorser. As Walter Benjamin has made clear, mass production has loosened objects from the context of production. Since authenticity, defined by Benjamin as the original object's essence, cannot be found with a mass produced good, it must be stamped with a new "aura," which is accomplished in most cases through marketing and advertising that creates identifiable brands. Celebrities give the product their aura, helping to create a brand identity. The choice of celebrity also demonstrates who the consumers of the brand should be. The endorsement must be aligned with the brand's image or there is a strong possibility that the product's associations will become too loose and, therefore, meaningless as a method of creating specific identities. In deciding who to use as celebrity endorsements for FUBU, John explained that their focus was on:

> whoever was a hot artist or sports player or stuff like that, who lived that life that we were talking about... we would align ourselves with [them] by

> putting the product on them in the videos or using them in our advertising campaigns...Those artists and sports figures...who felt that they fit the FUBU model would come to us also. We would all thrive off of each other.[40]

This mutually beneficial association demonstrates how the founders positioned FUBU as a lifestyle. The celebrities do not necessarily have to be involved in hip-hop, but they must be "hot" and representative of a certain lifestyle defined by fame, wealth, and a particular sense of style. While John's description seems to suggest an extremely broad view of the right celebrity for FUBU endorsements, the celebrities that FUBU uses help the company toe the line between the hip-hop market and the mass market, as none are particularly controversial.

FUBU's most prominent endorser has been longtime rapper LL Cool J, who grew up in the same neighborhood as the FUBU founders. In the world of hip-hop, there are few rappers who have the longevity of LL Cool J. Becoming a sensation in 1984 at the age of sixteen with his song "I Got A Beat," Cool J has managed to bounce back from a string of poor-selling albums to craft an image as a hip-hop sex symbol and mainstream celebrity who has appeared in movies and his own TV show. As I noted earlier, the relationship between Cool J and FUBU began in the mid-1990s, but it has continued consistently since then. Cool J has been featured not only in FUBU print advertisements but also has been photographed wearing FUBU at numerous public events. Even more interesting is the fact that Cool J continued to wear FUBU even when appearing in a 1997 television commercial for the Gap, a mainstream clothing brand. In the ad, Cool J wore Gap jeans and a FUBU logo hat while rapping "the Gap is for us, by us."[41] In this less-than-subtle ploy, Gap attempted to draw from FUBU's street credibility while FUBU was given free television advertising that distributed its image more widely than ever.[42]

While FUBU's association with LL Cool J accords it a certain hip-hop authenticity, this is further linked with a tough masculinity, an image that is repeated throughout most FUBU and other hip-hop fashion advertising. Young men are asked to emulate a confrontational, authoritative masculinity, demonstrated primarily through muscularity and the adoption of a "cool pose."[43] While the first advertisement that featured Cool J (figure 8.2) photographed him in a way that did not call particular attention to masculine authority, in later advertisements this becomes a central theme. For example, in an ad that appeared in the September 1997 issue of *The Source*, the viewer sees Cool J from the waist up, with his head tilted down and to the right, almost completely hiding his face with a FUBU hat. One hand reaches over to pull up the sleeve of his shirt, revealing the other arm, which is heavily muscled and emblazoned with a tattoo of a microphone topped with a crown, which stretches from shoulder to wrist. On the bicep appear the words "Mr. Smith." The tattoo emphasizes his muscularity and links him with a cultural style that, until very recently, was seen as lower class. Again, this ad trades on hip-hop insider knowledge. The only absolute method of knowing that this is LL Cool J is through knowledge of this tattoo and the fact that he is a FUBU endorser. While the earlier ad focused solely on Cool J's face, suggesting a desire for viewers to connect with the endorser, this image draws all the attention to the muscularity of the arms in hopes of imbuing the product with the association of tough hip-hop masculinity. This connection is further underscored with the use of other celebrities, such as boxer Lennox Lewis, who appeared in FUBU ads in 1999. Even when FUBU ads do not feature tough hip-hop celebrities, they utilize well-muscled male models who pose in similar ways. This is in direct contrast to the male models that appeared in the Tommy Hilfiger advertisement described earlier (figure 8.1). FUBU's hip-hop world is constructed as a dangerous one where black men must be constantly on guard and ready for potential confrontation, while Hilfiger's upper-class America is a realm of security and comfort.

Yet this hip-hop masculinity is only one part of the story. As I have argued FUBU has been successful due to its ability to create an aspirational hybrid that brings together urban hip-hop masculinity with the upwardly mobile image of the founders, who have come to be celebrities in their own right, and, as such, endorsers of the brand. While Hilfiger, Polo Ralph Lauren, and Nautica reiterate images of American flags and multicultural gatherings, FUBU references American mythology through the FUBU creation story. While John has repeatedly emphasized that the FUBU founders did not try to capitalize on their "hip-hop Horatio Alger"[44] story, their marketing campaigns suggest otherwise. Since 1999 the FUBU Web site has contained a biography of each of the founders that details their adolescence in New York and subsequent economic success. The Web site further stresses that even with their success the four men have remained tied to their community. As one of the founders said on *The Montel Williams Show* "Growing up we didn't have a lot of... business role models to let us know there were other ways to get out of the community in a positive manner, so we go back to the churches and the schools and we feel that its only right to give back where you came from."[45] The founders, therefore, become an important source for FUBU's credibility. As John noted, "we put ourselves out there so there was a face behind the brand, so let's say in case our celebrity didn't do as well or he changed, some people would like the rags to riches story, some people would like just to see who they're getting the product from."[46] The idea of a face behind the brand is critical. While the fortunes of various celebrity endorsers can shift, the founders' identity is stable. They are the ultimate endorsers of the brand.

Allowing consumers to see "who they're getting the product from" is the goal of certain FUBU advertisements (figure 8.3). The image in figure 8.3

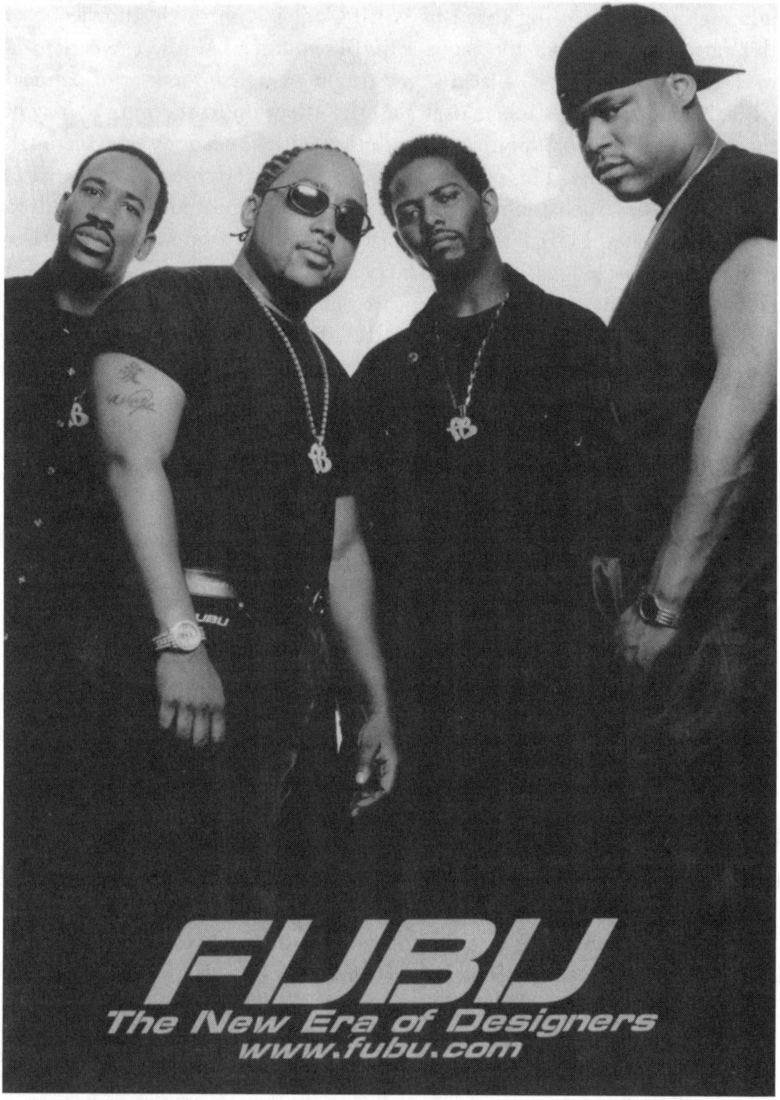

Figure 8.3 FUBU advertisement featuring founders.

Source: *The Source*: *The Magazine of Hip Hop, Culture and Politics* (October 1998).

shows the four founders looking directly at the viewer with the same uncompromising attitude and tough masculinity as LL Cool J and Lennox Lewis. The personal styles of the founders emphasize their connection with hip-hop culture: through their dress, the backward-turned baseball cap on Keith Perrin, and Daymond John's cornrowed hair. The racialized and classed meaning of the founders' image is underscored in a story told by Daymond John. He recounted how one "major department store" wanted FUBU to remove their hang tags, which featured this image. The store representative's rationale was "we want to sell to forty-year-old white people, and they won't buy it if they see those guys on there."[47] This department store recognized that the founders' image connoted hip-hop and a lower-class confrontational black masculinity that could potentially repel the wealthiest customers.

However, FUBU's 2005 press kit contained a new image of the founders. The founders (figure 8.4) are posed similarly to the earlier photograph, but are wearing suits from FUBU: The Collection. While the confrontational facial expressions remain, both John's and Perrin's hands are clasped making them less ready for physical confrontation and suggesting a controlled masculine body emphasized by the suits. Most important, however, is the upward mobility suggested in these two images. The ideal consumer, prepped through media stories about FUBU and their earlier advertisements, recognizes that this current image represents change over time. While the original goal of the brand was to reinterpret aspirational clothing items for street use, here we see the founders posing in expensive suits. Emulation moves from being directed toward a hip-hop celebrity or athlete who represents street authenticity and hypermasculinity (though also a wealthy lifestyle) to upward mobility through business. While this image personalizes American mythology, it follows logically from the development and marketing of hip-hop fashion, which has often utilized Americana as a selling point. For example, a series of FUBU ads showed a male model wearing work clothes posed in front of a stylized American flag. This dual approach, which is undergirded by the founders' ability to successfully argue that they are highly knowledgeable about hip-hop, has allowed FUBU to be mass marketed while remaining popular within the hip-hop subculture. In fact, FUBU was the first black-owned fashion company to have its own window in Macy's flagship department store in New York. While this was seen as a coup for the black business community, it could have suggested the movement of the brand away from its street roots. FUBU has been generally able to navigate around these shoals. As I have argued, this is directly related to FUBU's use of celebrity endorsements to create a fashion brand that is an aspirational hybrid, fusing hip-hop authenticity to American imagery, in the same way that the development of hip-hop style in the early years paired upscale and more common clothing items.

Figure 8.4 FUBU advertisement featuring founders. 2005 FUBU press kit.

Conclusion

The development of hip-hop fashion into a major sector of the fashion industry demonstrates a shift in consumer culture toward a conception of identity as a matter of commodity choice. While hip-hop began as a localized subculture that sampled the culture of mainstream America to speak to the concerns of urban youth of color, within twenty years it has *become* mainstream American youth culture, sold to a wide crosssection of youth. Yet, as I have shown, the development and marketing of hip-hop fashion through the 1980s and 1990s has been undergirded by a "love and theft" relationship between the subculture and mainstream popular culture. Hip-hop fashion began as a bricolage of upscale and common clothing items. As it became an industry, the images that marketed the clothing further underscored these seemingly contradictory pairings, as fantasy images of elite whiteness were paired with fantasy images of ghetto blackness.

FUBU's early marketing efforts branded it as part of a localized, historicized black community, intimately tied to an urban hip-hop milieu. At this time, the "for us" of the acronym seemed to mainly include those consumers who were heavily involved in hip-hop. In hopes of widening its popularity, the company created ads that utilized celebrity testimonials. By using these celebrities, FUBU implicitly asked its potential consumers: do you belong with "us" or are you part of "them"? In asking this question, FUBU was emphasizing the critical importance of identifying a subcultural community. This community was defined, on one hand, by the celebrities themselves, who represented urban hip-hop and an aggressive masculinity and who the consumers were told to emulate. The community was also defined, however, by images of the four founders and their story of upward mobility. The site specific politics that accompanied early hip-hop and which still inform much of hip-hop music, especially that of underground musicians, have been removed for a universalized presentation of possible identities. Race and class identities are decontextualized, presented instead as commodities through the use of lifestyle marketing techniques. While the spread of hip-hop fashion, especially gangsta style, brought controversy in the early 1990s for its potentially counterhegemonic mixing of racial and class identities, by the early twenty-first century it is clear that a new identity can be bought off the rack.

Notes

1. Jancee Dunn, "How Hip-Hop Style Bum-Rushed the Mall," *Rolling Stone* (March 18, 1999).
2. Donette Dunbar, "Gear Factor," *Daily Variety* (November 8, 2002), B4.
3. "Black Style Now" exhibit. Museum of the City of New York. September 9, 2006 through February 19, 2007.
4. William Julius Wilson, *The Truly Disadvantaged: The Inner City, the Underclass, and Public Policy* (Chicago: University of Chicago Press, 1990).
5. On punk, see Greil Marcus, *In the Fascist Bathroom: Punk in Pop Music, 1977–1992* (Cambridge, MA: Harvard University Press, 1999). On disco, see Carolyn Hilary Krassnow, "The Development of Aesthetic Ideology in

Popular Music: Rock and Disco in the Nineteen Seventies" (Ph.D. Diss., University of Minnesota, 1999).

6. George Lipsitz, *Dangerous Crossroads: Popular Music, Postmodernism and the Poetics of Place* (New York: Verso, 1994), 36.
7. Eric Lott, *Love and Theft: Blackface Minstrelsy and the American Working Class* (New York: Oxford University Press, 1993), 6.
8. Dick Hebdige, *Subculture: The Meaning of Style* (London: Methuen, 1979).
9. While logos and haute couture labels were extremely important to hip-hop style in this era, there was a reaction to this trend. Politically charged black nationalist musical groups such as Public Enemy and the Jungle Brothers traded brand names for kente cloth, Africa medallions, and paramilitary gear.
10. A spate of newspaper and magazine articles linked gang activity and hip-hop fashion in the early 1990s, including "Fashion Flares: Back-to-School Shopping Comes with Warning Signals," *The Los Angeles Times* (August 18, 1994); "'Saggin': A Boxer Rebellion in Fashion," *Orange County Register* (August 14, 1994); "The Costumes are all a Part of the Process," *The Santa Fe New Mexican* (May 1, 1994); "Kids and Gangs," *Newsday* (December 11, 1993); "Gang Colors," *Chicago Tribune* (April 13, 1992); and "Vulnerable Teens: Fashion's Messages in Media Pander to Gang Wannabes," *Seattle Times* (December 31, 1992), among many others.
11. Quote from rapper Ice Cube, found in Robin D. G. Kelley, *Race Rebels: Culture, Politics and the Black Working Class* (New York: The Free Press, 1996), 190.
12. Shane White and Graham White, *Stylin': African American Expressive Culture from Its Beginnings to the Zoot Suit* (Ithaca, NY: Cornell University Press, 1998), 6.
13. Richard J. Powell, "Sartor Africanus," in *Dandies: Fashion and Finesse in Art and Culture*, ed. by Susan Fillin-Yeh (New York: New York University Press, 2001): 217–242.
14. George Lipsitz, *Rainbow at Midnight: Labor and Culture in the 1940's* (Chicago, IL: U. of Illinois Press, 1994), 84.
15. "Colour Me Cross," *The Source* (January 1993).
16. According to *Newsweek*, even former President Bill Clinton occasionally wears Russell Simmon's hip-hop fashion company Phat Farm's sweaters. Johnnie L. Roberts, "Beyond Definition," *Newsweek* (July 28, 2003), 40.
17. Simmons discussed in "Beyond Definition," *Newsweek*. "To further widen their appeal many urban designers are moving away from using the label 'urban wear' and moving toward 'contemporary' or 'metropolitan'" says Ellzy of the Fashion Association. "The word 'urban' has grown outside that definition," says DNR's Romero. "The lines of what can be considered for those particular markets have been blurred. It started with the oversize denim and basic T-shirts, and has evolved to tailored clothing for men and women's wear collections." Leslie E. Royal, "Hip Hop on Top," *Black Enterprise* (July 2000), 40.

18. Lisa Lowe, *Immigrant Acts: On Asian American Cultural Politics* (Durham, NC: Duke UP, 1996), 30.
19. Tommy Hilfiger, *All-American: A Tommy Hilfiger Style Book* (New York: Universe Publishing, 1997), 14.
20. Dunn, 56.
21. Daymond John, interview by the author, tape recording, New York, NY, May 18, 2005. Many thanks to Leslie Short, President of Marketing at FUBU, who arranged for me to interview FUBU CEO Daymond John by phone in May 2005. Talking to John about issues of emulation, lifestyle marketing, and style have enriched this essay greatly and added a layer of analysis that I am extraordinarily grateful to have received.
22. Elena Romero, "FUBU Gets Ball Rolling," *Daily News Record* (January 25, 1999).
23. Sloane Lucas, "For Us, Forever—Marketing of Urban apparel maker FUBU," *Brandweek* (October 11, 1999).
24. Lan Nguyen Chaplin and Deborah Roedder John, "The Development of Self-Brand Connections in Children and Adolescents," *Journal of Consumer Research* 32, 1 (June 2005), 125.
25. Daymond John, interview by the author, tape recording, New York, NY, May 18, 2005.
26. Justin Dini, "FUBU Starts Talks with Shops," *Adweek* [*Eastern Edition*] (October 12, 1998).
27. For more on lifestyle marketing, please see Philip Kotler, *Marketing Management*, 8th ed. (Englewood Cliffs, NJ: Prentice Hall, 1994).
28. Bernd H. Schmitt, *Experiential Marketing: How to Get Customers to SENSE, FEEL, THINK, ACT, and RELATE to Your Company and Brands* (New York: The Free Press, 1999), 165.
29. Joshua Levine, "Badass Sells," *Forbes* (April 21, 1997).
30. Jack Schwartz, "Men's Clothing and the Negro," in *Dress, Adornment and the Social Order*, ed. Mary Ellen Roach and Joanne Bubolz Eicher (New York: John Wiley and Sons, 1965) 168.
31. Kobena Mercer, *Welcome to the Jungle* (London: Routledge, 1994), 120.
32. Sean Gregory, "Sean Combs," *Time* (December 17, 2004).
33. Daymond John, interview by the author, tape recording, New York, May 18, 2005.
34. "Fashion, the Mainstream & Us: A Good Combination?" *The Source* (January 1993).
35. Daymond John, interview by the author, tape recording, New York, May 18, 2005.
36. "FUBU Challenges Rivals," *Knight-Ridder/Tribune Business News* (November 11, 1996).
37. Leslie Royal, "Hip Hop on Top," *Black Enterprise* (July 2000), 91.
38. Fubu press kit, Company Profile. May 2005.
39. Daymond John, interview by the author, tape recording, New York, May 18, 2005.

40. Daymond John, interview by the author, tape recording, New York, May 18, 2005.
41. Lauren Goldstein, "Urban Wear Goes Suburban," *Fortune* (December 21, 1998), 169–171.
42. Melba Newsom and Gerda Gallop-Goodman, "Mad Marketing Skills," *Black Enterprise* (December 1999).
43. Richard Majors and Janet Mancini Billson, *Cool Pose: The Dilemmas of Black Manhood in America* (New York: Touchstone Press, 1993).
44. This phrase appears in Sloane Lucas, "For us, forever—marketing of urban apparel maker FUBU," *Brandweek* (October 11, 1999).
45. "FUBU" *The Montel Williams Show* (April 16, 1999).
46. Daymond John, interview by the author, tape recording, New York, May 18, 2005.
47. Leon Wynter, *American Skin: Pop Culture, Big Business and the End of White America* (New York: Random House, 2002), 186–187.

Notes on Contributors

Vicki Howard, the author of *Brides, Inc.: American Weddings and the Business of Tradition* (University of Pennsylvania Press, 2006), is currently working on a book about the small-town and small-city American department store. She is an Assistant Professor of History at Hartwick College in Oneonta, New York.

Stephen Johnson is Director of the Graduate Center for Study of Drama at the University of Toronto, where he teaches performance theory and the history of popular performance. His publications include the book *Roof Gardens of Broadway Theatres* and articles in a range of journals, including *The Drama Review*, *Canadian Theatre Review*, *Theatre Topics*, and *Nineteenth Century Theatre*, as well as *Theatre Research in Canada*, which he (co)edited for ten years. His database and Web site on blackface minstrelsy in Britain is available at link.library.utoronto.ca/minstrels/. He is a full member of the Playwrights Guild of Canada and the Writers Union of Canada.

Marina Moskowitz is Reader in History and American Studies at the University of Glasgow. She is the author of *Standard of Living: The Measure of the Middle Class in Modern America* (Johns Hopkins University Press, 2004) and coeditor of *Cultures of Commerce: Representations and American Business Culture, 1877–1960* (Palgrave, 2006). Her current research on the intersection of commerce and horticulture has been funded by the ESRC-AHRC Cultures of Consumption Research Programme, the Kluge Center of the Library of Congress, the Smithsonian Institution, and a variety of other fellowships and grants.

Dominique Padurano received her Ph.D. from Rutgers in 2007 and teaches at Horace Mann School in New York City. Currently she is writing a cultural biography of fitness icon Charles Atlas—born Angelo Siciliano in Calabria—to explain changes in American culture, masculinity, ethnicity, sexuality, and childhood during the first half of the twentieth century.

Michael Pettit is an assistant professor in the Department of Psychology at York University, where he is affiliated with the graduate History and Theory of Psychology and Science and Technology Studies programs. His work has appeared in *Isis, The Journal of the History of the Behavioral Sciences,* and *History of Psychology.* His current research is a cultural history of deception in American science and commercial life.

Mary Rizzo, who received her Ph.D. in American Studies from the University of Minnesota, currently serves as the Associate Director of the New Jersey Council for the Humanities, and teaches in the Women's and Gender Studies Program at the College of New Jersey. Her research interests include public history, class identity, fashion and the role of appropriation in twentieth-century American consumer culture. Her work has also appeared in *Dixie Emporium: Tourism, Foodways and Consumer Culture in the American South* (University of Georgia Press, 2008) and *Eating in Eden: Food and American Utopias* (University of Nebraska Press, 2006).

Marlis Schweitzer is Assistant Professor of Theatre Studies at York University. She is the author of *When Broadway Was the Runway: Theater, Fashion, and American Culture* (University of Pennsylvania Press, 2009), which explores how collaborations between the twentieth-century Broadway theatre and fashion industries contributed to the development of modern American consumer culture. She has also published work in *Theatre Journal, American Quarterly,* the *Journal of Women's History,* the *Journal of American Drama and Theatre,* and the edited collection *Producing Fashion: Commerce, Culture, and Consumers* (University of Pennsylvania Press, 2007), edited by Regina Blaszczyk.

Edward Slavishak, Associate Professor of History at Susquehanna University, is the author of *Bodies of Work: Civic Display and Labor in Industrial Pittsburgh* (Duke University Press, 2008). He is preparing a study of photography, tourism, and dereliction in the Appalachian Mountains.

Index

Note: *Page numbers in italics refer to figures.*

A. A. Marks Company, 96, 99, 101–2, 104, 106–15
A. and F. Pears Ltd., 124–25
actresses, 7–9, 12, 17, 123–49. *See also* celebrity endorsements
"Actresses, Cosmetics, and the Middle-Class Market," 17, 123–49
Adidas, 210–11
advertising agencies, 7–10, 16–18, 127–28, 141–42, 155–56
advertising campaigns
  examining, 10–12, 23–42, 51–70, 79–92, 95–117, 123–43, 151–67, 173–99, 207–27
  examples of, *4*, *8*, *39*, *126*, *131*, *139*, *158*, *159*, *196*, *197*, *215*, *216*, *224*, *226*
  history of, 23, 55
Advertising Progress, 10
Advertising to Women, 154
"After a Season of War," 15–16, 79–94
"Age of Barnum," 51–78
agrarian economies, 81–82
Aguilera, Christina, 221
Alger, Horatio, 174–75, 195, 223
American Artificial Limb Company, 99–100, 111
American Goliah, The, 56, *57*, 58
American Notes, 14, 32
amputations, 95–117
Anglin, Margaret, 138
Anzolut, Albino, 190, 194
Apgar, John T., 99, 102–3, 106, 108–10, 112–15
Archbald, Anne, 138
artificial limbs, 16, 95–117
"Artificial Limbs and Testimonials at the Turn of the Twentieth Century," 16, 95–121
Atlas, Charles, 18, 173–205
Autobiography, 175
"average consumers," 3, 9, 18, 133
Ayer, Harriet Hubbard, 125

Banes, Margaret Illington, 123–24, 132, 142
Barnum, P. T., 27, 33, 42, 51–78
beauty magazines, 128–30, 136
beauty products, 17, 123–43
Becker, Leo, 194, 198
Beckham, David, 5
Bederman, Gail, 175
Beecher, Henry Ward, 84
Bell, J. J., 86
Belletto, Steven, 57
Belmont, Alva, 9, 156
Benjamin, Walter, 221
Bernhardt, Sarah, 125
Beyoncé, 5
Bibb, George M., 28
Bird, Larry, 9
blackface minstrelsy, 14, 25–41
black hypermasculinity, 18–19
Black Panther Party, 212–13
Blink, 12
Bliss Company, 80, 86, 90
Bly, Douglas, 99
bodybuilding, 18, 173–205

Body-building, or Man in the Making, 178
bodybuilding ad, *196*, *197*
Bonaco, David, 194, 198
Boyle, Robert, 53–54, 64
"Boz's Juba," 14, 31–36, 40–42
Bragg, B. L., 83
brand identity, 2, 221
branding, 2, 5–6, 10, 70, 221
brand loyalty, 7, 82
brand names, 2–5, 127, 132, 152, 162, 210–11
Brand New, 10
Brandweek, 217
Brandy, 18, 220
bridal industry, 17–18, 151–71, 158, 159
bridal magazines, 17, 151–52, 160–67
bridal testimonials, 17–18, 151–71
"Bridal Testimonials and the Rise of Consumer Rites, 1920s–1950s," 17–18, 151–71
Bride's magazine, 17, 160, 164–66
Briggs Company, 80, 83–84, 88
Britton v. White Manufacturing, 67–68
Broach, William, 111
Brown, Carl, *226*
Buist, Robert, 86, 88–89, 92
Buist Company, 80, 83–84, 86
Bunyan, John, 174
Burke, Billie, 138, 140
Burpee, W. Atlee, 89
Burpee Company, 83
Business and Economic History, 12
Busta Rhymes, 221
Byrne, John, 101

Calhoun, John C., 28
Capra, Frank, 195
Cardiff Giant hoax, 15, 55–59, *57*, 70
cartomania, 124
Catalogue of Artificial Limbs, *97*
celebrity endorsements, 8–10, 18, 135, 207–27. *See also* advertising campaigns
celebrity testimonials, 124–35, 141, 227. *See also* testimonial advertising
Chaplin, Lan Nguyen, 218
"Charles Atlas, American Masculinity, and the Bodybuilding Testimonial, 1894–1944," 18, 173–205
Chauncey, George, 193
Chauvenet, Caroline Louise, 157
Chicago Tribune, 112
Chiovitti, J., 197
Chrisley, Charles, 108
Christ in Concrete, 195
Civil Rights Movement, 210, 213
Civil War, 15–16, 79–80, 85, 95, 100–1, 105, 111, 152
Clarke, John, 57
"co-brand," 5
Collins, Isaac, 102
Combs, Sean, 219, 221
commercial culture, 12, 52, 59, 62–63, 69, 152
Comstock, Anthony, 60–61
consumer behavior, 2–3, 16–17, 62, 124
consumer experience, 3
consumption patterns, 16–17
Coote, Charles, 37
Corbett, G. A., 101
Corgan, W. L., 110
corporate identification, 10. *See also* branding
cosmetics industry, 17, 123–43
Cosmopolitan, 129
Cowl, Jane, 137
Créme Nerol, 138–40, *139*
Criterion of Fashion, The, 130
"Culture and the Practice of Business History," 12
"Culture of Emulation," 207–30

Darrow, Clarence, 66
Davenport, Fanny, 125
"Dear Friend," 18, 173–205
deception, 51–53, 58–62, 66–69

de Cordova, Richard, 130
Def Jam Records, 210
Deily, Bertha, 110
Delineator, The, 137, 138
Democrat (Rochester), 88
Dempsey, Jack, 189
Dickens, Charles, 14–15, 32–34, 36–37, 42
Diddy, P., 219
DiDonato, Pietro, 195
Diesel, 208, 209
Diorio, F. G., 194
display advertisements, 83. *See also* advertising campaigns
DKNY, 208, 209
Douglass, Frederick, 212
Dreer, Henry, 86
Dry Goods Economist, 153
Dubner, Stephen, 12
Duchess of Marlborough, 155
Duke of Wellington, 30, 31
Dunn, Harry, 111
Dynamic Tension (DT), 173–77, 182, 188–89, 191–94, 197–99

Ecklund, Virginia, 162–63
Edward VII, 125
Ehrlin, Adam, 102
Elliott, Maxine, 130–32, *131*, 137, 138
emulation, 1–22, 207–30
endorsements, 2, 8–10, 18–19, 135, 207–27. *See also* advertising campaigns
Engelman, Elysa, 60
epistolary form, 80, 87–92
Ernst, Robert, 179
Esquire, 189
Ethiopian Serenaders, 27–42
Evans, Janet, 9
eyewitness testimonials, 15, 32, 36, 52–59, 64–70. *See also* testimonial advertising

"50 Cent," 221
Fables of Abundance, 10
Face Beautiful, The, 139
Facebook, 13
Farrar, Geraldine, 138
fashion industry, 207–30
fashion magazines, 128–30, 136
Fatio, L. C. F., 28
Federal Trade Commission (FTC), 1, 9, 189
Feick, William, 99
Feick Brothers, 99, 101, 106, 113, 116–17
female consumers, 16–18, 129. *See also* bridal industry; cosmetics industry
feminine identity, 151–52, 165
Fiske, Mrs., 138
Ford, George, 79–80, 83
Ford, Henry, 195
"For Us, By Us," 18–19, 207–30
Foster, D. R., 91
Foy, John P., 191
Franklin, Benjamin, 174, 175, 186, 198
Freakonomics, 12
Frederick, Christine, 154
FUBU apparel ad, 215–17, *216*
FUBU ("For Us, By Us"), 18–19, 207–30
FUBU founders, 223–26, *224*, *226*
Fuller, George, 99–100

gangsta rap, 211. *See also* rappers
gangsta style, 211, 213, 227
Garbarini, Louis, 197
Garden, Mary, 130, 137, 140
Garden Manual and Almanac, 88
Garland-Thomson, Rosemarie, 106
Garnica, Luis, 194
Garvey, Ellen Gruber, 160
Geddes, George, 57–59
George Fuller Company, 99–100
Germon, Frank, 28
Gilded Age, 53, 59–62, 175
Gioseffi, Andrew, 190, 194
Gladwell, Malcolm, 12
Godfather, The, 211

Goldstein, William, 193, 194, 197, 198
Gordon, Lady Duff, 134–35
Grapes of Wrath, The, 195
Gray, Dorothy, 163
Green Book Album, The, 132
Gucci, 210

Hammond, E. H., 101
Harper's Bazaar, 129, 131, 133
Harper's Weekly, 62, 84
Hastings, Herman, 108
Haywood, "Big Bill," 65
Helburn, Mrs. William P., 157
Held, Anna, 138, 142
Heth, Joice, 52
Hill, Thomas, 91
"Hip-Hop Fashion, Commodity Blackness and the Culture of Emulation," 18–19, 207–30
hoaxes, 15, 51–52, 55–60, 70
Holt, Douglas, 10
"Honestly—If Possible," 69
Horowitz, Daniel, 152
horticulture, 15–16, 79–94
Howard, Vicki, 17, 151, 231
How Brands Become Icons, 10
Hull, George, 56, 59
humbuggery, 51–52, 57, 60
Humbugs of the World, 51, 60
Hurd, Charles W., 127
hypermasculinity, 18–19, 225

"I am Kay and I Prefer Modern," 17–18, 151–71
Ice Cube, 211
identity
  brand identity, 2, 221
  feminine identity, 151–52, 165
  masculine identity, 175–76, 193, 199, 212
  racial identity, 166, 209
Ielardia, Antonio, 107
illusions, 62–63
industrial economies, 81–82
Iyer, K. V., 194

Jackson, Janet, 221
Janis, Elsie, 137, 141
Jastrow, Joseph, 62
Jenner, Bruce, 9
Jessop, William, 102, 112
Jewelers' Circular, The, 153
jewelers trade, 153–54
J. F. Rowley Company, 96, 98–99, 101, 107, 111, 113–16
John, Daymond, 208–9, 217–21, *225*, *226*
John, Deborah Roedder, 218
John Bull, 31
Johnson, Stephen, 14–15, 23, 231
Jones, Carl, 213
Jordan, Michael, 5
"Juba and the Legitimization of American Blackface Minstrelsy in Britain," 14, 23–49
J. Walter Thompson Company, 2, 7–10, 141–42, 155–56

Kasson, John, 178
Kelczewski, T., 197
Kelley, Robin D. G., 211
Keohn, Nancy, 10
Kerns, Ben, 61
Klein, Naomi, 5, 10
Kournikova, Anna, 5
Kraus, Charles, 197
Krolok, Paul, 197

LaChapelle, David, 221
Ladies' Home Journal, The, 129, 141, 157, 161
Laird, Pamela, 10
Lane, William Henry, 14
Langtry, Lily, 125, *126*
Lavater, Johann Kaspar, 65
Lears, Jackson, 10
Leavenworth, Elias, 58, 59
Leeper, David, 61
Lehr, Lew, 189
letters of testimonial. *See* testimonial letters
letter-writing manuals, 5, 87–89, 91–92

Levitt, Steven, 12
Lewis, Annabel, 87
Lewis, Lennox, 220–21, 223, 225
Lewis, Sinclair, 69
Liberty, 135
Liederman, Earle, 173–74, 180–81, 189, 194, 198
lifestyle marketing, 215–27
Lipartito, Kenneth, 12
Livingston, J. W., 194
LL Cool J, 18, 207, 216, 217, 222–23, 225
Loev, Sidney, 197
Lott, Eric, 209, 210
Louis Vuitton, 210
Lowe, Lisa, 214
lower-class culture, 209, 214, 225
Lux Toilet Soap, 7–8, *8*, 155, 167

Macfadden, Barnarr, 186
MacFadden, Bernard Adolphus, 179–80
Macfadden, Bernarr, 176, 179
Madison, Dolley, 28
Mad Men, 1, 11
"Mad Search for Beauty, The," 17, 123–49
magazines
- for brides, 17, 151–52, 160–67
- for men, 173, 176, 179–87, 189
- for women, 17, 128–30, 135–36, 151–52, 157, 160–67

Mahin, John Lee, 62
mail-order business, 6, 87–92
mail-order courses, 18, 173, 176, 186–87, 198
male consumers, 18, 173–205, 207–27
Man, Jacob, 197
Manliness and Civilization, 175
Manners, Diana, 155
Manual of Artificial Limbs, 115
Manual of Social and Business Forms, 91
Marchand, Roland, 70, 160, 190
marketplace definition, 11
Marlowe, Julia, 138, 140
Marshall, Edward, 112
Martin, J. Alexander, *226*
masculine identity, 175–76, 193, 199, 212
masculinity, 18–19, 173–205, 225
Mason, J. Y., 28
Massimo, Clevio, 194
Mayhew, Henry, 30
McCall's, 157
McCann v. Anthony, 67
McClure's Magazine, 64, 65
McCuaig, C. B., 69
McDougall, E., 59
McLean v. Fleming, 67
mechanical objectivity, 54, 64
medicines, 59–60
Melba, Nellie, 132
menswear, 207–27
middle-class audiences, 14, 17, 27–28, 38–42, 57
middle-class market, 123–43, 152–55
middle-class models, 210–13
middle-class publications, 59, 135
middle-class success, 213
minstrel show testimonials, 28–34
minstrel show tour, 27–32
minstrelsy, 14, 25–41
Mitchell, Margaret, 195
M'Mahon, Bernard, 82, 88
Modern Bride, 17, 160–67
Montel Williams Show, The, 223
Montgomery Ward Company, 6
moral character, 15, 55, 58, 61–62, 64
Morrison, H. P., 87
Moskowitz, Marina, 1, 15, 79, 231
"Mrs. Consumer," 151, 154, 162, 167
Mr. Smith Goes To Washington, 195
MTV, 211
Müller, Friedrich Wilhelm, 177–79. *See also* Sandow, Eugen
Münsterberg, Hugo, 63–66, 68–70
Mutschler, Carl, 190, 194, 198
MySpace, 13

Naether, Carl, 154
Nautica, 208, 209, 223
Newell, William "Stubbs," 56, 59

New Parlor Letter Writer, 87
New Yorker, The, 184–85
New York Times, 125, 177
New York World, The, 137
No Logo, 10
N'SYNC, 221
NWA, 211

objectivity and reliability, 53–55, 64, 68–70
Olden, J. C., 179
Olds, Edward A., 127
Onondaga Giant, The, 56
On the Witness Stand, 63
Opp, Julie, 138
optical illusions, 62–63
Orchard, Harry, 65, 70
Otto, Lenn, 191

Padurano, Dominique, 18, 173, 231
Palmer, Frank, 99–100, 111
Paltrow, Gwyneth, 5
Park, Roberta, 178
Patti, Adelina, 127
Pavlova, Anna, 141
Pears Ltd., 124–25
Peiss, Kathy, 128
Pell, G. W., 24, 29–32, 34–37
Perrin, Keith, 225, *225*, *226*
personal experiences, 12–14
Perthshire Constitutional, 37
Pettit, Michael, 15, 51, 232
Photoplay, 7
Physical Culture, 173, 176, 179–87, 189
Pickford, Mary, 129
Pilgrim's Progress, 174–75
Pinkham, Lydia E., 59–60
playbills, 38–41, *39*
Pocket Letter Writer, 87, 89
Polo Ralph Lauren, 214, 223
Pond's Cold Cream, 9, 140–42, 146–49, 155–56, 160, 167
Pope Leo XIII, 3, *4*
Porter, Theodore, 54
posters, 40–41, 136
Potter, Cora Brown, 125
Powell, Richard J., 212
Powers, C. S., 103
Prince Albert, 30, 36–37
Prince Charles, 6
Prince Philip, 6
Printers' Ink, 68–69, 83, 128, 130–31, 134–35, 154
print technology, 2, 6, 82
Progressive Era, 53, 63
prosthetics, 12, 16, 95–116, 133
psychologists, 62–69
"Puff Daddy," 219
Pullen, Forrest D., 138, 140

quantification, 54
Quantrell Raid, 79
Queen Elizabeth, 6
Queen Latifah, 221
Queen Victoria, 30, 32, 36

racial identity, 166, 209
Ralph Lauren, 214, 223
rappers, 207–11, 216–19, 222
Raymond, C. S., 91
Reader's Digest, 1
reality TV, 13
"Reconstruction-Era Landscape," 15–16, 79–94
Reed, Abijah, 90
Regan, Margaret, 162
Reilly, Alan C., 127
reliability and objectivity, 53–55, 64, 68–70
reliability and truth, 59–70
"Reliability in Marketing, Science, and Law at the End of the Age of Barnum," 15, 51–78
reliable witness, 53–55, 58–59, 64–70
Resor, Helen Landsdowne, 141
Resor, Stanley, 2–3, 5, 7, 19
Rice, T. D., 25
Rideing, William, 95–96
Rigaud, V., 130, 140
Rizzo, Mary, 18, 207, 232
Robertson, Chris, 221
Rohan, Patrick J., 191–92

Roman, Charles, 173, 186, 187
Romero, Hector, 197
Roosevelt, Eleanor, 9
Roosevelt, Franklin D., 189
Rospigliosi, Giambatistta, 155
Royal Family, 6, 30–31, 36–37
royal warrants, 5–6
Run, Reverend, 210
Run DMC, 210
Russell, Lillian, 125, 133, 137

St. Louis Globe-Democrat, 100
Sandow, Eugen, 174, 176–81, 185, 198
Santillo, Phil, 197
Saturday Evening Post, The, 129, 184–85
Scanlon, Jennifer, 161
Scarface, 211
Schaffer, Simon, 53
Schmitt, Bernd H., 218
Schorer, Eleanor, 137
Schwarzenegger, Arnold, 198
Schweitzer, Marlis, 1, 17, 123, 232
science and testimonials, 15, 53–55, 68–70
scientific observer, 53–55, 68–70
Scott, Walter Dill, 62, 68–69
Sean John, 219
Sears, Roebuck and Company, 6, 95, 134
seed trade, 15–16, 79–94
Selling Mrs. Consumer, 154
Shapin, Steve, 53
"Sharing Horticultural Success in the Reconstruction-Era Landscape," 15–16, 79–94
Sheridan, Ann, *8*, 9
Short, Leslie, 208
Siciliano, Angelo, 176, 179, 182–87, 194. *See also* Atlas, Charles
silk souvenirs, 23–24, 38–40
Simmons, Russell, 210, 213–14
Sing, Cheng Liang, 194
Slavishak, Edward, 16, 95, 232
Smith, Will, 18, 220
Snyder, Robert, 179
social networking, 13, 194
"society agents," 9
Source: The Magazine of Hip Hop, Politics and Culture, 214, 216, 222
Sparks, William, 110
"Spirit of Emulation, The," 1–22
Spitz, Mark, 9
sports endorsements, 9–10, 19. *See also* celebrity endorsements
Stage, Sarah, 60
Star-Beacon, 189
Starr, Frances, 138, 141
Steinbeck, John, 195
stereotypes, 18–19
Sterling Journal and Advertiser, 37
Stewart, Edward, 110
Stilgoe, John, 82
Stirling Observer, 36
Strongfort, Lionel, 179
Surowiecki, Jim, 12
Susman, Warren, 175
Swiencicki, Mark, 104
Swift and Co., 130–31

"tainted testimonials," 9, 125, 127
Taliaferro, Mabel, 138
Taylor, Laurette, 137
Taylor, Robert, 185
"Ten Year Club, The," 16, 95–121
"Testifying Subject, The," 15, 51–78
testimonial
- benefits of, 12
- origins of, 1–2
- success of, 2
- types of, 2

testimonial advertising
- examining, 10–12, 23–42, 51–70, 79–92, 95–117, 123–43, 151–67, 173–99, 207–27
- examples of, 4, 8, 39, 126, 131, 139, 158, 159, 196, 197, 215, 216, 224, 226
- history of, 5–13, 52–53

testimonial letters
appeal of, 15–16, 80–92, 178–81, 190–94
inclusion of, 81, 86–87, 90–92
testimonial marketing, 3–6, 12–15. *See also* testimonial advertising
testimonial networks, 98–100, 104–5, 112–13, 160–61, 164
testimonials, tainted, 9, 125, 127
"Testimonials in Silk," 14, 23–49
Tetrazzini, Luisa, 138
Theory and Practice of Advertising, 62
Tia, M., 194
Tiffany, Mrs. Charles, 9
Tipping Point, The, 12
Tommy Hilfiger, 208–10, 214, 215, 223
trademark infringement, 62, 66
trademarks, 2–3, 134
True Story, 161
truth and reliability, 59–70
"Truth in Advertising" campaign, 68–69
Tucker, D. W., 115
Tyler, John, 28

Unger, Max, 179
unwary purchasers, 61–62, 66–68
upper-class culture, 157, 208–9, 214, 223
urban wear, 207–30

Vanity Fair, 130, 133
Vauxhall Gardens, 23–24, 34–36
"Vauxhall Silk, The," 23–24
Veblen, Thorstein, 212
Vick, James, 79, 82–84, 87–92
Vick Company, 80, 83–84, 87, 91
Vick's Annual Catalogue and Floral Guide, 79–80, 81, 87
Vin Mariani ad, *4*
Virginia Serenaders, 25, 27, 29
visual deception, 62, 67
visual imagery, 2, 208
Vogue, 130, 131, 133, 138, 141

Waggoner, R. H., 84
Walker, Aida Overton, 129
Walsh, William, 115
Wardell, Mr., 34
Warner, Anna, 84
Washington, George, 52
Wayans Brothers, 18, 220
wedding industry, 17–18, 151–71, 158, 159
Weinsoff, Herman, 193, 194, 198
Wellman, Francis, 66
Wharton, Edith, 153
White, Graham, 212
White, Shane, 212
Wickliffe, Charles, 28
Wigmore, John, 66
Williams, Hype, 221
Williams-Searle, John, 105
Wisdom of Crowds, The, 12
Withrow, C. S., 197
Witmer, Lightner, 64
women's magazines, 128–30, 135–36, 157, 160
Wood, Otis F., 134–35
"Woodbury bride," 157–60
Woodbury soap, 156–60
Wood vs. Lucy, Lady Duff-Gordon, 135
Worch, Michael S., 197
Wynter, Leon, 208

Ziegfeld, Florenz, 138
Zimmerman, J. W., 91
Zolotow, Maurice, 185